D0153405

O'Meara

CAMBRIDGE TEXTBOOKS IN LINGUISTICS

MORPHOLOGY

In this series:

B. COMRIE *Aspect*

T. BYNON *Historical Linguistics*

R. M. KEMPSON *Semantic Theory*

J. ALLWOOD, L.-G. ANDERSON, O. DAHL *Logic in Linguistics*

MORPHOLOGY

AN INTRODUCTION TO THE THEORY OF WORD-STRUCTURE

P.H.MATTHEWS

PROFESSOR OF LINGUISTICS

UNIVERSITY OF READING

CAMBRIDGE UNIVERSITY PRESS

CAMBRIDGE

LONDON·NEW YORK·MELBOURNE

Published by the Syndics of the Cambridge University Press
The Pitt Building, Trumpington Street, Cambridge CB2 1RP
Bentley House, 200 Euston Road, London NW1 2DB
32 East 57th Street, New York, NY 10022, USA
296 Beaconsfield Parade, Middle Park, Melbourne 3206, Australia

Library of Congress Catalogue Card Number: 73-91817

ISBN 0 521 20448 8 hard covers
ISBN 0 521 09856 4 paperback

First published 1974
Reprinted 1978

Printed in Great Britain at the
University Press, Cambridge

CONTENTS

PREFACE

This was first conceived as a partial editio minor of my recent *Inflectional Morphology* (in the 'Cambridge Studies in Linguistics'). But it has become, I think, a little more interesting. I hope that it will be of value to specialists in particular European languages, as well as to postgraduate and undergraduate students of general linguistics.

I am very grateful to my colleagues R. W. P. Brasington, D. Crystal, G. C. Lepschy, F. R. Palmer, K. M. Petyt and Irene P. Warburton, who read the book in typescript and have helped me to make a number of corrections and improvements. I look forward with pleasure to a fresh collaboration with the University Printers, who set my first book so beautifully.

July 1973 P.H.M.

PRINCIPAL REFERENCES

Note: When a statement requires scholarly backing, or a book or passage needs immediate identification, I have supplied it in a footnote. But each chapter also has an appendix called 'Related Reading'; this refers the reader both to fuller or more marginal treatments, and also to corresponding passages (often fairly brief) in other introductions which a student will be required or encouraged to read. The following is a list of abbreviations which I have used where necessary.

BLOCH & TRAGER = B. Bloch & G. L. Trager, *Outline of Linguistic Analysis* (Supplement to *Lg*: Baltimore, 1942).

BLOOMFIELD = L. Bloomfield, *Language*, British edition (London, 1935).

BOLINGER = D. L. Bolinger, *Aspects of Language* (New York, 1968).

CHOMSKY, *Structures* = N. Chomsky, *Syntactic Structures* (The Hague, 1957).

CHOMSKY, *Aspects* = N. Chomsky, *Aspects of the Theory of Syntax* (Cambridge, Mass., 1965).

CHOMSKY, *Mind* = N. Chomsky, *Language and Mind*, 2nd ed. (New York, 1972).

CHOMSKY & HALLE = N. Chomsky & M. Halle, *The Sound Pattern of English* (New York, 1968).

FL = *Foundations of Language: International Journal of Language and Philosophy* (Dordrecht, 1965–).

FUDGE = *Phonology: Selected Readings*, ed. E. C. Fudge (Harmondsworth, 1973).

GLEASON = H. A. Gleason, *An Introduction to Descriptive Linguistics*, 2nd ed. (New York, 1961).

GOODWIN = W. W. Goodwin, *A Greek Grammar*, 2nd ed. (London, 1894).

HARRIS = Z. S. Harris, *Methods in Structural Linguistics* (Chicago, 1951). Also in paperback under the title *Structural Linguistics.*

HILL = A. A. Hill, *Introduction to Linguistic Structures: from Sound to Sentence in English* (New York, 1958).

Historical Linguistics = *Directions for Historical Linguistics*, ed. W. P. Lehmann & Y. Malkiel (Austin, 1968).

HOCKETT, *Models* = C. F. Hockett, 'Two models of grammatical description', *Word*, **10** (1954), pp. 210–31. Reprinted in *RiL*, pp. 386–99.

HOCKETT, *Course* = C. F. Hockett, *A Course in Modern Linguistics* (New York, 1958).

HOUSEHOLDER = F. W. Householder, *Linguistic Speculations* (Cambridge, 1971).

IJAL = *International Journal of American Linguistics* (Baltimore, 1917–).

Inflectional Morphology = P. H. Matthews, *Inflectional Morphology: a Theoretical Study Based on Aspects of Latin Verb Conjugation* (Cambridge, 1972).

JL = *Journal of Linguistics* (London, 1965–).

LEPSCHY = G. C. Lepschy, *A Survey of Structural Linguistics* (London, 1970).

LEWIS = G. L. Lewis, *Turkish Grammar* (Oxford, 1967).

Lg = *Language: Journal of the Linguistic Society of America* (Baltimore, 1925–).

Lingua = *Lingua: International Review of General Linguistics/revue internationale de linguistique générale* (Amsterdam, 1947–).

LYONS = J. Lyons, *Introduction to Theoretical Linguistics* (Cambridge, 1968).

MANSION = *Harrap's Standard French and English Dictionary*, ed. J. E. Mansion, Vol. 1, *French–English* (London, 1934).

MARCHAND = H. Marchand, *The Categories and Types of Present-Day English Word-formation: A Synchronic-Diachronic Approach*, 2nd ed. (Munich, 1969).

MARTINET = A. Martinet, *Éléments de linguistique générale* (Paris, 1960). English translation, *Elements of General Linguistics*, by Elizabeth Palmer (London, 1964).

New Horizons = *New Horizons in Linguistics*, ed. J. Lyons (Harmondsworth, 1970).

NIDA = E. A. Nida, *Morphology*, 2nd ed. (Ann Arbor, 1949).

OED = *The Oxford English Dictionary*, ed. Sir James Murray *et al.*, reissued with Supplement (Oxford, 1933). New Supplement, Vol. 1, *A–G*, ed. R. W. Burchfield (Oxford, 1972). Shorter edition, 3rd ed. by C. T. Onions (Oxford, 1944).

PALMER = F. R. Palmer, *A Linguistic Study of the English Verb* (London, 1965). A new version, *The English Verb*, is now in the press.

PAUL = H. Paul, *Prinzipien der Sprachgeschichte*, 5th ed. (Halle, 1920). English adaptation (of the second edition), *Introduction to the Study of the History of Language*, by H. A. Strong *et al.* (London, 1891).

PIKE = K. L. Pike, *Language in Relation to a Unified Theory of the Structure of Human Behavior*, 2nd ed. (The Hague, 1967).

QUIRK *et al.* = R. Quirk, S. Greenbaum, G. N. Leech & J. Svartvik, *A Grammar of Contemporary English* (London, 1972).

REYNOLDS = *The Cambridge Italian Dictionary*, ed. Barbara Reynolds, Vol. 1, *Italian–English* (Cambridge, 1962).

RiL = *Readings in Linguistics I*, ed. M. Joos (Chicago, 1966). Formerly *Readings in Linguistics* (1st ed. New York, 1957).

RiL II = *Readings in Linguistics II*, ed. E. P. Hamp, F. W. Householder & R. Austerlitz (Chicago, 1966).

ROBINS = R. H. Robins, *General Linguistics: an Introductory Survey* (London, 1964).

SAPIR = E. Sapir, *Language* (New York, 1921).

SAUSSURE = F. de Saussure, *Cours de linguistique générale*, 5th ed. (Paris, 1955). English translation, *Course in General Linguistics*, by W. Baskin (New York, 1959).

TCLP = *Travaux du cercle linguistique de Prague* (Prague, 1929–39). Vol. 8 has been reprinted under its own title, *Études phonologiques dédiées à la mémoire de M. le Prince N. S. Trubetzkoy* (University, Ala., 1964).

TPhS = *Transactions of the Philological Society* (Oxford, 1842–).

TRUBETZKOY = N. S. Trubetzkoy, *Grundzüge der Phonologie* (Prague, 1939) (*TCLP* 7). French translation, *Principes de phonologie*, by J. Cantineau, with additional articles (Paris, 1949). English translation, *Principles of Phonology*, by Christiane A. M. Baltaxe (Berkeley/Los Angeles, 1969).

ULLMANN = S. Ullmann, *Semantics* (Oxford, 1962).

WARTBURG = W. von Wartburg, *Problèmes et méthodes de la linguistique*, revised edition in collaboration with S. Ullmann (Paris, 1963). English translation, *Problems and Methods in Linguistics*, by Joyce M. H. Reid (Oxford, 1969).

Word = *Word: Journal of the Linguistic Circle of New York* (New York, 1945–).

I
Why study morphology?

Morphology as the study of 'forms of words'; current lack of interest in morphological theory; reasons for this in Chomskyan and other schools; practical importance of morphological description.
Theoretical preliminaries: double articulation; grammatical and phonological levels; formatives and morphemes; 'word formation'; limits of morphological analysis.
Importance of morphology for general issues: semantics and historical linguistics; theories of language universals; variety of morphological models.

In the traditional view of language, words are put together to form sentences. The words differ from each other in both sound and meaning: *clock* and *gong*, for example, refer to different sorts of object and are distinguished by different consonants at the beginning and end. Hence the sentences will also differ in sound and meaning, *The clock has been sold* being distinguished from *The gong has been sold* as a function of *clock* versus *gong* in particular. However, not only the words but also the construction and the 'forms of words' will vary from one individual sentence to another. For example, *The gong has been sold* has a Passive construction with *the gong* as Subject, while *He has sold the gong* has an Active construction in which it appears as Object. Moreover, in both these sentences the Noun is in its Singular form *gong*, and in the Passive the Auxiliary word *has* is in the Singular to match; contrast *The gongs have been sold* or *He has sold the gongs*, where both *have* and *gongs* are in the Plural. In such examples, the choice between different forms of words – between the endings of *gongs* and *gong* on the one hand and *have* and *has* on the other – varies independently of the variation in construction (Passive versus Active). But in other cases the construction itself requires that a word should be in one form rather than another. For example, in *He hit them*, the word *them* is Object and must therefore appear in what is traditionally called the 'Accusative' Case. Contrast *They have sold the gong*, where the same Pronoun is Subject and must therefore appear as the 'Nominative' *they* instead. In describing a language all four varying facets – sounds, constructions, meanings, and forms of words – have to be given due attention.

In the same spirit, the field of descriptive theory may be divided into four major subfields. The first is concerned with the study of speech sounds, a subject which in modern structural linguistics is handled on two theoretical levels. Of these the level of **phonology** is concerned with the functioning of sound-units within the systems of individual languages, whereas that of **phonetics** is concerned with the nature and typology of speech sounds in themselves. The second major subfield is that of **syntax** (from a Greek word meaning a 'putting together' or 'arranging' of elements), which traditionally covers both the constructions of phrases and sentences and also the features of meaning which are associated with them. For example, the Interrogative (*Has he sold the gong?*) is different both in construction and in meaning from the Non-Interrogative or Declarative (*He has sold the gong*). The third subfield of **semantics** then reduces to the study of word meanings – to which perhaps we may add the meanings of idioms (see the end of Ch. II) or of special phrases generally. Traditionally, the problems of semantics have often been relegated to the dictionary. However, the oppositions of word meanings also lend themselves to structural analysis, most notably in specific 'semantic fields' such as those of kinship, colour terms, occupations, types of skill and knowledge, and so on. In addition, the limits of syntax and semantics have frequently been disputed both within and between the various structural schools. According to some, constructional meanings would also belong to semantics – syntax being then reduced to the formal distribution of words or other units. According to others, some features of word meaning would also belong to syntax: for example, the potentiality of a given Verb (e.g. *sell*) to combine in the Active with a Human subject (e.g. *he*) rather than a Non-Human or Inanimate. At the time of writing the debate continues in full vigour.

The last major subfield is that of **morphology**, and it is this that forms the central theme of this book. The term itself is a Greek-based parallel to the German *Formenlehre* (the 'study of forms'), and like many linguistic terms is nineteenth-century in origin, the first references for this sense in the *OED* being from the 1860s (s.vv. 'morphology', 'morphological', 'morphologically'). As a biological term it is older by at least thirty years (the first references for English in the *OED* being to 1830), and its linguistic sense was at first conceived in the same intellectual framework. It must be remembered that the science of language was at that time influenced by the evolutionary model of Darwin's *On the Origin of Species* (published in 1859). But the parallel between linguistics and biology is now seen as spurious. Philologists have long given up the hope (expressed so seductively in Max Müller's Oxford lectures of 1889) that by studying the 'evolution' of words in Indo-European, and their 'four or five hundred' basic roots in particular, the 'world-old riddle of the origin of language' can be solved.[1] On a less fanciful level, the history of individual languages is no longer seen in a Darwinian framework; nor indeed is morphology (or linguistics in general) seen as a specifically historical discipline. 'Morphology', therefore, is simply a term for that branch of linguistics which is concerned with the 'forms of words' in different uses and constructions. What precisely this means will be distinguished more carefully in the middle paragraphs of this chapter.

The analysis of words is a subject which is momentarily out of fashion in linguistic theory: few theorists have devoted books to it in recent years. To the layman it might seem surprising that this should be so. The word is a linguistic unit familiar at all levels of our culture: words are things that a schoolboy or typist can spell correctly or incorrectly; words can be used grammatically or ungrammatically in sentences; choosing the 'right word' can take agonies of time. In a more restricted context, learning the diverse forms of words (the paradigms of Latin or German, the 'principal parts' of irregular Verbs, the rules for forming one form of a word from another) is the most traditional and ritualised aspect of mastering a foreign language. In our grammatical training, words are parsed or assigned to classes (Noun, Verb, Active Verb, Present or Past form of Verb, etc.) by a technique which goes back for two millennia. Far earlier than the nineteenth century, words were already the very foundation of language study.

The neglect of morphology would also have been surprising to any structural linguist of fifteen or more years ago. In Joos's well known *Readings in Linguistics* (an anthology of American writings from 1925 to 1956),[2] eight of the items selected for 1940 to 1955 are concerned predominantly or exclusively with morphological questions: this compares with about twelve for phonology, at most five for syntax and none for semantics. Morphology is also central to many of Joos's more general selections. In the eventual companion volume, *Readings in Linguistics II*,[3] there are various European contributions of equal importance. Still in Europe, the programme of the VIth International

[1] F. M. Müller, *Three Lectures on the Science of Language and its Place in General Education* (Repr. Benares, Indological Book House, 1961), p. 32.

[2] *RiL* in our list of abbreviations.

[3] *RiL* II.

Congress of Linguists (Paris, 1948) was based on the replies to three fundamental questions, of which the first bears directly on our topic in Ch. XI, and the second will indeed be taken as the starting point for our own discussion in Ch. IX. The same concern for morphology is shown in the general works and textbooks of that time: for example, in Harris's *Methods in Structural Linguistics*, a work of fundamental importance in the development of North American linguistics, the relevant chapters form over a quarter of the book (HARRIS, Chs. 12–14). The leading practical introduction to word analysis (NIDA in our list of abbreviations) belongs to the same creative period.

Nevertheless, interest has undoubtedly slackened since the mid 1950s. In part this is for a very laudable reason. If the 1930s were for structural linguistics above all a decade of phonology, and the 1940s and early 1950s a period of apparently parallel progress in morphology, the 1960s in particular have been a decade of syntax. The main inspiration has come from Chomsky's brilliantly original *Syntactic Structures* (CHOMSKY, *Structures*), a work which at the end of the 1950s seemed to open quite new fields to structural analysis. But at the same time other groups of linguists also made important contributions to syntactic theory. In France, Tesnière's *Éléments* was published posthumously in 1959.[1] Again in North America, the tagmemic theory of Pike and his disciples bore fruit in numerous monographs and articles from 1960 onwards.[2] In Britain, Halliday's 'Scale and Category' theory (itself very similar to Pike's in many of its basic insights) received its first exposition in 1961.[3] In the wake of this interest in syntax, the latter part of the decade also saw a fashionable if perhaps (so far) less profitable concentration on semantics. The study of meaning above all had been neglected in the immediate post-war period. As these trends developed, it is not surprising that morphology attracted less attention.

However, there were also more specific reasons in the nature of the theories themselves. In Chomsky's account of language, the basic syntactic relations (relationships of Subject and Object, of modifying and subordinate structures to their dominating elements, of simple sentences to complex sentences, and so on) are handled at a 'deep' level (referred to further in Ch. X) which is too abstract for the word to serve any useful purpose. Let us take for illustration the English sentence

[1] L. Tesnière, *Éléments de syntaxe structurale* (Paris, 1959).

[2] Though the leading work (PIKE) was not published in its final version until later.

[3] M. A. K. Halliday, 'Categories of the theory of grammar', *Word* **17** (1961), pp. 241–92.

They are trying hard. In terms of words – on the 'surface', Chomsky would say – we may talk among other things of a relationship within a Verb phrase between *are* and *trying*. But if we compare this 'phrase' with other possible 'phrases' (*have tried, have been trying*, and so on), a quite different division of units soon emerges. Firstly, the *are* and the *-ing* part of *trying* can be opposed as a whole to, for example, the *have* and *-ed* parts of *have tried*; the evidence is that one cannot say either *have trying* or (in the same Active construction) *are tried.* By the same token, the more complex *have been trying* may be analysed into the three interlocking members *try-*, *be* and *-ing*, *have* and *-en*. The reason, again, is that in standard English one cannot say [*They*] *have being trying* (replacing *-en* in the member *have* + *-en* with *-ing*), or *have be trying* (dropping *-en* altogether), or *been trying* (dropping *have* but holding everything else constant), and so on. *Have* and *-en, be* and *-ing* are pairs of dependent variables.

This analysis is natural on semantic grounds also. In *are trying*, the *are* and *-ing* together mark what may be called the 'Present Progressive' Tense, as opposed, for example, to the Simple or Non-Progressive Present in *They try hard.* Likewise, the *have* and *-ed* of *have tried* mark what is normally called the 'Present Perfect', and in *have been trying* we have a combination of the Auxiliaries, with associated *-en* and *-ing*, that marks both 'Perfect' and 'Progressive' together. At an abstract level it is these concepts of Tense ('Present', 'Progressive', 'Perfect') that the analyst is above all concerned with. But at the same time the Verbal element *try-* or *tri*(*e*)- (*trying* and *tried* shorn of their endings) may be linked on its own with the separate word *hard. Hard* is an Adverb that sits easily with *try-*, whereas others (e.g. *mellifluously* or *away*) sit with difficulty at best; this fact is independent of the remainder of the Verb phrase, *They have tried away* being as awkward as *They are trying away*, but *They have gone away*, by contrast, being as natural as *They are going away*. The rest of the phrase may even be absent in certain Non-Finite constructions ([*We have made them*] *try hard*), coordinate structures ([*They'll try, and*] *try hard*), and so on. One cannot find a converse case in which *try-* is dropped from the phrase instead (*are -ing hard* or *are hard-ing*). Now *try-* and *hard* must, of course, be recognised as independent variables. But in a weaker sense they still go together against *are* and *-ing*.

We now have an analysis which cuts clean across the 'surface' boundaries between words. The construction is no longer *were* + *trying* +

hard (two-word Verb phrase and Adverb *hard*), but rather [*are -ing*] + [*try- hard*] or – we might be tempted to say – '*try hard*' in the Present Progressive. The precise way of handling these units varies in successive recensions of Chomskyan grammar: for many of his pupils, the foregoing remarks might still be excessively 'near the surface'. But at some level deeper than surface structure such are the 'facts' which a grammar would be obliged to express. At the superficial level, the word will, of course, continue to be an important unit. Furthermore, there must be rules or statements which relate the 'surface representation' of a sentence to its strictly phonetic representation – the features of the 'phonetic signal' which the speaker utters. Here morphology, or what is sometimes called 'morphophonology' (see Ch. XI), has a potential rôle. But the word is no longer the basic unit of syntactic statement, as it has been (with qualifications) for the whole of the grammatical tradition until well into this century. Given such analyses, it is only natural that morphology should seem of diminished interest.

The 'deep' decomposition of the phrase is a feature characteristic of Chomsky's theory in particular. But the theories of Pike and Halliday have depreciated the word for equal if for different reasons. For these scholars, *trying* and *are* would certainly be syntactic units. Together the two words (units at 'word level' in the grammatical hierarchy of English) form a phrase *are trying* (one unit at the 'phrase level'); in the same way *they*, *are trying* and *hard* (three one- or two-word phrases, at least in Halliday's treatment) together form the 'clause' *they are trying hard*, and this, in turn, is the only unit in a one-clause sentence. So far, therefore, we are basically in tune with the tradition: these statements belong to syntax, while statements about *are* and *trying* as such could still belong to morphology. But why, these scholars would ask, should such a division actually be made? Just as *are trying* consists (as we have seen) of two grammatical units *are* and *trying*, so *trying*, at least, can be said to consist quite clearly of *try*- and *-ing*. This division of a word into smaller units (such theorists would insist) does not require a form of statement which differs essentially from the division of phrases, clauses, and so on. We shall return to this thesis later in this chapter; we shall also develop it further at the beginning of Ch. V, by which stage the arguments for it will be initially more persuasive. But if we were to accept it, there would indeed be no reason to divide our statements between morphology (concerned just with the bottom rung in the hierarchy) and syntax (concerned with all the remainder). There is one unitary branch of GRAMMAR, which can be distinguished as a whole from phonology and phonetics on the one hand, and semantics or the lexicon on the other.

In addition (it would be emphasised) there are at least some languages which do not HAVE 'words'. That is, they do not have a unit of grammar which is distinct from the minimal unit on the one hand (the unit represented in English by *try-* or *-ing*), and also from the phrase on the other, and which generally has the properties which can be ascribed to the word in European languages. We shall return to this later in this chapter (and more elaborately in Ch. IX). But for the moment the ensuing argument will be obvious enough. If some languages do not have words then the fact that others do is merely a descriptive observation. A theory proposed for language in general would be false if the notion 'word' was included as an obligatory feature. Hence one can build no general theoretical distinction upon it. Since morphology is traditionally 'that branch of linguistics which is concerned with the structure of words', and the word is not itself a theoretical entity, then a division between morphology and syntax has no theoretical status either. It is not merely objectionable for English and other languages which do have the word rung in their hierarchy, but plainly false for those which do not.

The above is a fair statement, the author would like to believe, of a position with which he does not himself agree. It is a very widespread view, with roots in certain aspects of Bloomfield's theory (although Bloomfield himself retained a morphology/syntax division), and also in that of Hjelmslev (who firmly rejected it). Well, let us accept this view for the sake of argument. The analysis of word structure is merely one 'area', let us say, in the grammatical description of a certain number of particular languages. Nevertheless it is often a very important area. In the latest structural grammar of Italian, over three hundred pages are devoted to morphology in the lexical and the inflectional sense (see Ch. III).[1] The recent *Handbook of Middle American Indians* includes a set of eight grammatical sketches (about twenty pages each in double columns), by American authors of varying background: under one heading or another the discussion of words varies from about a quarter to over half of each contribution.[2] In Bouquiaux's grammar of the Birom language of Nigeria, a thorough work remarkable for its detailed treatment of

[1] R. A. Hall, Jr, *La struttura dell'italiano* (Rome, 1971).

[2] Vol. 5, *Linguistics*, ed. N. A. McQuown (Austin, 1967), pp. 179ff.

syntax, the passages devoted to morphology as we understand it nevertheless form about a quarter of the description.[1] The same is roughly true of Hoffmann's more traditional account of Margi (another Northern Nigerian language).[2] In published grammars it is quite normal for the section on the Verbal word to be longer than the whole discussion of vowels and consonants; this is true of both the Margi and the Italian grammars referred to. All this is to say nothing of monographs and articles devoted to word-level analyses alone.

The reader may perhaps feel that counting pages proves nothing. We must justify our field by logical argument and not by appeals to the format or content of grammar books. But the theory of grammar should not become divorced from the exigencies of ordinary description. The analysis of words (under whatever heading we put it) is an important task facing the investigator of most little-known languages. It is only in favoured cases, where the morphology is simple or is already thoroughly explored, that a beginner can plunge straight into syntax. How DOES one plunge into syntax when one cannot identify or categorise the elements whose rôle and distribution is in question? In the teaching of linguistics this point is generally recognised. Morphology is often assigned a separate course of lectures, and as a part or extension of this course a student will normally be given a series of written exercises ('morphology problems') which instil a technique and frame of reference peculiar to this level of analysis. In most departments he will also attend a practical class with an informant; usually this involves a stage at which the word supplies the frame for grammatical and indeed for phonological investigation. But how are the techniques and frames of reference (the 'models', as we shall call them) to be justified and made explicit? There is a plain job of work which theorists of language have tended to pass by in recent years.

For this reason – a frankly practical reason if that is how the reader likes to see it – a new introduction to morphological theory needs no excuse. But the author also believes that even the purest theoretician (a scholar concerned with the nature of language quite independently of practical application) now has excellent reasons for looking at this 'area' of grammar closely. We shall return to this point in the final section of this chapter.

* * *

[1] L. Bouquiaux, *La langue Birom: phonologie, morphologie, syntaxe* (Paris, 1970), pp. 109ff., 189ff., 232ff., 297ff., 325ff.

[2] C. Hoffmann, *A Grammar of the Margi Language* (London, 1963).

So far we have largely taken the reality of our field for granted, assuming (as implied already by the subtitle of this introduction) that words do have a 'structure' about which a 'theory' may be formulated. But it is now time to define the subject more carefully, indicating, in rather more technical terms, the sort of patterning that is in question. To do this, we must again begin with a consideration of certain aspects of linguistic patterning in general.

One important property of human language, as most theoretical surveys and textbooks emphasise, is the one which we shall refer to as that of **double articulation**. Another way of putting this is to say that language has a **dual** structure, or that as a form of communication it has the property of **duality**. Any simple example in speech or writing will make this characteristic clear. If we take the first sentence of W. B. Yeats's 'Sailing to Byzantium':[1]

> That is no country for old men

we can say, first of all, that it consists of seven words, *that*, *is*, *no*, and so on. These combine to form phrases: *old men* is one phrase, and according to most writers would itself be part of a larger phrase *no country for old men*, which forms the Complement of the clause or sentence as a whole. Such phrases and clauses are articulated according to definite rules. If we put the final Noun into the Singular:

> That is no country for old man

the result can be understood and could conceivably be poetry, by some standards. But strictly the Singular phrase (*old man*) ought to have an Article. The sentence could be intuitively corrected – say to the form:

> That is no country for an old man

– and that would be more in accordance with English syntax. It is the job of the linguist to discover and elucidate these rules, distinguishing them from patterns of style etc. and testing their adequacy against the actual facts of usage.

This is the first level of organisation – the **first** or **primary articulation** of language – in which words or similar elements are related to each other in syntactic patterns. It is this that is referred to as the level of syntax or of grammar – the term 'grammar' being used here in the most restricted of its senses in linguistics. But the words *that*, *is* and so

[1] From *The Tower* (1928); in *Collected Poems*, 2nd ed. (London, 1950), p. 217.

on have another internal organisation of their own. *That* consists of four separate letters *t*, *h*, *a* and *t*; when spoken, [ðæt], it can be analysed into a consonant, vowel and further consonant which are assigned to the phonemes symbolised by 'ð', 'æ' and 't'.[1] Likewise *is* [iz] may be analysed into two letters or two phonemes, and so on for the remainder. The units which are basic to the primary articulation of language are thus distinguished and identified by combinations of smaller units, letters or phonemes. Moreover, these combinations are in turn subject to rule. A native English word cannot begin, for example, with the consonants *cv* [kv], although it could begin with *cl*, *qu* [kw] or the like. It is not merely that a word such as *cvab* ([kvæb] or [kvɔb]) does not happen to exist. To the author's knowledge *quab* does not exist either, but there is no reason why it should not do so in the future. It is not an elegant acronym, and perhaps not the word to choose for a new soft drink or washing powder. But if an embarrassed reader were to tell me that it is in fact a four-letter word, which for some reason I have not encountered even on National Service, I could just believe him. A colleague also suggests that it would be a suitable name for a weed-killer! We can react in these ways because it is a possible English word, and we can sense its resemblance to other words. But if someone were to blush at *cvab* I would wonder whose army he had been in.

These smaller patterns of organisation form a **second** or **secondary articulation** of language – the level of phonology if, as normally, we are talking of sound-structure and not in terms of the spelling. Now perhaps some might wish to argue that it is phonology that is properly 'primary' and grammar that is properly 'secondary'; insofar as this is an issue of substance it need not concern us here. The important point is that the levels are distinguished, and it is this property which is referred to as that of duality or double articulation. For some scholars the distinction of units alone (words or the like on one side, phonemes etc. on the other) is a central 'design feature', serving to set human language apart from the communication of animals, or so-called 'natural languages' apart from many artificial 'languages' (the 'language' of arithmetical formulae, for instance).

[1] Spoken forms in English (Southern English RP or Received Pronunciation) will normally be cited in the phonetic transcription of Daniel Jones; see, most conveniently, his *English Pronouncing Dictionary*, of which I have used his last (11th) edition (London, 1956). These will normally be put in square brackets; occasionally, as in Ch. v, it will be necessary to distinguish square brackets (for 'sounds' or 'phones') and solidi (for phonemes), but, as will be clear when we come to Ch. xi, I have no wish to commit this book to any one specific phonological theory.

If that were all, there would be no place for morphology. We would simply state which combinations of phonemes could form words, and list in a dictionary those which actually were words; there would be no other sense in which a notion of 'word-structure' would be meaningful. But of course it is not all. If we take a little more of Yeats's poem:

> The young
> In one another's arms, birds in the trees
> – Those dying generations – at their song,
> The salmon-falls, the mackerel-crowded seas,
> Fish, flesh, or fowl, commend all summer long
> Whatever is begotten, born, and dies.

we at once find several words with parts which function separately. *Arms*, *birds*, *trees*, *generations*, *-falls* and *seas* share an ending *s* ([z]) by which, as Plural Nouns, they are distinguished from the corresponding Singulars *arm*, *bird*, and so on. This *-s* is an example of what we shall usually call a **formative** or element entering into the 'formation' of words (more specifically an **inflectional formative** – see Ch. IV). Similarly, *dies* has a formative *-s* which distinguishes it from *dying* (with a different formative *-ing* or [iŋ], and also from *die* (with no corresponding formative) or *died*; compare *tried*, *trying* and *try* in our earlier illustration. In general, then, we may proceed to specify the structure of this set of words by saying that any member (*bird* or *birds*, *dies*, *die* or *dying*) consists of a minimal Noun or Verb, followed either by no formative at all (*bird* or *die*) or by whichever of the series of formatives for Plural, '3rd Singular Present', etc., suits.

According to a common proposal one would then say that it is not words, in fact, that form the basis of the primary or grammatical articulation. In *birds in the trees* there are not four basic units but six (or five with one appearing twice). The words *birds* and *trees* are themselves combinations of units – the second unit being identified by the letter '*s*' or the phoneme symbolised by 'z' – in much the way that, as we said, the phrase *old men* is a combination of *old* and *men*. If we could tear ourselves away from word spelling a student of grammar might find it more convenient to write the example as follows:

bird s in the tree s

– the smaller grammatical units distinguished in this way being generally, though not universally, referred to as **morphemes**. It is this conclusion that underlies the grammatical theories of Pike and Halliday which we discussed earlier. For them the morpheme is the minimal, indivisible or primitive unit; the word is merely one of a hierarchy of complex or non-minimal units including the phrase, the clause, the sentence, and maybe others still larger.

We will return to the morpheme and to this view of word-structure in another chapter (Ch. v). But for the moment there is one important point which has to be noted. We said that morphemes are identified BY combinations of phonemes (or of other elements). We did not say, and it would have been wrong to say, that they are identified AS combinations of phonemes. From the grammarian's viewpoint *men* is the Plural corresponding to *man* and *those* the Plural corresponding to *that*. But the phonemic differences are not the same as in the case of *seas* and *sea* or *arms* and *arm*. If we looked at the regular Plurals alone we might be tempted to say that the second morpheme is 'composed of' the letter *s* or the phonetic [z], just as, it would seem, the element *sea* is composed of the letters *s*, *e* and *a* or the phonemes represented by [si:]. What then would we say of *men*? It has no ending *-s* or [z], and indeed does not have this structure at all. Should we say, perhaps, that only one of our minimal grammatical elements is involved? If so, then it is 'composed of' *m*, *e* and *n* in just the way that that other grammatical element *man* is composed of *m*, *a* and *n*. But for syntactic purposes this is nonsense. These grammatical elements are wanted precisely as the elements of grammar. It is accidental to their rôle whether they can be spelled out as letters or phonemes or not. As grammarians, we obviously want to say that the proportion *men*:*man*, *those*:*that*, *these*:*this*, etc., is part of the same proportion as *seas*:*sea*. 'Plurality' is identified by different phonemic variations in different cases: by a contrast of vowels in the first pair, by the complex of contrasts between final [ouz] and [æt] in the second, by the presence or absence of *-s* in the majority. But Plural, the morpheme of 'Plurality', remains constant.

Similar points can be made for the Verbs in the same passage. In the line:

> Whatever is begotten, born, and dies

there are two words, *begotten* and *born*, which grammarians traditionally classify as 'Past Participles'. If we then cite the final couplet of this verse:

> Caught in that sensual music all neglect
> Monuments of unageing intellect.

we find another, *caught*, and in the corresponding lines of the second verse:

> And therefore I have sailed the seas and come
> To the holy city of Byzantium.

there are two more, *sailed* and *come*. But if we examine the whole proportion *sailed*:*sail*, *born*:*bear*, *begotten*:*beget*, *caught*:*catch*, and so on, we cannot say that the 'Past Participle morpheme' is identified as or composed of any constant combination of phonemes. *Sailed*:*sail* has the regular pattern; compare *died*:*die* or *tried*:*try*. But there is a different ending in *born* and *begotten*, and moreover the preceding vowels are different: [bɔː] plus [n] versus [bɛə], [bigɔt] plus [n] versus [biget]. *Caught* [kɔːt] versus *catch* [kætʃ] shows a more extended contrast similar to that of *those* versus *that*. Finally, the pair *come*:*come* shows no contrast at all. In *I have sailed . . . and come* the word is identified as a Past Participle only by the syntactic construction.

It is with such variations that morphology is, in part, concerned. However, this is still not the whole of word structure; there are other aspects, often referred to under the heading of 'word formation' (Ch. III), which shade away into patterning of finer and finer subtlety. In Yeats's poem, *unageing* consists of *ageing* and a formative element *un-*, on the face of it in much the sense that *died* consists of *die* and *-d*. The latter has *-d* as its ending, whereas the former has *un-* as its 'beginning'. But is it quite the same sort of case? We will normally think of *died* and *die* as forms of the 'same word' (see Ch. II for this sense of 'word'). We would not expect them to have separate entries in a dictionary, and a statement about the meanings and syntactic uses of '*die*' would be taken to cover the Past Tense as well as the Present. We would likewise identify forms of the word '*age*' in both *It has aged* and *It will age*. But do we want to say that *unageing* is merely another form of the same word – the Negative form of the Participle, as it were, in contrast to the Positive *ageing* (e.g. in *He is ageing*)? Surely the answer is No. Indeed, whatever we think of *ageing* or *dying* in a Verbal construction of the type *He's ageing* or *He's dying*, do we still want to say that they are forms of the Verbs '*age*' or '*die*' when they appear in the phrase *his ageing father* or in Yeats's *those dying generations*? Again, a dictionary provides a rough practical test of our intuitions. We would certainly expect entries for *dying* and *undying*, and at least in a full dictionary for *ageing* and *unageing* also. The reader will find, for example, that the first pair have separate headings in the *Shorter OED*, and all four are in the *OED* proper. With many other forms in *-ing* the issue is even plainer: thus the Adjective *trying* which appears in *a trying day* is obviously not the same as the form of the Verb '*try*' which we analysed in *They are trying hard.*

Nevertheless they are related. We cannot say that *a trying day* has nothing whatever to do with the use of *tries* in *I find this weather tries me very hard*, or that *dying generations* and *unageing intellect* have nothing whatever to do with '*die*' and '*age*'. Moreover, it is a relationship of meaning as well as form: it is not simply that *dying* or the like are Adjectives which happen to have a Verbal sort of ending. If we now take the word *generations* it is formally no more than a Noun. It has the Plural ending of *trees*, *arms*, etc., and in a phrase such as *three generations ago* it may function as a straightforward time word, as such just a little more imprecise than *five decades ago* and much more so than the potentially exact *fifty years ago.* In *the modern generation* or *later generations* it is still a straight Noun, though of a slightly different class. But at the same time it is related in form to the Verb *generate*, and may be used with a definite Verbal nuance: thus *Electricity is clean, but its generation makes a mess* (effectively with Object *it* = *electricity*; compare *generating it*), or less explicitly in *the act of generation.* In Yeats's poem this relationship is clearly exploited. Although *those dying generations* has the syntactic construction of *later generations*, *that sensual music*, and so on, the underlying Verbal sense of *generate* may still be caught and put in opposition to the sense of '*die*' in *dying*. Similarly, the Adjective *sensual* (in the last couplet of this verse) has a formal and semantic connection with *sense* (compare *the gratification of the senses*) which brings it closer to its opposite *intellect* (compare *intellectual*). Yet an Adjective it remains.

Naturally, there are limits beyond which such analyses cannot be pushed. In one of Aldous Huxley's stories, a character feels like saying 'Bow-wow-wow!' when he hears the word 'cynic'.[1] Here (as often in Huxley's work), the resources are purely etymological – *cynic* being from a Greek Adjective formed from the word for 'dog' (κύων *kýɔːn*, Genitive κυνός *kynós*). So far as English is concerned, there is neither a formal nor a semantic connection between *cynic* on the one hand and *dog* or any comparable Noun on the other. But what of the other English Nouns in *-ic*? *Music* in Yeats's poem has an etymological connection

[1] 'The Gioconda Smile', *Collected Short Stories* (London, 1957), p. 93.

with *Muse*, just as *panic*, for example, is connected with *Pan*. The latter pair have no link in modern English, and indeed the god Pan will mean little to many speakers. But are *Muse* and *music* entirely divorced? There is certainly a morphological formative *-ic*, in Adjectives such as *horrific* or *melancholic*. Admittedly, no Nouns in *-ic* have a truly transparent analysis. But if a writer invokes an interplay between music and the Muses can we say with absolute confidence that it is etymology and not word structure that he is playing with?

The limits of morphological analysis can be illustrated with more humdrum examples. In *farmer* or *actor* we recognise a formative element *-er* or *-or* (phonetically both [ə]); the words have an obvious relationship to *farm* and to at least one sense of *act*. Well, let us go along the High Street. The *baker* is in origin someone who 'bakes', the *banker* runs a 'bank', the *furniture remover* 'removes furniture', and so on. What then of the *butcher*, the *grocer*, or the *ironmonger*? One answer might be that *butcher*, for instance, is indeed *butch-* plus *-er*; since this '*butch-*' is not connected in meaning with any other '*butch*', it would be established as a (so-called) 'partially independent' element, distinct from *-er* but nevertheless unable to enter into any other combination. Likewise *groc(e)-* and *mong-* would be extracted as elements which are restricted to *grocer*, *groceries*, *ironmonger*, and the like. The other answer, of course, is that words such as *butcher* are morphologically simple; but why, one then asks, do even simple 'occupation' Nouns so often end in *-er*? One can fruitlessly prolong the discussion of this kind of patterning.

But there will come a point at which no analyst will wish to pursue the chopping-up process further. Let us consider the points of the compass: *East*, *West*, *North* and *South*. The first two are opposite to each other on the dimension of longitude, and the words both end in *-st*. The others are opposite on the dimension of latitude, and both end in *-th*. Shall we therefore divide each into successive parts: an ending *-st* or *-th* for the 'East/West' or 'North/South' coordinate, preceded by four 'partially independent' elements *Ea-*, *We-*, *Nor-* and *Sou-*? Indeed shall we say that *Sou-* (phonetically [sau]) recurs independently in *Sou-wester*? In fact, we will not support such analyses. Even if there is something here worth saying, the pattern is too restricted to fall profitably within the morphological domain. Another case that is often discussed is that of phonaesthetic (loosely onomatopoeic) groupings: to take a well known example, is the *-mp* or *-ump* of *bump*, *thump*, etc., a separable element? If we separated it consistently, any attractions the analysis might have would rapidly dissolve. But can one say with precision where the domain of morphological analysis should end? If these are limiting cases, then are there general criteria by which the line is drawn? On the face of it, each of the cases which we have mentioned raises slightly different problems.

* * *

The reader will begin to agree, perhaps, that the study of morphology is important because it is there – a facet of language which, in itself, is the source of interesting problems. But it also impinges on more fashionable topics. In the past few years, much attention has been given (and rightly) to the boundary and interrelationships of grammar and semantics. But how can this be discussed unless the problems of *generation* or *sensual*, of certain compounds (see Chs. II and III), and of 'word formation' generally are taken into account? As we shall see in Ch. X, this branch of morphology has led to important controversies in Chomskyan syntax. The problems of language change have also returned to the forefront of linguistic theory, after a period of relative neglect in North America especially. But for the historical linguist too morphology is a central topic, partly because the reconstruction of formatives is an essential element in establishing genetic relationships, and also because the nature of morphological change is a fascinating field for the exploration and application of structural concepts. We cannot conveniently include historical morphology in this introduction (though see the references at the end of this chapter). But it can be expected to return to the forefront of discussion soon.

Another major topic is that of language universals. There are certain general features that appear to be common to all languages: double articulation is one, and 'creativeness' in all its various aspects (see Ch. XII) is another. These are among the 'design features', as we remarked, which set off human language from other sorts of 'language' either actual or possible. But some authors (notably Chomsky and his pupils) have advanced a multitude of much more detailed hypotheses. These concern the possible oppositions within a phonological system, the technical organisation of rules of syntax, the way that one such rule must hang together with another, the basic construction of sentences, and so on. Many proposals are so specific that one has to be well advanced in linguistics before one can understand them. As part of this programme, Chomsky has suggested that children would be genetically disqualified to learn a 'language' (a system of communication which could be a 'language' in some general sense of that term) which did not fall within the class that universal features of this sort are intended to delimit.

We are not concerned with the merits or demerits of this suggestion here. But it is advanced as an explanatory hypothesis: languages, it is said, ARE similar and this genetic restriction would explain why. It is therefore important that the universalist should look at areas in which no other explanation would be forthcoming. Phonetics and phonological oppositions will not do, since we can generally account for the evidence by physiological and auditory factors. It is hardly surprising that no language has a consonant articulated with the lower lip against the uvula; more seriously, there are known reasons for the close relationships of labials and velars in many systems, for such restrictions as exist on velarisation, retroflection and pharyngealisation, for the incidence of nasalisation with respect to vowel quality, and so on. Most semantic categories will not do either: again, it is no surprise if in all languages one can say something, by one mode of expression or another, about the location of an object in space. It is for such reasons that the technical study of grammar has assumed particular importance, and it is on his detailed theory of syntax that Chomsky has principally rested his case.

Morphology, however, is prima facie something of a challenge to the universalist hypothesis. In the nineteenth-century tradition, languages were said to be of strikingly different types. In some, grammarians speak of a 'word' without internal grammatical structure: according to the first typologies these were 'isolating' languages – Chinese and Vietnamese (Ch. IX) being notably of a near-isolating type. In others the word is a central, tightly knit, and often complex unit, carrying in itself many of the basic grammatical categories. Here the extreme cases form the 'inflecting' type, Spanish and Italian being modern examples and their parent Latin perhaps the most familiar to most educated Europeans. In others again the word is complex but more loosely knit, and categories are not so closely associated with the words individually. These form a third 'agglutinating' type, Turkish (see Chs. V and IX) being a stock example. This typology has since been criticised and elaborated; moreover, there are many languages (such as English) which stand between the extremes. But the extremes have not been seriously disputed. In some languages all grammarians will take the word as the basic unit of syntax, but in others (as we remarked earlier) it does not exist. Some are said to have a very complex morphology; others none at all. Now this is a level at which, once again, a set of universals is not to be expected on a priori phonetic or semantic grounds. If they WERE IN FACT discovered, it would be hailed as significant evidence bearing on the genetic hypothesis. But then it is surely suspicious if, to all appearances, there are none. Why should languages vary so widely, in such a fundamental aspect of their grammatical articulation, if (as alleged) they are all cut to the same template?

At the same time linguists have tended to describe morphology with the aid of markedly different theoretical 'models'. In an important article of the mid 1950s, Hockett pin-pointed three models of grammatical analysis in general – three different 'frames of reference' (to adapt his words) within which an analyst might 'approach the grammatical description of a language and state the results of his investigation' (HOCKETT, *Models*, init.). One was the 'Word and Paradigm' model, which we will begin to elucidate in Ch. IV. Another he labelled 'Item and Arrangement', referring to an approach based on the morpheme which we will expound in Ch. V particularly. The third he called 'Item and Process', its starting point being the processes discussed in Ch. VII. We will return to these models in Ch. XII, by which time all the relevant points will have been illustrated. But is each model just as suitable, in fact, for any group of languages? In practice, different types will often be described in different ways, and not merely through inculcated theoretical prejudice. Again, can the universalist show that the same model or template suits them all?

This is for the most part not an argumentative work, and we will not be able to pursue the topic of universals systematically. But if one model could indeed be justified – justified and not imposed by fiat, naturally – it would be a major contribution to the intellectual debate. For that reason too, it is unfortunate that morphology has been relatively neglected in the past fifteen or more years.

RELATED READING

For Chomsky's treatment of the English Verb see CHOMSKY, *Structures*, pp. 38–42, but 'deep' and 'surface' structure are later (see Reading for Ch. X). For the semantic categories see PALMER, though he reserves 'Tense' for Present versus Past in particular.

For Pike's and Halliday's theories see also Reading for Ch. V. For Hjelmslev's views on morphology/syntax see L. Hjelmslev, *Prolegomena to a Theory of Language*, 2nd ed. (Madison, 1961), pp. 26, 59, but his positive conceptions are more accessible in *Language: an Introduction* (Madison, 1970), both works being in very clear translations by F. J. Whitfield. Bloomfield's account of morphology (BLOOMFIELD, pp. 207ff.) rests on his account of the word (see below, Ch. IX).

For the first and second articulations see MARTINET, §1.8, but Martinet's term 'moneme' (for a unit of the first articulation: MARTINET, §1.9) is not general. For double articulation generally see A. Martinet, *La linguistique synchronique: études et recherches* (Paris, 1965), Ch. 1 (largely reprints of important articles). The term 'duality' is that of Hockett (e.g. HOCKETT, *Course*, p. 574); to distinguish this from the 'duality' of sound and meaning, perhaps 'duality of patterning' (as in Hockett's index) or 'duality of structure' (e.g. Lyons in *New Horizons*, p. 12) is preferable. For 'design features' or 'key properties' of language see HOCKETT, *Course*, p. 574; valuable discussion by HOUSEHOLDER, Ch. 3.

The term 'morpheme' has been used in many senses; for the most important distinction see ROBINS, p. 203, for more detail the other references in *Inflectional Morphology*, pp. 41^6, 42^2. The usage here is effectively that of the Post-Bloomfieldian school; see Reading for Ch. V below. 'Formative' is not an established term; for my usage see *Inflectional Morphology*, pp. 57^2, 185.

For 'partially independent' elements see HARRIS, p. 177; the stock example, discussed by various authors, is the *cran-* of *cranberry*. For phonaesthesis, onomatopoeia or sound symbolism generally see ULLMANN, pp. 82ff.; O. Jespersen, *Language: its Nature, Development and Origin* (London, 1922), Ch. 20. For *bump* or *thump* type examples see BLOOMFIELD, pp. 244–6, BOLINGER, pp. 15, 242f.; also more generally in D. L. Bolinger, *Forms of English: Accent, Morpheme, Order* (Tokyo, 1965), Part 2, Chs. 2–5 (selected papers edited by I. Abe and T. Kaneyiko). For the limits of analysis in general see Bolinger's 'On defining the morpheme' (*Ibid.*, Part 2, Ch. 1), but note that his distinction of 'formative' and 'morpheme' is different from mine.

For the role of morphology in reconstruction and comparison see A. Meillet, *La méthode comparative en linguistique historique* (Oslo, 1925), Ch. 3: for morphological change *Ibid.*, pp. 91ff., 100ff.; also WARTBURG, §§2.3–4. The leading student of diachronic morphology is Jerzy Kuryłowicz; although there is no easy introduction, important papers are reprinted in *Esquisses linguistiques*, 2nd ed. (Munich, 1973) and general points are included in *The Inflectional Categories of Indo-European* (Heidelberg, 1964). Other learned papers of interest include C. E. Bazell, 'A question of syncretism and analogy', *TPhS*, 1960, pp. 1–12; Y. Malkiel, 'The inflectional paradigm as an occasional determinant of sound change', in *Historical Linguistics*, pp. 21–64.

For Chomsky's theory of language universals see CHOMSKY, *Aspects*, Ch. 1; CHOMSKY, *Mind*, especially Ch. 2; also J. Lyons, *Chomsky* (London, 1970), Chs. 9–10. For morphological typology see ROBINS, pp. 331–8, LYONS, pp. 187ff.; for the history Jespersen, *Language*, Book 1, passim. The main twentieth-century contribution is that of SAPIR, Ch. 6.

II
Word, word-form and lexeme

Different senses of 'word': words and lexemes; homonymy and syncretism; lexical homonymy; words and word-forms.
Practical illustrations: counts of word frequency; concordances and collocations.
Phonological words and grammatical words; lexemes, compounds, idioms.

The reader may have noticed that the term 'word' has been used in two, or perhaps three, different senses. We said, first of all, that the opening sentence of Yeats's poem:

That is no country for old men.

was made up of seven words, and that each of these was made up of varying numbers of letters or phonemes. Likewise in a Horatian tag about a river:

Labitur et labetur in omne volubilis aevum.

'It glides past and will continue to glide past, rolling on for all time' (*Epistles*, I, 2. 43) we will distinguish a seven-letter word *labitur* '[it] glides', a two-letter word *et* 'and', and so on. The ancient grammarians would already have analysed the line in this way, saying more precisely that *labitur* was built up of the three syllables *la*, *bi* and *tur*, and that it was these in turn which were built up of the letters *l*, *a*, etc. Similarly, the English word *country* could, in the first instance, be divided phonetically into the syllables [kʌn] and [tri], with stress on the first. In all this we are describing a 'word' in terms of phonological units: syllables and ultimately letters or phonemes, considered as the primitives or minimal elements (in the Ancient Greek philosophers' term the στοιχεῖα) of the secondary articulation of language. Let us refer to this, for the moment, as a characterisation of the 'word' in sense I.

At the same time we said, for example, that *dies* and *died* (two different words in sense I) are nevertheless varying forms of the SAME word '*die*'. Similarly, *man* and *men* are two different forms (Singular and Plural) of the one word '*man*', and in the line of Horace which we have cited there are two different forms *labitur* 'glides' and *labetur* '[it] will glide', of the one word which we look up in the dictionary as '*labor*' ('slip', 'glide', etc.). The distinction is perhaps more familiar in Latin than in English, since we are used to thinking of the forms of Latin words (the forms being the 'words' in sense 1) as set out in paradigms for learning purposes. We will look up '*amo*' ('love') in the dictionary, but we know that this subsumes a battery of forms which may be classified as 1st Person, 2nd Person and 3rd Person (*amo* 'I love', *amas* 'you [sg.] love', *amat* '[he] loves'), and then again as Present or Perfect (*amo* 'I love', *amavi* 'I loved, have loved') and so on. So, if we came across a particular form such as *amat* or *amavi* in a particular passage of literature we might ask 'What exactly is the force or significance of "*amo*" here?', meaning not the individual form *amo* (the word in sense 1), but the dictionary word '*amo*' to which it and *amat*, and *amavi*, and many other variant forms belong.

The words which we have been writing in inverted commas ('*amo*', '*labor*', '*die*' or '*man*') are plainly words in a different sense from that in which our assemblages of syllables, letters or phonemes (*died*, *labitur*, *man* or *amo* specifically) are words. Let us, for the moment, simply refer to this as the 'word' in sense 2. It should be obvious that the word in sense 2 is not, as such, composed or built up of any kind of smaller element. It is instead an ABSTRACT unit. It belongs to the grammatical or primary articulation of language, and when we talk about its properties they are most usually characteristics of syntactic classification (for instance, the word '*die*' is a Verb) or of meaning (for example, '*die*' is in one sense opposite in meaning to '*live*'). Again, if we say that '*man*' and '*die*' are very common words in English the statement is neutral not only between the variants *man* or *men*, *die* or *died*, etc., but also between the written forms *man* etc. (which are analysable in terms of letters), and the spoken [mæn] etc. (which are analysable in terms of phonemes).

This point may perhaps need underlining. When we look up '*amo*' or '*labor*' in a Latin dictionary we do, of course, expect to find them in alphabetical order. We therefore open the book at the beginning or towards the middle and scan the page headings for '*a*' or '*am*', for '*l*', '*lab*', and so on. And perhaps we are mildly narked if we look up the Adjective '*volubilis*' (as in our Horatian example) and find that it has been printed '*uolubilis*', with the modern letters '*v*' and '*u*' conflated together. In this practical sense it may seem that '*labor*' and '*volubilis*' or '*uolubilis*' are indeed composed of letters. However, this is a property of the symbol (the way the object is represented), not of the object itself which is being symbolised. In talking about Latin it has always been the custom to refer to words in sense 2 by means of the Nominative Singular of Nouns (e.g. the word '*mensa*', meaning 'table'), and the 1st Singular Present Indicative of Verbs. In talking about French or Italian, however, the accepted usage is to refer to Verbs by the Infinitive instead: the Verb '*aimer*' or the Verb '*amare*' (both 'love' once again). For some other languages, such as Sanskrit, dictionaries are organised by stems or roots (see Chs. III and IV); this is like taking '*am-*' as the heading for the dictionary entry for '*amo*', '*mens-*' for that of '*mensa*', or '*lab-*' for that of '*labor*'. But whichever symbolic convention we adopt, the object which we are talking about will remain the same. If we did happen to refer to French Verbs by the 1st Singular or to Latin Nouns by the root it would not affect their identity, as such, in the slightest.

In order to reinforce this abstract status it will be helpful to make a small change in the way the symbol is written. So far we have been trying to do this with inverted commas, but they are untidy and the lower case letters still suggest too close a connection with the individual forms in sense 1. From now on we shall therefore follow a convention by which the word in sense 2 is represented by small capitals: thus Latin AMO, English LOVE, French AIMER, and so on. At the same time, it is also convenient to have a new term for the 'word' in this sense. Linguists are notorious for introducing new terms as soon as they can detect the finest distinction, and often their coinages last no longer than they deserve. But in this case it does seem genuinely helpful. We shall therefore refer to the word in sense 2 as the **lexeme** – the fundamental unit (compare other terms in '-eme' such as 'phoneme' and 'morpheme') of the lexicon of the language. This is a usage which is beginning to establish itself in linguistic writings, and which can be related to other senses of the term going back over roughly thirty years (compare the end of this chapter). So, to sum up, we will say that *dies*, *died*, *dying* and *die* are forms of the lexeme DIE, that *man* and *men* are the Singular and Plural of MAN, that the lexeme MAN is a Noun but DIE a Verb, likewise in Latin that *amo* and *amat* are both forms of the lexeme AMO, that *mensa* is the Nominative Singular of the Noun MENSA, that AMO 'love' is contrary in meaning to ODI 'hate', and so on.

Having distinguished the lexeme in this sense, we might then reserve the term 'word' for our original sense 1. So, conversely, MAN would have as its forms the two words *man* and *men*, and the paradigm of AMO would comprise the words *amo* 'I love', *amas* 'you love', and so on. But there is still another distinction which is implicit in some of our discussion in Ch. I. In the case of *a trying day*, we remarked that the Adjective '*trying*' is not the same as the other '*trying*' which appears in *They are trying hard*. We will now say, of course, that two different lexemes are involved: an Adjective TRYING in the first example but the Verb TRY in the second. However, this is not quite enough, since we still want to say that the first '*trying*' as such is a different word from the second '*trying*', likewise as such. In more technical terms we have two different units (one a form of TRYING, the other of TRY) which are nevertheless **homonymous**. The notion that words may be homonymous will be familiar to most readers. But in what precise terms should homonymy be defined?

Similar identities can be demonstrated for forms of the same lexeme in most languages. In *He came* and *He has come* we distinguish a Past Tense *came* and a Past Participle *come*, both of which belong to the lexeme COME. In *He tried* and *He has tried* the first '*tried*' must again be Past Tense and the second again the Past Participle; for TRY (as for most English Verbs) the two forms are identical both in spelling and in phonetics. The term 'syncretism' (in origin a term in diachronic linguistics) is often applied synchronically to this situation. In English there is regularly a **syncretism** (according to some writers a 'neutralisation') between the Past Tense and the Past Participle endings. On the other hand, while TRY has no distinction here, the forms of COME exhibit a much less usual pattern of homonymy in which the Past Participle (the '*come*' of *He has come*) is identical with the Present form (the '*come*' of *They come*). Grammatically, the two words are again as different as *tried* and *try*. In a language such as Latin regular syncretisms leap to the eye in sets of paradigms. The most cited case is in the Nominative and Accusative of Neuters. In Horace's phrase *in omne . . . aevum* 'for all time' the words *omne* 'all' and *aevum* 'time' are Accusative, this being the construction required by the Preposition *in*. But in other constructions identical forms would appear as the Nominatives of the same lexemes. The distinction of Nominative and Accusative endings is **syncretised** (or, again, 'neutralised') in any Neuter paradigm.

In all these statements it is evident that we are again using the term 'word' in two different senses. Our original 'word in sense I' was described as an assemblage of syllables and phonemes (or syllables and letters). Accordingly, two such words can be said to differ if and only if their composition differs. *Tries*, *trying* and *tried*, *came* and *come*, etc., all differ in one or more elements, but *tried*, *trying* or *come* are in this sense three words and three words only. Similarly, *omne* is the one disyllable built up of *om-* and *-ne*, and *aevum* the one such unit built up of *ae-* and *-vum*. Homonymy then arises when a single word as it appears on the basis of phonology or spelling (sense I) nevertheless corresponds to more than one word in another, essentially grammatical, sense. Thus, as we have seen, there are two words in this other sense – sense 3, let us provisionally call it – which correspond to the one written or spoken word *come*. In more technical terms, homonymy is one particular facet of the discrepancies between the two articulations of language (see Ch. I).

This situation can be shown within or across the paradigms of lexemes, as we have seen. But naturally we can have the further case where two whole paradigms are homonymous at every point. If we compare the examples *I struck a match* and *I had to strike two matches* with *He won the match* and *He only won two matches* we might distinguish two separate '*match*' lexemes. Dictionaries usually give them separate headings (if only because they have different etymologies!), and following common dictionary notation we can distinguish them as MATCH^1 and MATCH^2. But each form of MATCH^1 (e.g. Singular *match*) is homonymous with the corresponding form of MATCH^2. This is the clearest sort of instance in which we would normally speak of 'lexical' homonymy: a reasonable abbreviation is to say that the lexemes themselves are formally identical. But of course there are others, in appearance at least. In many instances our conventions force us to head two dictionary entries with the same 'word', even though, in fact, there are distinctions elsewhere in the paradigms. For example, we also have a Verb which appears in *They match beautifully* – MATCH^3 we will have to call it. But we could make a distinction without superscripts if the tradition was to represent Verbs by Participles (MATCHING) instead. Many such instances may be seen more exactly in terms of the homonymy of roots or stems (*match-*) in the sense of Chs. III and IV below.

But for the moment we are still concerned with words. This third sense of the term – the word in sense 3 – may also be approached from another angle. One sort of 'word analysis', as we have seen, is in terms of syllables and phonemes. So English [bi'gɔtn̩] *begotten* may be analysed into three syllables [bi], [gɔ], [tn̩], with stress on the second. The corresponding synthetic statement – a statement of synthesis as opposed to analysis – is that phonemes are 'built up' to form syllables and syllables built up to form the word (in sense 1) as a whole. But words may also be analysed, as we saw in Ch. I, in terms of the primary or grammatical articulation of language. For the student of grammar *begotten* is not a primitive. It has an analysis involving at least two elements, one of which we will now refer to as the lexeme BEGET and the other the element 'Past Participle' which we earlier referred to as a morpheme. What, then, is the corresponding statement of synthesis at this level? As we have seen, the minimal elements of grammar are not identified as combinations of phonological units – the bits, as it were, of the word in sense 1. The unit which is 'built up' of BEGET and 'Past Participle' is a 'word' in another sense, and obviously our sense 3 precisely. In our Western grammatical tradition, this unit would be identified by a verbal formula of the type 'the Past Participle of BEGET': more elaborately, we will say that *begotten* or [bigɔtn] (the word in sense 1) 'is' – i.e. is the written or phonetic form taken by – the Past Participle of this lexeme. It is this verbal formula (which we will discuss more precisely at the beginning of Ch. VIII) which distinguishes the word in the sense we are now concerned with. Similarly, to go back to our homonyms, we will say that *tried* is either 'the Past Participle of TRY' or 'the Past Tense of TRY' instead. There is at least one other way in which the structure of the word in sense 3 might be expressed (see Ch. V), but for the moment this traditional style is perfectly adequate.

The distinction which we have just drawn is naturally neither crucial nor relevant on all occasions. When we are concerned with the syntax of a sentence and we say, for example, that in Horace's *in omne volubilis aevum* 'rolling on for all time' the Preposition *in* governs the 'words' *omne aevum* (these words being in the Accusative and not, as in some other constructions with *in*, in the Ablative), our reference to the Cases 'Accusative' and 'Ablative' makes clear that we are talking of words in sense 3. We must be, since we are analysing the phrase at the grammatical level. But it would be stupid not to represent the words we are talking about by their ordinary written forms. To say that the Preposition IN governs the Accusative Singular Neuter of OMNIS followed by the Accusative Singular of AEVUM (however strictly it derives from our principles) would lead to a cumulatively rather tiresome grammar. It is equally obvious, when we speak of phonemes in 'word-final' position or in the position 'before the word-boundary', that we are talking of words in sense 1. Again, we may say that Horace's line has 'seven words', meaning either words in sense 1 or words in sense 3 (since here – though see later in this chapter – there is no practical consequence of discriminating between them). For this reason, it would be pedantic to impose a distinction of terms – 'word^1' and 'word^3', as it were – and insist on following it throughout. The distinction of words in general (senses 1 or 3) and lexemes (sense 2) is the one which has to be maintained most consistently.

Nevertheless, it is useful to be able to make the terminological opposition where we need it. One obvious way of doing so would be to call the word in sense 1 the 'phonological' (or 'orthographic') word, and the word in sense 3 the 'grammatical word'. These are the terms adopted in one widely used textbook (LYONS, p. 196; also in *New Horizons*, p. 22). But it is in morphology that the difference must most frequently be drawn, and it is perhaps a little awkward to have to use qualifiers. Furthermore, there is another slightly different sense for which this terminology may be reserved, as we shall see in the final section of this chapter. A neater alternative is to refer to the word in sense 1, where the distinction is necessary, as the **word-form**. Thus it is the word-form *tried* or [traid] which is analysable in terms of letters or phonemes. An additional convenience of this usage, it will be seen, is that we can use the same term 'word-form' whether we are speaking of phonetic forms or of writing. The term **word** may then be reserved, in the strictest usage, for sense 3. Thus the word-form *tried* is the form of the word which we call 'the Past Participle (or the Past Tense) of TRY'. Again, we would say that the first sentence of Yeats's poem has six monosyllabic word-forms (*this*, *is*, *no*, *for*, *old* and *men*) out of seven, the remaining word-form (*country*) being a disyllable. On the other hand, we will not say that word-forms are, as such, Nouns or Verbs or Participles, etc.

* * *

At this stage, some readers may possibly be beginning to feel that we are being over-careful. Must we really say, for instance, that in *a trying day* the word-form *trying* corresponds to the word '*trying*' and this happens to be the only member of the paradigm of the lexeme TRYING? Although we have given reasons – comparing this '*trying*' with that of *They are trying hard* – is it not rather tiresome for this one Adjective in isolation? Well, perhaps if we concentrate on the individual case we do seem to be multiplying entities beyond necessity. But the distinctions which we have made can often be very important. How, for example, do we go about 'counting words' for statistical analysis? When we say that *x* is a commoner word than *y* or that in *A*'s writings the word *x* appears more often than in *B*'s, we are usually implying that *x* and *y* are lexemes. But it would be as well to check and make clear that this is so. If we say that English has more monosyllabic words than Latin, or that there are proportionately more such words in Yeats's later poetry than in Joos's *Readings in Linguistics*, we are instead talking strictly of word-forms. In still other cases we may want to count words in our specifically grammatical sense. Again, it would be important to decide precisely what we were doing.

A concrete illustration may help to bring home the pitfalls. Let us suppose, first of all, that we want to count the number of times that individual Verbs occur in Henry James's novels. We might want to compare the figures with those for some other novelist, or to compare figures for earlier and later works to elucidate the way in which James's style developed. Even cruder 'indices' have been computed for some literary purposes (to prove, as it were, that *The Wings of the Dove* and *The Europeans* cannot possibly have been written by the same man!). Now we will, of course, decide to make our counts by computer. To be precise, we might ask our programmer to print out a complete list of all the different words which appear in any particular novel (we will call these the word **types**, following a fairly normal usage), and to set against each the total number of occurrences in that novel (the total number of **tokens**). We can then look at the list of types ourselves, and pick out whichever words (e.g. Verbs) we happen to be interested in.

Well, let us begin by feeding in the first chapter of *The Portrait of a Lady*. What exactly will the computer do? It should be obvious that if this is all we have said it is liable to do some very silly things. Our programmer will naturally have taken 'words' to mean 'sequences of letters between spaces'. If not, he would have thrown the problem back at once and asked how on earth he is supposed to get the machine to discriminate. So, for a start, different forms of lexemes will be taken as different types; in the dialogue:

> 'Does it mean that . . .? or does it simply mean that . . .?'
> 'Whatever else it means, it's pretty sure to mean that, . . .'

we would have three tokens of the type *mean* and one of the type *means*.

This might not greatly matter; we could just add up the totals at the end. But in two earlier passages we have two other tokens of this second type *means*: 'She chiefly communicates with us by means of telegrams'; 'Because you have – haven't you? – such unlimited means'. We do not want these conflated with the first '*means*', but how can our machine do otherwise? How do we then know, when we get our output, which tokens of *means* were forms of the Verb MEAN and which were not?

A glance through James's text, or through any other text in English for that matter, will show that there are many word-forms that are orthographically homonymous between one part of speech and another. Very often there is a semantic connection: for example, the forms *mind*, *house* [haus], *perfect* ['pəːfikt], *close* [klous], *man*, or *mellow* (which are among those appearing as Nouns or Adjectives in the novel's first paragraph) are more or less closely related to the Verb-forms *mind*, *house* [hauz], *perfect* [pə'fekt], *close* [klouz], etc. But there are others (harder to spot!) where there is none. Still in James's first paragraph, the *rest* of 'the rest of the set', the *object* ['ɔbdʒikt] of 'the most characteristic object', the *still* of 'still to come', or the *long* of 'the shadows were long upon the . . . turf' have nothing at all to do with Verbal *rest*, *object* [əb'dʒekt], and so on. To pursue *long* a little further, it appears Adjectivally three times on the first two pages of my copy. After all, it is a pretty common epithet. But the Verb LONG, as in *I always long for silence*, is not so ordinary. Our figures would be meaningless if the two were conflated.

What do we do then? We have got our novel on tape, and we hardly want to waste the investment. Perhaps we will pause and think: what if we can get the computer to assign parts of speech labels automatically? All it needs (we will say) is a few ingenious routines for automatic syntactic analysis, and we will get accuracy at least to a respectable percentage. And so we must embark on a quite new task which has nothing whatever to do with the one we originally had in mind. If we had thought carefully at the outset – and had still decided we wanted to count Verbs in James's novels! – we would have realised that we are concerned with the tokens of lexemes and not of word-forms, and that the simplest way of indicating forms of Verbal lexemes is to mark them in the text by hand. If we had grasped that we might never have brought in the computer at all.

This may seem a naive little parable. But to any reader who had contact with the field of computational linguistics in the early 1960s it will not ring entirely false. Various projects foundered or ran into greater trouble and expense because the investigators did not first respect these seemingly pedantic distinctions. One field where real progress has been made, however, is in the automatic preparation of concordances or indexes. If we do want to provide a tool for studying an author's use of words, we would be wise to think of this sort of project. But it is again worth asking: what exactly do we mean by indexing the set of 'words' which a writer employs?

It will be obvious that the WORD-FORM is not the sort of 'word' in which the user of a concordance is most likely to be interested. As in a dictionary, our headings will ideally be LEXEMES; we might like to follow some standard dictionary in determining when lexemes are the same or different. But will the user be interested in WORDS, in the strictly grammatical sense, as well? Perhaps it might be instructive to study which Verbs, let us say, are used most frequently in 'Progressive' or 'Continuous' Tenses (e.g. the Latin or Italian Imperfect) and which in 'Non-Progressive'. Or is it rather that we should show, in general, how the individual LEXEMES are USED grammatically? Certainly, there are general grammatical distinctions which a user might want to take into account. So, for example, in Merguet's set of concordances for Cicero the entries for Verbs distinguish between an Absolute and a Transitive construction, and in the detailed volumes they also note which particular Nouns appear as the Object in individual instances.[1] This was a concordance made by hand by a specialist. But by a well-planned collaboration between hand-sorting and machine-sorting (e.g. by marking forms in the text before computation or by finer clerical work afterwards) we could in principle get the same results.

The answers will at least bear thinking about. For one particular application let us consider the problem of studying the significant co-occurrences – the collocations, to use a widespread term – of one 'word' with another. Now, of course, the co-occurrent pairs will not always be adjacent in the text; for example, in the following imaginary dialogue:

'What do you do with potatoes?'

'Well, you can just boil them, or you can bake them in the oven, or you can roast them – you know, in a pan with fat – or you can chip them, or sauté them (that means boiling them and then slicing them and frying them), or you can mash them', etc. etc.

[1] H. Merguet, *Lexicon zu den Reden des Cicero*, 4 Vols. (Jena, 1877–84), *Lexicon zu den philosophischen Schriften Cicero's*, 3 Vols. (Jena, 1887–94).

a student of cooking vocabulary would be interested in the collocations of FRY and POTATO, MASH and POTATO, SAUTÉ and POTATO, etc., regardless of the distance between them in the text. Since many concordances only show the immediately adjacent forms they would not, perhaps, be the perfect basis for this inquiry. But in general they are an excellent starting-point – even if (as in this example) we might be forced to check back to the original.

Here we have identified the collocations in terms of the lexemes FRY, SAUTÉ, POTATO, etc. But we would need to consider carefully whether this is always the right thing to do. Let us suppose, for example, that we want to investigate the co-occurrence ranges of Adverbs. In *He'll make it very badly* we have the pair *make* and *badly*. In *He made it very badly* we have *made* and *badly* instead. The Tense does not appear to be significant and we will therefore say that in both we have the same collocation of BADLY and the lexeme MAKE. But the Tense is not insignificant in the case of Time Adverbs. If we found an instance of *He made it soon* (Full stop: not, e.g., *He made it soon afterwards* or *He soon made it*) it would be just the sort of usage that should engage our attention. As a native speaker, asked in vacuo whether the Past Tense with final SOON is 'correct' or not, I find I cannot reasonably give an answer. We would likewise be interested if we found anything of the type *He was making it suddenly* (Note, not *He was suddenly making it*). In these cases, therefore, we would not want to register collocations of lexeme with lexeme. Indeed, this is a relationship which is not strictly between words either, but between the whole Time-expressions (which will often be phrases, *next week*, *come the Autumn*, etc.) and the categories of Verb phrases. If we want to study the lexical patterns by which 'words go together', we had better start by making clear what we mean by 'words'.

This last illustration leads us to the theoretical problems of meaning. It is part of the meaning of SAUTÉ, at least in the author's non-technical speech, that it collocates with POTATO only. Restrictions on the collocability of SOON or SUDDENLY at least reflect, and are thus important evidence for, the meanings of these lexemes. Here we are concerned with the semantic relationships which words and lexemes can contract within a text or spoken discourse. In Ch. I we have already referred to the problem of semantic relationship within the lexicon itself: the relations between GENERATION (as we will now represent it) and GENERATE, between SENSUAL and SENSE, and so on. There too the analyst of meaning may sometimes have to consider particular members of the paradigm (the Plural form in *the senses*, for example). It is hardly surprising that the terminological distinction between word and lexeme (in our present sense) was first brought to the fore in one of the few studies of the 1960s to achieve a real progress in semantic theory.[1]

* * *

At first sight, one way of summing up this chapter would be to say that we have distinguished words at three linguistic levels: the word in phonology or orthography (the word-form), in grammar (the word proper) and in the lexicon (the lexeme). But we ought to end by looking at one or two qualifications. In the first clause of Virgil's *Aeneid*:

Arma virumque cano 'I sing of arms and the man'

(Word by word 'arms' – 'man–and' – 'I sing of'), *virumque* is a 'word' in the conventional sense of orthographic spacing. Moreover, these spaces have a sound justification in Latin phonetics. In the classical period the accent or stress was predictable, given the word-boundaries so indicated and the form of the next to last syllable. By the same general rules *labitur* in the line of Horace was stressed on the first syllable *lá-*, *labetur* (which has a long vowel in the next to last syllable) on that syllable *bé-* and *virumque* as *virúmque*. Purely for phonological reasons, therefore, it is possible to establish a hierarchy of three successively larger units: the phoneme (roughly corresponding to letters), the syllable (divided into at least two different types), and the word as it is conventionally demarcated. *Virumque* is one instance of this largest unit.

But, as the gloss 'man–and' may already have suggested, this is not so satisfactory when we turn our attention to the level of grammar. Just as the 'word' in Latin phonology is marked by the accentual pattern, so in Latin grammar it is marked by the patterns of inflectional endings. From this viewpoint *virumque* is an anomaly. The *-que* element ('and') is not an 'ending' in the sense of an inflectional formative. It is not specific to any particular class of lexeme, but can be attached to anything (Noun, Verb or whatever) if it is syntactically appropriate. Let us just say that it is a particular sort of 'Particle'. At the same time *virum* is a word or word-form in itself, which can appear separately in *virum cano* 'I sing of the man' or in other constructions. No classical

[1] J. Lyons, *Structural Semantics* (Oxford, 1963), p. 11.

scholar would accept that *virumque* as a whole is simply one member of a Nominal paradigm: 'the Conjunctional Accusative Singular of VIR' or the like. Although the phonologist must say that *virum-* is not here a separate 'word' in his sense (though in *virum cano* of course it is), the grammarian has equally good reasons for saying that it is one in his.

This discrepancy is evidently different from our earlier discrepancies between words and word-forms. There we were talking, in particular, of homonymies within or across the paradigms of a language. Here we are concerned with two divergent analyses of a specific phrase or sentence. In the phonology we establish one hierarchy, in which the 'word' is distinguished from the phoneme and the syllable as smaller units and also from larger units which might be set up as the domains of intonational features. In grammar we then establish another, in which it is distinguished from larger units such as the phrase and clause and perhaps from smaller units such as the morpheme (Ch. I). Now of these various units the syllable and morpheme would not correspond in Latin and still less in English. In some languages it is even difficult to establish anything corresponding to the word on purely phonological grounds. French is a notorious instance (see Ch. IX): in the sentence *Je ne la connais point* 'I don't know her at all' the student of grammar may wish to say that at least *connais* and *point* are words in his sense, but for the phonologist the whole piece [ʒənlakɔnɛ'pwɛ̃][1] is a unitary sequence of syllables. In Latin, however, a discrepancy of 'words' arises only with the two Conjunctions *-que* 'and' and *-ve* 'or' and an Interrogative Particle *-ne*. Where the correspondence is as close as this, substantially the same unit can be said to enter into both the phonological and the grammatical hierarchies.

Nevertheless, the 'words' in phonology and grammar are not quite co-extensive. It is in this context, therefore, that we can perhaps best use the qualified terms **phonological word** and **grammatical word** (which, as the reader will recall, we rejected for 'word-form' and 'word' earlier in this chapter). So, if the point has to be made, *virumque* is allotted to the phonological word as a unit in the hierarchy at that level. That is, it is a 'word' established ultimately by phonological criteria. The word-form, though also describable in terms of phonological units, is in case of argument identified by criteria drawn from grammar. That

[1] French will be transcribed following Harrap's dictionary (MANSION).

is, it is the written or phonological form representing a 'word' established as part of the grammatical hierarchy. We will naturally continue to use the unqualified term in this latter sense, since it is that unit which is central to the morphological investigation.

A quite different discrepancy arises between the lexeme as considered from the grammarian's viewpoint, and a 'lexeme' which might be posited on strictly 'lexical' grounds. In the phrase *a block of ice* the word *ice* belongs to the lexeme ICE, and in *a jug of cream* the word *cream* belongs to the lexeme CREAM. But what of *ice-cream* in *I want some ice-cream*? In this last example *ice* and *cream* are certainly 'words' in one sense. In the author's speech (though not that of all speakers) the pattern of stress is identical to that of a normal Adjective plus Noun construction: e.g. *I want some fresh cream.* But the semantic relationships are different. In *some fresh cream* the Adjective functions as the Modifier of the Noun, both being freely replaceable by forms of other lexemes. We could say *some thick cream* or *some sour cream*, or alternatively *some fresh milk* or *some fresh lemonade*, and in either case the meaning of *cream* or *fresh* would remain constant. But in *some ice-cream* there is no modification: we are not talking of a particular sort of 'cream' ('ice cream' as opposed to 'thick cream' or 'double cream', and so on) but of a separate commodity which is 'ice-cream' specifically. This meaning cannot be predicted from those of ICE and CREAM as such, and the dictionary writer must therefore give it in a separate entry (as in the *OED*) or in a special subentry under '*ice*' or '*cream*' or both. '*Ice-cream*', that is to say, is a distinct unit from the semantic or the lexicographical viewpoint.

It is in such a case that some writers have found the term 'lexeme' particularly appropriate. Although in one sense or at one level *ice-cream* remains, as at first sight, *ice* plus *cream*, nevertheless in another sense or at another level it is simply one more unit in the lexical inventory of the language. So far, of course, we may happily go along with this: ICE-CREAM, we can say, is a **compound lexeme** related by a process of 'composition' or 'compounding' (see further Ch. III) to the simple lexemes ICE and CREAM. But how far should we go? *He made up his mind* has a meaning which is not predictable from those of MAKE, UP, MIND and so on. *He pulled his socks up* has one meaning which is not predictable (compare the equally metaphorical *He pulled himself together*) alongside another which is (He literally 'pulled up his socks'). A dictionary writer would ideally like to list these as 'idioms' ('*to pull one's* *socks up*', '*to make up one's mind*') under one entry or another: one need only dip into the detailed Harrap's dictionary for French and English (MANSION) to see how important this is for a foreign user in particular. Should we accordingly extend the term 'lexeme' to cover idioms also? If we were operating by purely semantic criteria it would not seem unreasonable that we should do so. But is this, in fact, the same sort of case as the one already exemplified by *ice-cream*?

From the grammarian's viewpoint there are good reasons for saying that it is not. In *He pulled his socks up* the form *pulled* is still the Past Tense of the Verb PULL, and as such contrasts with other Verbal forms (*He must pull his socks up*, *He's showing signs of pulling his socks up*, etc.) regardless of whether the idiomatic or literal sense is intended. Again, *his* is specifically the Possessive form of HE, replaceable by a form of THEY in *They pulled their socks up*, by a form of another Pronoun SHE in *She'll have to pull her socks up*, and so on. Of course, the idiom brings with it certain restrictions: *socks* cannot be replaced by the Singular *sock* (*He must pull his sock up* can only be understood literally), and there must be agreement between the Subject of PULL and the Possessive (I cannot say of my pupil that *I shall have to pull his socks up* for him). But all this is stated in terms of the lexeme PULL, a particular form of the lexeme SOCK, of particular members in a construction of Verb + Possessive + Object, and so on, and not in terms of a unitary 'PULL SOCKS UP' element. By contrast, ICE-CREAM can be handled like any normal lexeme of its Nominal class. It can have its epithets and modifiers like any other Noun: *nice fresh creamy ice-cream* alongside *nice fresh creamy milk*, and so on. Nor does the student of syntax have to say anything specifically about either its '*ice*' or its '*cream*' member.

This distinction can often be registered more sharply in a richly inflecting language. The Latin form *liquefacit* '[he] makes [something] liquid' is analysable into forms relatable in some way to *liquet* 'is liquid' on the one hand and to *facit* 'does, makes' on the other. Yet inflectionally it is constructed like any ordinary Verb-form. Just as *facit* may be turned into the Plural by a mere alteration of the ending (compare *faciunt* 'they do, make'), so *liquefacit* may be turned into *liquefaciunt* 'they make [something] liquid' without any alteration of the *lique-* part or of any other feature of the word-form. For this reason we will establish a single compound lexeme LIQUEFACIO, grammatically just another Verb (meaning 'make liquid'), alongside the simple FACIO 'do, make', LIQUEO 'be liquid', and so on. But there are other 'lexical units', sometimes called 'compounds' in the earlier tradition, which are made up of separately inflectable members. The Roman *tribunus militaris* (to cite the Nominative Singular) was an officer of a specific military rank: the precise meaning cannot be deduced from those of TRIBUNUS 'tribune' and MILITARIS 'military' any more than that of *ice-cream* can be deduced from those of ICE and CREAM. '*Tribunus militaris*' is therefore a special item for any conscientious lexicographer. But for the grammarian it is still two words: if we turn it into the Plural (*tribuni militares* 'military tribunes') or the Accusative (*tribunum militarem*) the endings of both the Noun *tribunus* and its modifying Adjective *militaris* have to be altered.

Perhaps it does not greatly matter how this discrepancy is handled in our terminology. We ourselves will say that *tribunus militaris* displays an **idiomatic use**, in a particular Noun with Modifier construction, of the lexemes TRIBUNUS and MILITARIS. We will not say – as the student of meaning might perhaps prefer us to say – that 'TRIBUNUS MILITARIS' is itself a single composite Noun. Similarly, '*to pull one's socks up*' or '*to make one's mind up*' display an idiomatic use of PULL, UP, SOCK (or more precisely Plural *socks*), MAKE, MIND, and so on – again in a construction which has non-idiomatic functions also. Only LIQUEFACIO and ICE-CREAM, of the examples which we have given, are composite or compound lexemes (composite 'WORD lexemes', might one say?) in a grammarian's sense.

Whatever terms we use, the discrepancy is there. The real problem, in a sparsely inflected language such as English, is to determine where the boundary between the relevant 'word lexemes' (compounds) and the 'idiom lexemes' (idiomatic uses of words or lexemes) should be drawn. Can it indeed be drawn as neatly and as conclusively as we might wish? We will return to these problems at the end of Ch. X.

RELATED READING

'Lexeme', 'word-form' and 'word' are distinguished as in *Inflectional Morphology*, pp. 160f. For the substance of the distinctions see LYONS, pp. 196f. (also *New Horizons*, pp. 21f.) but, as already noted in the text, the last two = Lyons's 'phonological word' and 'grammatical word'. In a work on semantics now in progress, Lyons defines 'word-form' as here, and 'morphosyntactic word' as the word in grammar; for 'morphosyntactic' see below, Chs. IV and VIII. Again the substance is not affected.

In reading other introductions, note that Martinet's 'lexème' (MARTINET, §4.19) is a lexical 'monème' (corresponding more exactly to our 'morpheme') rather than a lexical 'word'. Hockett's usage (HOCKETT, *Course*, p. 170) is also different (and entirely personal). For other references for this term, relating in particular to the end of this chapter, see *Inflectional Morphology*, p. 161[3].

'Type' and 'token' (in the James illustration) are from C. S. Peirce: see LEPSCHY, pp. 30f., also Barbara M. H. Strang, *Modern English Structure*, 2nd ed. (London, 1968), p. 10. I cannot leave Henry James without referring to S. Chatman's most interesting study, *The Later Style of Henry James* (Oxford, 1972) – an example of how a linguist may study style properly. For automatic concordancing see D. G. Hays, *Introduction to Computational Linguistics* (New York/London, 1967), Ch. 10; R. A. Wisbey, 'The analysis of Middle High German texts by computer – some lexicographical aspects', *TPhS*, 1963, pp. 28–48.

For phonological and grammatical words see general references for the word in Ch. IX. For the separation of hierarchies see, for example, the beginning of J. T. Bendor-Samuel's 'Some prosodic features of Terena', in *In Memory of J. R. Firth*, ed. C. E. Bazell *et al.* (London, 1966), pp. 30–9. On idioms there is little theoretical discussion: ROBINS, pp. 69f. is sound but brief; Hockett uses the term extensively (HOCKETT, *Course*, pp. 171–3, Ch. 36) but in a personal and wider sense. For more technical treatments see W. L. Chafe, *Meaning and the Structure of Language* (Chicago, 1970), Ch. 5 and elsewhere; U. Weinreich, 'Problems in the analysis of idioms', in *Substance and Structure of Language*, ed. J. Puhvel (Berkeley/Los Angeles, 1969), pp. 23–81. For compounds v. idioms and syntactic constructions see Reading for Ch. X.

III
Lexical and inflectional morphology

Inflections and 'word-formation', derivation and composition; lexical roots and stems, lexical formations and formatives; the term 'derivation'.
Criteria for lexical v. inflectional formations: alteration of 'parts of speech'; syntactic determinability (Gender of Italian Nouns and Adjectives); determinability not sufficient (Number, Grade of Comparison, English *-ion*); substitutability of derived and simple stems; criteria of regularity and meaning; relative nature of criteria.
Historical perspectives: fluctuations of derivation and inflection; derivation v. composition; derived forms v. simple; learned borrowings.

Generate and *generation* are related in form and have certain features of meaning in common (see Ch. I). Nevertheless they are forms of two different lexemes, GENERATE and GENERATION. Again, the Adjectives TRYING and DYING (*a trying day*, *his dying wish*) are related in both representation and meaning to the Verbs TRY and DIE, and in the line of Horace which we cited at the beginning of Ch. II the Latin Adjective VOLUBILIS 'rolling' would be connected similarly with the Verb VOLVO 'roll'. Nevertheless a dictionary will again insist that these are separate lexemes; Adjectives and Verbs will be listed with their own distinct entries or subentries, with their own distinct definitions. By contrast, forms such as *beget* and *begotten* are merely different members (Present and Past Participle) of the paradigm of a single lexeme (BEGET); a dictionary will have one entry and one set of definitions, merely adding (perhaps) that the forms *begat* and *begotten* are irregular. Similarly *tries*, *tried* and the Verbal *trying* (*He's trying hard*) are all forms of the single lexeme TRY, and in Latin *volvitur* 'is rolling' and *volvetur* 'will roll' would be two different forms of the one Verb VOLVO. Whereas in *generate* and *generation* we are faced with relationships between lexemes (items which traditionally have their own separate paradigms), here we are faced with relationships between words or word-forms (traditionally with the oppositions within the paradigms themselves).

Such a distinction will be familiar to any student of modern or Indo-European philology (among others). According to the most usual division of subjects, the field of morphology in general is divided into two major subfields: one concerned with processes of **inflection** (for example, with the rôle of the English Verbal endings *-s* or *-en*), and the other with what are usually referred to as processes of **word-formation**. This latter field is then divided in turn into two smaller subfields, of which one is concerned with processes of **derivation** (for example, the derivation of '*generation*' from '*generate*' or Adjectival '*trying*' from Verbal '*try*') and the other with processes of **composition** or compounding. Under this last heading one would talk, for example, of the formation of the compound '*ice-cream*' from the simple '*ice*' and '*cream*' or of the Latin compound '*liquefacio*' from (let us provisionally say) '*liqueo*' and '*facio*' (compare the end of Ch. II). The grounds for dividing composition from derivation will be sufficiently clear: in the case of *ice-cream* both *ice* and *cream* can represent words in their own right, whereas in *generation* the *-ion* is a purely formative element (a 'bound morpheme' – see Ch. IX) which has no status as a 'word' on its own. The higher division between inflection and word-formation (the latter covering, as we say, both derivation and composition) is defined precisely by the distinction between 'forms of the same paradigm' (*beget* versus *begotten*) and 'forms with separate paradigms' (*generation* versus *generate*) which we have already referred to.

This terminology is well established and perhaps it will seem unhelpful to disturb it. But the notions of 'word formation' and of the 'derivation' of 'words' are both potentially confusing. If the formation of 'words' means the formation of 'lexemes' (the lexical 'word' as distinguished in Ch. II) then the expression is close, perhaps, to what is involved. Nevertheless it is not strictly so. The lexeme is in an important sense an abstract, indivisible entity – simple, compound or 'derived' alike. The morphologically 'derived' UNKIND or UNHEALTHY are semantically opposite to KIND and HEALTHY in the same general way that the morphologically simple BAD or NASTY are opposite to GOOD and NICE. The relationships are contracted equally by all four pairs of items, regardless of whether they are contrasted formally (by the *un-* of the forms *unkind* and *unhealthy*) or not. In many cases, formally related and unrelated pairs enter into even tighter meaning correlations. Thus Italian ZIO 'uncle' is to ZIA 'aunt' partly as PADRE 'father' is to MADRE 'mother', and again CUGINO 'male cousin' is to CUGINA 'female cousin' much as FRATELLO 'brother' or 'male sibling' is to SORELLA 'sister' or 'female sibling'; nevertheless ZIO/A and CUGINO/A are connected overtly while the others are not. From this viewpoint the 'lexical word' is simply a lexeme full stop. It is in that sense that the unit was distinguished from other possible sorts of 'word' in Ch. II.

This is not to deny the morphological relationship: CUGINO and CUGINA, KIND and UNKIND, and so forth are in another sense closer than FRATELLO and SORELLA or GOOD and BAD. The meaning relationship has a marker and so, up to a point, a form of overt guarantee. But this is not so by virtue of the lexemes themselves, but rather of the forms (*cugino/a*, (*un*)*kind*, etc.) by which they are realised. Would it therefore be more correct, one asks, to interpret the 'formation of words' to refer to the word-form (the 'word in sense I' of Ch. II)? Again it seems clear that it would not. When we say that Latin VOLUBILIS or '*volubilis*' is related in form to VOLVO or '*volvo*' we are talking of 'forms' maybe, but we are still speaking in abstraction from the particular members of the Verbal 'roll' paradigm on the one hand (*volvo* 'I roll [something]', *volvitur* 'is rolling, is being rolled', etc.) and the particular members of the Adjectival 'rolling' paradigm (Nominative Singular *volubilis*, Neuter Plural *volubilia*, etc.) on the other. Likewise in the case of LIQUEFACIO one is not saying that the form *liquefacio* 'I make liquid' is derived, as such, from the corresponding 1st Singulars *liqueo* and *facio*. In English the point is perhaps less striking, but nevertheless in the case of GENERATION any statement which we make will be independent of the opposition between Singular *generation* and Plural *generations*, or between Past Tense *generated*, Present Participle *generating*, and the other forms of GENERATE. Although the relationship lies between forms rather than lexemes, it does not lie between word-forms specifically. Is it strictly appropriate to speak of the formation of 'words' at all?

What we ARE concerned with will by now be clear. The paradigm of a lexeme such as VOLUBILIS is built on a common stock or base form (*volubil-* at least on first appearances) upon which the several inflectional endings (*-is*, *-ia*, Nominative/Accusative Plural *-es*, and so on) are appropriately grafted. Similarly, a form *volv-* may be abstracted from the entire paradigm of VOLVO: *volv-o*, *volv-itur*, *volv-etur* '[it] will roll', and so on. A relationship between *volubil-* and *volv-* may then be elucidated by reference to the Participle *volutus* 'rolled'. This too is part of the paradigm of VOLVO, but the monosyllabic form *volv-*

(in *volvo* etc.) is now transformed to a disyllable – phonetically with long *u*, [wolu:] – before the Participial inflections *-tus* (Masculine Nominative Singular), *-ta* (in the corresponding Feminine *voluta*), and so on. In *volubil-* we find the same disyllable (the form being phonetically [wolu:bil]), from which it is clear that just as *volutus* equals *volv + tus* so also *volubil-* can be said to equal *volv + bil-*. It is between 'forms' such as these (*volubil-* and *volv-*), and not between the 'words' in any of our senses ('*volubilis*' and '*volvo*') that the morphological relationship truly holds. Likewise in the case of English GENERATION (we may argue) the relationship lies not between *generate* and *generation* as word-forms, but rather between the stocks on which their respective paradigms (*generates*, *generate*, *generated*, *generating*; Singular *generation*, Plural *generations*) are inflectionally based.

From the viewpoint of inflectional morphology, a form such as *volv-* of *volubil-* functions as the **root** of the lexeme (VOLVO or VOLUBILIS) from whose paradigm it is abstracted. This rôle of the root in inflections will be made more precise at the end of Ch. IV. In accordance with such usage, one possibility would be to say that *volv-* is a morphologically **simple root** (a root which is not itself based on any more elementary root), whereas *volubil-* is a **complex root** which is morphologically 'derived', from the base *volv-*, by the 'derivational' element *-bil-*. Similarly, the lexeme LIQUEFACIO 'make liquid' would have a **compound root** (*liquefac-*, let us say) which we may derive more precisely from a form *liqu-* (serving most simply as the root of LIQUEO 'be liquid') and another form *fac-* (serving as the root of FACIO 'make'). Many linguists, however, would prefer to reserve the term 'root' for a form which is not only inflectionally unanalysable, but 'derivationally' and compositionally unanalysable also. In this sense *volv-* would be a root and so would *fac-* or *liqu-*, but *volubil-* or *liquefac-* would not. If this usage is accepted, then the usual practice is to speak of the **stems** of lexemes instead. So, for our present purposes, we will say that the Verbs VOLVO, FACIO and LIQUEO have the **simple stems** *volv-*, *fac-* and *liqu-* (stems, that is, which consist of a root alone with no additional elements or modifications). By contrast, the Adjective VOLUBILIS and the Verb LIQUEFACIO have a **complex** or **'derived' stem** (*volubil-*) and a **compound stem** (*liquefac-*) respectively. If we want to speak more precisely, we will refer to stems in this sense as **lexical stems** as opposed to 'inflectional stems'; the reason for this qualification will again become clear at the end of Ch. IV.

This is an area in which the terminology is very fluid. Once the concepts are grasped it is easy to be consistent in one's own usage; but whatever precisely one takes to be 'stems' or 'roots' it will be possible to find other writers who are consistent in a different way. In any scheme, however, it seems misleading to speak of the 'formation of words' ('*volubilis* from *volvo*', '*liquefacio* from *liqueo* and *facio*', and so on) in a case where the 'formation of stems' or the 'formation of roots' would be more appropriate. Fortunately, there is a natural alternative which already appears in the title of this chapter: namely, to refer to the two main branches of morphology as **inflectional morphology** (as before) and **lexical morphology**. *Volubil-*, we will accordingly say, is a stem which exhibits a **lexical formation** (the addition of *-bil* to the stem of a Verb), whereas the form *volubilis* itself exhibits an 'inflectional formation' (see again Ch. IV) with the ending *-is*. Similarly, the English Noun *generation* (or strictly the lexical stem of this Noun) belongs to a lexical formation in which the formative element *-ion* is added, with an accompanying change of stress and consonant modification, to the stem of a Verb. Thus *generate* (phonetically, ['dʒenəreit]) combines with *-ion* to form [dʒenə'reiʃn]. In the same spirit, the 'derivational' elements *-bil* or *-ion* will be referred to as **lexical formatives** (formatives by means of which one lexical stem is derived from another). Another lexical formative is the *-e-* which joins together the separate *liqu-* and *fac-* in the formation of *liquefac-*.

In all this the terms 'derived' and 'derivational' have been put in inverted commas. Again, they are well established and perhaps it is better if we let them stand. But here too there is a possibility of misunderstanding. According to one view of inflectional morphology (see Chs. IV and VII), a form such as *tried* or *generations* would also be 'derived', from the base forms *try* or *generation*, by a process of adding [d] or [z]. A 'derivational' technique would be used in both branches, only the lexical versus inflectional status of the 'derivations' making the difference. According to an opposite theory of morphology (that of Ch. V) a 'derivation' would equally be involved in neither. In *I'm trying hard* the grammatical elements identified by *try-* and *-ing* can be seen to stand in a certain grammatical construction. In *a trying day* they simply stand in another construction, forming an Adjectival word instead of a Verb. In brief, the notion of 'derivation' would not enter into this branch of morphology either. A few theorists might, perhaps, be tempted to reject our division of branches altogether. But no one would actually DEFINE 'derivational morphology' merely as the subfield in which forms are 'derived' from other forms.

Of course, the motives for the term are obvious when it is seen within the context of philology or historical linguistics. If I suddenly use a form such as *culturist* (*No I'm not a racist, damn you, I'm a culturist*) I am momentarily, at least, deriving something new from the existing resources of the language. You may be pedantic and ask me if there 'is' such a word; although it is intelligible (I hope) I could not support it even from the latest supplement to the *OED*. Alternatively, you may pick it up and it might even become established (for example, as a new term of abuse). If so the language is enriched with a 'new' lexeme 'derived' from a sense of the 'existing' lexeme CULTURE. But if someone then uses the Plural *culturists* (*Oh, naturally, we're all culturists if that's what you mean*) there is nothing new and no further process of creative 'derivation'. The Plural is merely a mechanical consequence of the Singular. Although this distinction is not as clearcut as the example may suggest (compare the scientific forms in *-ate* and *-ation* referred to later) it is easy to see why, in the process of history, a 'derivation' must be posited in one sort of case but not the other.

But to see the motivation for a term is not necessarily to accept that it is appropriate. One objection is that creativity in this sense (see Ch. XII) does not characterise the 'derivational' subfield specifically. It is also a feature of many compounding formations – a form such as *girl-hater* or *schoolgirl-hater* (*I'm not a woman-hater, just a schoolgirl-hater*) having the same feel of a 'new word' or 'non-word' about it. If anything, therefore, the term in this sense should be used for lexical morphology as a whole. In addition, can one always say that lexeme *a* is synchronically prior to lexeme *b*? In most cases one can: for example, the form *unsightliness* is derived by the addition of a formative *-ness* to the base *unsightly* (note that there is no form *sightliness*) and the latter in turn is derived, by the addition of the formatives *-ly* and *un-*, from the simpler base *sight* (again, there is no form *sightly*). But is it right to speak of 'derivation' in the case of our Italian pair CUGINO and CUGINA ('male cousin' and 'female cousin')? If one had to decide one would doubtless say that the Masculine stem (*cugin-*) served as a base for the Feminine stem (also *cugin-*); semantically, there are grounds for saying that the Masculine Gender is the neutral or 'unmarked' member (see more generally Ch. VIII) in the opposition. But is that criterion morphologically relevant? So far as the stems are concerned, it seems more revealing to say that CUGINO/CUGINA, ZIO/ZIA are terms in a perfectly symmetrical or 'equipollent' relationship.

Despite this we will have to stick with the term 'derivational', simply because (to the writer's knowledge) there appears to be no natural and viable alternative. Like 'morphology' itself, it is an old term which has persisted into a different intellectual climate. But the reader must bear in mind that it is simply a term, meaning 'that branch of lexical morphology which is concerned with formations other than those of compounds'. Any special implications of the root 'derive' should be consciously set aside.

* * *

Let us now leave the problems of formulation, and return to the substance of the lexical/inflectional dichotomy. So far we have largely referred to our intuitions and to the practice of lexicographers: we expect, and find, that *generate* and *generation* have separate definitions. Another way of saying this is that they are not, to our feeling, members of the same paradigm. However, our established dictionaries and paradigms have not been handed to us on tablets of stone. Why do we not say, instead, that there is a single lexeme under which both 'GENERATION' and 'GENERATE' are subsumed? *Generations*, let us say, would be its 'Nominal Plural' as opposed to 'Nominal Singular' *generation*, *generated* its 'Verbal Past Tense' or 'Past Participle', and so on. Similarly, for another such pair, we would say that *automation* was the 'Nominal Singular' and *automate* the 'Verbal Present Tense' (excluding '3rd Singular') of a single lexeme which subsumes both 'AUTOMATE' and 'AUTOMATION'. What is the reason for putting one sort of morphological proportion (*generate*:*generation*, *automate*:*automation*, etc. – compare Ch. I) on a different footing from the others?

An initial answer might be that *generate* and *generation* belong to different 'parts of speech': the latter, as we have said, would be classed as 'Nominal' and the former as 'Verbal'. But this in itself will certainly not do. Firstly, our traditional parts of speech have not been handed to us on tablets of stone either. Why, we would have to ask, is the distinction between a Nominal and a Verbal class of 'words' on a different plane from that between a Singular class and a Plural, or a Present Tense class and a Past? Secondly, there are many cases in which this criterion would fail. According to our grammatical tradition, the Latin form *volvitur* 'is rolling' is a Verb whereas the form *volutus* 'rolled' is a Participle; Verbs and Participles are said to be different parts of speech. Nevertheless they are learned as members of the same paradigm, both *volutus* and the Finite *volvi* 'I rolled [something]' being included in the 'Principal Parts' (see Ch. IV) of VOLVO 'roll'. Conversely, 'words' such as English *duke* and *duchess*, *waiter* and *waitress*, Italian *cugino* and *cugina*, *zio* and *zia*, and so on are accepted as separate dictionary items. Nevertheless they are all Nouns. Why do we not say, for example, that Italian has a single lexeme meaning 'cousin' of which *cugino* is the 'Masculine Singular' and *cugina* the 'Feminine Singular'?

Let us begin with the Italian example, which in one sense is particularly tricky. In Italian the distinction between Nouns and Adjectives cannot be determined merely by the endings of their word-forms: the same endings (*-o*, *-a*, etc.) appear in both. On the one hand there are many Adjectives which distinguish Singular and Plural only. The pattern in this case is one which can be illustrated with the paradigm of FELICE 'fortunate' or 'happy':

Singular	felice
Plural	felici

in which the stem or root (*felic-*) is accompanied by the endings *-e* and *-i*. But the same pattern is also found in many Nouns, for example MONTE 'mountain':

Singular	monte
Plural	monti

with the lexical stem *mont-*. From the paradigms alone it is impossible to assign these lexemes to two different classes.

In another class of Nouns we find the same semantic opposition (Singular versus Plural), but with two more major patterns of inflection. These may be illustrated with the 'Masculine' LIBRO 'book' and the 'Feminine' TAVOLA 'table':[1]

	'book'	'table'
Singular	libro	tavola
Plural	libri	tavole

in which the roots (*libr-* and *tavol-*) are accompanied by the endings *-o* and *-i* in one case and *-a* and *-e* in the other. However, these same

[1] Also Masculine TAVOLO (see below); but let us take the leading dictionary form to start with.

endings also mark a second major class of Adjectives, in which both Number and Gender (Masculine versus Feminine) are distinguished. For illustration we may cite the paradigm of NUOVO 'new':

	Masculine	*Feminine*
Singular	nuovo	nuova
Plural	nuovi	nuove

which shows that the root (*nuov-*) is accompanied by 'Masculine' endings *-o* and *-i* on the one hand and 'Feminine' endings *-a* and *-e* on the other.

How then do forms such as *cugino* and *cugina* fit into these patterns? The range of endings is identical with that of NUOVO. Since they are also parallel in meaning, we could apparently set up an isomorphic paradigm:

	'Masculine'	*'Feminine'*
Singular	cugino	cugina
Plural	cugini	cugine

in which the Masculines and Feminines are again distinguished by the Singular *-o* and *-a*, the Plural *-i* and *-e*. We are left with the root *cugin-*, belonging to the single lexeme meaning 'cousin'. To sum up, therefore, we might say that the lexemes MONTE, FELICE, etc., fall into two main classes or 'parts of speech'. In the first class the paradigms distinguish Number only: within this class some members make this distinction with the endings *-e* and *-i* (FELICE, MONTE), others with *-o* and *-i* (LIBRO) and still others with *-a* and *-e* (TAVOLA). In the second class Gender is distinguished also: the endings are the same for all members (NUOVO, the lexeme for 'cousin', and so on). It is this division (we might say) which reflects a true analysis of the word-forms, not the traditional division between Nouns and Adjectives.

Of course, we will not in fact say anything so silly. The reasons why have to be sought first in the syntax of the forms which we have analysed. In the phrase *un libro nuovo* 'a new book' the Adjective, as one may see, is Masculine; in *una tavola nuova* 'a new table' it is Feminine. But in such a construction the choice between *nuovo* and *nuova* is entirely determined or predictable. One could not say either *un libro nuova* (substituting *-a* in the first example) or *una tavola nuovo* (substituting *-o* in the second). No more, indeed, could one switch the Articles (*un* and *una*) and say *una libro nuovo* or *un tavola nuova*; there is a rule requiring that both Adjective and Article should agree in Gender with the Masculine *libro* or the Feminine *tavola*.[1] It follows that the difference between *nuovo* and *nuova* cannot in itself bear any difference in meaning. To distinguish the phrases from one another we need merely point to the choice of Nouns: LIBRO versus TAVOLA. To distinguish them from other phrases we need merely add that the Nouns are in the Singular (not Plural), that there is an Indefinite Article (not Definite, Demonstrative, etc.), and that the specific lexeme NUOVO acts as Modifier. Everything else (the Number and Gender of the Adjective, the Number and Gender of the Article) then follows automatically.

The Gender of the Nouns LIBRO and TAVOLA is, however, a quite different matter. The phrase *una libra nuova* would not be a mistake, as it were, for *un libro nuovo*; there is no rule of grammar which it contravenes. It simply contains a different Noun (LIBRA 'balance') and accordingly means something different. Nor is *un tavolo nuovo* a 'mistake' for *una tavola nuova*. Rather it is an alternative way of saying the same thing; according to the author's information, the general meaning 'table' may be expressed as readily by the Masculine 'TAVOLO' (more strictly by the paradigm forms *tavolo* Singular and *tavoli* Plural) as it may by the Feminine 'TAVOLA' which we have considered hitherto. In neither case, therefore, is there a general rule by which the choice of Gender is determined. In one it is simply part and parcel of the choice of lexeme (LIBRO 'book' rather than LIBRA 'balance', MONTE 'mountain', and so on and so forth), and in the other the lexeme itself varies freely between one paradigm class ('TAVOLA') and the other ('TAVOLO'). All this will be familiar to students of Italian or of most other European languages. For the Nouns, Gender is in principle inherent in the individual lexeme: LIBRO is Masculine whatever the construction it happens to appear in, and in TAVOLO/A it is the individual Noun itself that varies. The same point may be made for the paradigms in *-e* and *-i*: the Noun MONTE 'mountain' is inherently Masculine (hence the Masculine Article and Adjective in *un monte bello* 'a beautiful mountain'), whereas SIEPE 'hedge' is inherently Feminine (*una siepe bella* 'a beautiful hedge'). All this must be given in the dictionary. For the Adjectives, however, the Gender is determined by grammatical

[1] The general rule has exceptions, as my colleague Dr Lepschy reminds me, in metonymic compounds of the type [*una*] *terz'anno* '[a] third-year [female] student'. The syntactic peculiarity points, of course, to the compositional nature of the construction (compare Ch. x).

or otherwise by general rule. If '*monte*' is Masculine and '*siepe*' Feminine then which, one might foolishly be tempted to ask, is '*felice*'? For an Adjective the question is meaningless: sometimes it stands in a construction with a Masculine (*un uomo felice* 'a happy man'), and sometimes the opposite (*una donna felice* 'a happy woman').

We now have a better classification in which, regardless of the paradigms of endings, lexemes such as BUONO and FELICE have one sort of characteristic and lexemes such as LIBRO, MONTE, TAVOLA or TAVOLO another. How then do the words for 'cousin', 'uncle' or 'aunt', etc., fit into this pattern? The answer is again supplied by the syntax of the phrases. In *un mio cugino* 'a cousin [specifically 'male cousin'] of mine' the Gender of *un* 'a' and *mio* 'my, of mine' are determined by the same grammatical rule that we have considered already; the only additional point is that the Possessive Adjective normally precedes the Noun, whereas in our earlier examples the Descriptive Adjectives *nuovo* and *nuova* followed. So, one could no more say *una mia cugino* than one could say *una mia libro* for 'a book of mine'. Conversely, one could not say *un mio cugina* instead of *una mia cugina* 'a female cousin of mine' – any more than one could say *un mio tavola*, with the Feminine form for 'table'. But there is no further rule which, in turn, can determine the Gender of *cugino* and *cugina*: the difference between *un mio cugino* and *una mia cugina* lies precisely in the choice of either a Masculine in *-o* or Feminine in *-a* to serve as the determining element for the remainder. The same observation holds for every construction in the language: although it is puzzling if one says, for example, *Giovanni è una mia cugina* 'John [i.e. a man's name] is a female cousin of mine', nevertheless there is no rule of grammar requiring the Gender of Subject and Complement to agree. Masculine and Feminine throughout inhere, once again, in the forms '*cugino*' and '*cugina*' themselves.

For this reason the 'cousin' words are grouped with LIBRO or with TAVOLA and not, as appeared originally, with NUOVO, MIO, and so on. It does not matter that the roots *cugin-* and *nuov-* are accompanied by the same formal range of endings; syntactically, their status is not the same. By the same token the 'cousin' words belong to the class of Nouns, and by the same token again their forms are divided between two different lexemes: a Masculine CUGINO in the subclass of LIBRO and a Feminine CUGINA in that of TAVOLA. Both the part of speech assignment (Noun not Adjective) and the morphological status of the Gender (lexical not inflectional) justify themselves within the framework of the same syntactic analysis. By contrast, NUOVO or MIO is a single Adjective, and the Gender difference between *nuovo* and *nuova*, *nuovi* and *nuove* has an inflectional status. A sufficient criterion, we surmise, is that *a* and *b* are in an inflectional opposition if (in at least some instances) the choice between them is determined by a general grammatical rule.

This is, of course, a natural criterion. To say that an opposition is 'lexical' means that the difference is stated in the lexicon or dictionary; it is therefore 'non-lexical' if, instead, its terms are in general selected by the grammar. Unfortunately, the converse is not a sufficient criterion for lexical or 'non-inflectional' status; for a grammatical opposition, too, the choice may sometimes be just as free. In the sentence *I miei cugini sono arrivati* 'My cousins have arrived' the Number of the Noun (*cugini* '[male] cousins' as opposed to *cugino* '[male] cousin') is no more determinable than its Gender. Both merely determine, in turn, the Gender and Number of *i* and *miei*, the Number of the Auxiliary *sono* (compare Singular *è*), and the Gender and Number of *arrivati* 'arrived'. Yet we will say that the Number of Nouns is inflectional (*cugini* being the 'Plural of CUGINO'), whereas their Gender is lexical (CUGINO being a different lexeme from CUGINA). Why so? For the Gender the supporting argument will perhaps be obvious enough. Its rôle in the construction (Noun with Modifying Adjective, Possessive, etc.) is paralleled by words which cannot but be independent lexemes: LIBRO and TAVOLA, MONTE and SIEPE. These last are overwhelmingly more numerous, and so establish a pattern into which CUGINO and CUGINA fit. Number, by contrast, is chosen freely for one element after another: *libro* versus *libri*, *tavola* versus *tavole*, and so on. Although there are a few for which it is normally fixed (Plural *cesoie* 'scissors' just like English *scissors*), they are not sufficient to disturb the pattern. Hence it MAY be inflectional. But we cannot say that it IS inflectional unless we introduce some criterion other than that of determinability.

For another example, we may turn to the opposition of Positive and Comparative in English. In the sentence *It's getting hot* we could also substitute the Comparative: *It's getting hotter.* There is again no grammatical rule which determines the choice of one word or the other. Do we say, then, that HOT and HOTTER are two different lexemes? According to some theoreticians we might; the category of Grade (Positive, Comparative and Superlative) is often cited as a borderline instance. But that would be contrary to the normal practice of lexicographers. In the *OED* there are entries for '*hotter*' (Sc. and north dial. 'to move up and down with vibration'), but not qua Comparative of '*hot*'; that is instead given under the 'forms of "*hot*"', just as the Plural *men* is given under the 'forms of "*man*"', the Past Tense *left* under the 'forms of "*leave*"', and so on. Again, why so? One point is that there are, of course, constructions in which the Positive and Comparative are not freely substitutable: one says *They are hotter than the others* but not *They are hot than the others*. Similarly, there are constructions in which neither the Positive nor the Comparative can appear in place of the Superlative: *the hottest of the lot* but neither *the hot of the lot* nor *the hotter of the lot*. Although the choices are not determined by other specific words in the construction (as the Masculine Plural *miei* was determined specifically by the Plural of the Masculine *cugini*), we could perhaps argue that they are determined by the nature of the construction itself. But would that be a sufficient reason for treating the opposition as inflectional?

The snag, unfortunately, is that the same argument could also be applied to our earlier examples GENERATE and GENERATION. In a 'Gerundial' phrase (*generating electricity*, *automating our work-processes*) the construction requires a form in *-ing*: one without *-ing* could not be substituted in the same sentence contexts (*They disapprove of automate factories*, and so on). Hence, we would say, the oppositions between *generate* and *generating*, *automate* and *automating* is inflectional rather than lexical. But equally the corresponding Nominal construction (*the generation of electricity*, *the automation of our work-processes*) appears to require the form in *-ion*. Again we cannot substitute the simple form (*the automate of factories*) while remaining within the rules of syntax. Do we accept, then, that forms such as *automate* and *automation* are also in an inflectional opposition? Of course, we do not; but why not?

This 'of course' is perhaps a little naughty. According to some linguists 'much of what is traditionally referred to as derivation can be, and ought to be, integrated with the syntactical rules of English' (LYONS, p. 196) in a way which we will examine later in Ch. x. For them the difference between AUTOMATE and AUTOMATION might indeed be removed entirely from the traditional lexicon. But what is the case in favour of our normal practice? One important point is that the forms in *-ion* can always be paralleled by other simple stem-forms: in *the generation of electricity* we can substitute *cost* to yield *the cost of electricity*, in addition to saying that *Automation is a good thing* we could also say that *War is a good thing*, and so on. In that sense the *-ion* is not properly to be considered part of the construction. It is merely part of the make-up of a certain class of Noun-forms (*generation* but not *cost*, *automation* but not *war*) which can function at a certain position within it. On the other hand, there is no indisputably simple form that can be substituted for *hotter* in *It's hotter than the others*. In this construction the only alternatives are more complex phrases: for example, *more* or *less beautiful* in *She's more/less beautiful than you*. Here then, at least, the Comparative is an essential part of the grammatical statement. To distinguish the construction properly one has to say that *than* is preceded either by an Adjective with *less* or (as the case may be) by an Adjective with *-er* or *more*.

Such is the case seen, as it were, from the grammarian's viewpoint. But the dictionary writer will have his own complementary arguments. It will not be enough simply to say that there are Verbs in *-te* and Nouns in *-tion*. For one thing, not all Verbs in fact have such a Noun corresponding: one can say *He dilutes his whisky* and *the dilution of whisky*, but not *The salution of officers is compulsory* as an alternative to *One must salute officers*. There are also a few Nouns in *-ion* without a corresponding Verb. *Elocution* seems to belong to this formation and indeed one could understand *She's elocuting marvellously*; but the author at least would be facetious if he said it. In such cases one is often in doubt. One could say of someone that *He pontificates about linguistics*, but would one also say *his pontification about linguistics*? It is not easy to be sure either that one would or that one would not.[1] Conversely, is there a Verb '*halate*' to match the photographer's term *halation*? The latter was coined as such from the base *halo*; the source (from 1859) is cited in the *OED*. In the intervening century a back-formation could plausibly have arisen (e.g. *These negatives are badly halated*). But it is not recorded in the 1933 supplement of the *OED* or in the more recent *Webster's Third International*. One doubts whether it has been used.

There would thus be a lack of regularity (to put it at its crudest) in any putative series of 'paradigms': *salute* but not *salution*, *elocution* but

[1] Mr C. J. Bosanquet, of the Press's editorial staff, has most aptly referred me to an example in *The Listener* (13 December 1956, p. 999) in which a correspondent refers to 'the endless pontification' that accompanies certain discussion (see also *Ibid.*, 10 January 1957, p. 66). Again, does this strike the reader as a fully established usage? I have shown the passage to one English speaker who said that of course there was such a word, but at the same time was unable to tell me what in fact it meant!

not *elocute*, *function* but not *funct*, and so on. These gaps are not predictable by general rule. There is no reason at all why there should not be a Verb HALATE except that, apparently, there isn't. The lexicographer must therefore show, in individual cases, whether both forms exist or not. However, he is also faced with semantic problems. A *delegation* is a collection of people who have been 'delegated', and a *selection* (of goods or what-not) will have been 'selected'. But an *election* is not a collection of people who have been 'elected', nor would one speak of a *diversion* or a *direction* of parcels (compare *an assignment of parcels*) arriving. ELECTION, DIVERSION and DIRECTION lack what one might call the 'Passive' sense. There are also a few which lack the converse 'Active' sense (that of *the generation of electricity* or *his delegation of the responsibility*). For example, one can say *He opted for apple-pie* but not *his option for* (meaning 'his decision to choose') *apple-pie*. Do our 'paradigms' have homonymous 'Active' and 'Passive' terms? If so, there are yet more gaps for certain of our putative 'lexemes'.

That, however, would still be far too crude. The 'Active'/'Passive' distinction is at best an overall criterion of classification, which must then be qualified and supplemented in numerous individual cases. Perhaps, the reader may say, our example OPTION does have a quasi-Active sense: for instance, *his option for* (meaning 'his option to purchase') *three tons of apple-pie*. But this is a quite specific business usage, which cannot be predicted from the general meanings of OPT as such. For our earlier example SALUTE one might be tempted to bring in the Noun SALUTATION; although there is no *-ion* form at least there is one in *-ation* instead. But again the senses of Verb and Noun do not precisely correspond: one could not say *the salutation of officers* either. Similar points can be made for most of the pairs which we have cited: DIRECTION has a largely unpredictable sense (vis à vis DIRECT) in the normal collocation *He was going in the other direction*, GENERATION (as we remarked in Ch. I) in *three generations ago*, and so on. It does not follow that Noun and Verb are semantically unrelated. But one cannot establish an overall correlation ('*option*' is to '*opt*' as '*direction*' is to '*direct*', as '*generation*' is to '*generate*', and so on), and simply leave it at that. The dictionary writer is forced to make separate statements (sometimes several special statements) about an individual item. By contrast, he has nothing special to say about the oppositions between Italian Singulars and Plurals or English Comparatives or Positives. Semantically, *cugino* is indeed to *cugini* as *monte* is to *monti* or *libro* to *libri*. Barring idioms perhaps, *hotter* is indeed to *hot* as *colder* is to *cold*, as *prettier* is to *pretty*, and so on.

Such criteria cannot be expected to give absolute results. Alongside the normal form *cesoie* 'scissors' which we cited earlier, the *Cambridge Italian Dictionary* (REYNOLDS) also gives the Singular *cesoia* with the translation 'shears' and the rubric 'eng[ineering]'. Here a correlation which is apparently inflectional does, nevertheless, require an occasional lexical qualification. Occasionally, too, an inflectional paradigm will show an unexpected gap. Still in Italian, one would expect SOCCOMBERE 'succumb' to have a Participle *soccombuto* (and, indeed, it is explicit or implicit in dictionaries); nevertheless speakers are not happy with it.[1] For a converse example, let us first pretend that there is an English Plural *gluds*: for example, *He's walking with his whopping great gluds all over my flower beds*. From this there follows automatically the Singular *glud*: *He came out with only one glud on*. This is a characteristic feature of inflectional oppositions, as we have already implied. But what of *He arrived gludless*? Its meaning is quite regular and if it seems facetious that may be in the nature of the construction itself. The formation in *-less* lies on the boundary between the automatic **productivity** of the Plural formation, by which any *X* yields Plural *Xes* (barring some general reason to the contrary), and what we will call the **semi-productivity** of the majority of lexical formations, by which new stems are formed sporadically by creative processes (see Ch. XII). Many scientific terms in *-ate* and *-ation* also stand in virtually mechanical relationships. Would one meet the term *chelation* before seeing a form of the corresponding Verb (say, *a chelating agent*)? Or would it be the other way round? Whichever is learned first, the other strikes one more as a 'variant' than as 'another word' to be learned individually.

Such examples do, let us admit, run contrary to the pattern which our lexicographical arguments have established. In general, therefore, a grammatical criterion may be preferred in cases where it proves decisive. But the exceptions are too marginal to impugn the normal dictionary writer's practice. Almost all Italian Singulars and Plurals do in fact form a regular correlation. Conversely, English forms in *-t(e)* and *-tion* are in general eligible to branch out on their own. It is quite explicable that some, particularly in technical or very recent usage, will remain more closely linked.

* * *

[1] Example suggested to me by Dr Lepschy.

In this discussion we have considered the problem synchronically and have assumed, moreover, that the boundary is sufficiently determinate in all cases. But in the history of languages the status of a formative may naturally vary between one stage and another. The Latin form *maturescit* 'it ripens' has a stem formed with the Inchoative element *-sc-* ('becomes, begins to, begins to become'). This is classed as a lexical formative, the Verb MATURESCO 'ripen' being a different lexeme from the Adjective MATURUS 'ripe'. Looking forwards in time, the same element (etymologically) appears in modern Italian *fini-sc-e* (phonetically [fi'niʃʃe]) '[he] finishes' or *appari-sc-o* [appa'risko] 'I appear'. Looking backwards, one may equally reconstruct an Indo-European **-sk-*, which is reflected most obviously by the comparison between Greek *gi-gnɔ́ː-sk-ɔː* (γιγνώσκω) 'I come to know' and the Latin *co-gno-sc-o*. But the rôle of this '*-sc-*' does not remain the same from one language-period to the next. In Indo-European one can argue, at least, for an inflectional status: forms in **-sk-* (or **-ē-sk-*) were characteristic not of a separate set of lexemes, but rather of a separate 'Inchoative' section in the range of Present forms of Verbs.[1] In Latin the formative was lexical, as we have said. In Italian it has become part of the paradigm entirely. *Finisce* and *apparisco* are ordinary forms of the lexemes FINIRE 'finish' and APPARIRE 'appear', the *-sc-* appearing only in certain forms of the Imperative, Present Indicative and Present Subjunctive, and then, moreover, for just a subclass of one of the major conjugations. Over the millennia, the same element has changed from probable inflectional to certain derivational status, and later back (so far as that distinction goes) to inflectional again.

Since rôles can shift historically, it is not surprising that the boundary can in fact be blurred at one particular stage. In the phrase *a crowded room*, CROWDED may reasonably be classed as a derived 'Participial Adjective' (and is so classed in the latest supplement to the *OED*). A common test is that it may be modified by *very*: *a very crowded room.* By contrast, *heated* in *a well heated room* remains the Past Participle of the Verb HEAT, among other reasons because one does not say *a very heated room.* Here (as in the case of the two forms '*trying*') an identical range of formatives (*-ed*, *-en*, etc.) has at present both an inflectional and a lexical rôle. Where then do we draw the boundary in individual cases? In *a written confession*, for example, is *written* a form of WRITE

[1] For the most recent discussion of this formative see C. Watkins, 'Hittite and Indo-European studies: the denominative statives in *-ē-*', *TPhS*, 1971, pp. 51–93.

or of a separate lexeme WRITTEN? We cannot say *a very written confession* (but, of course, there are Adjectives which cannot be modified by *very* for semantic reasons). Nor is a putative WRITTEN quite established in the Predicative construction: *if his confession had been written* is likely to be understood as a Passive (compare *if his confession had been finished*) rather than as the equivalent of *if his confession had been a written one*. Such tests might point to a continuing Verbal status. But against this a putative Participle would have restricted collocations in the Attributive construction: one does not talk of *a written book* nor, really, of *a written letter* (though one does say *He wrote a letter* or *He wrote a book*). Nor can *a written confession* be readily detached from a *hand-written* (or *typewritten*, or *unwritten*) *confession*, where there are certainly no Verbs HAND-WRITE, TYPEWRITE or (in the relevant sense) UNWRITE. These points suggest that we should recognise an Adjective. Diachronically, 'WRITTEN' (like others of its kind) is in the process of emerging from its Verbal origin. But synchronically, the decision is bound to be partly arbitrary. The class of Participial Adjectives is a notorious crux for those who are determined to chop too neatly.

Fluctuations and uncertainties can also be found in the case of derivation versus composition. The *-heit* of German *Freiheit* 'freedom' or *Gesundheit* 'health' is now a derivational formative, with etymological cognates in other Germanic languages (for example, *-hood* in English *boyhood* or *manhood*). But originally it was an independent lexeme entering into a compositional formation. Indeed it is still recorded as a word in certain dialectal phrases.[1] Synchronically, there will again be cases in which it is hard to see on which side of the boundary a formation falls. *Policeman* or *postman* originate, at least, in compounds with the second member MAN. But phonetically they have now lost the full vowel: [pəˈliːsmən] not -[mæn]. Moreover, there is another class of forms which do have [mæn], such as *insurance man* or (in the author's speech) *gas man*. Has the [mən] then broken away from MAN, making a lexical formation on its own? There are two possible objections. Firstly, the Plural (also [mən]) would then be slightly puzzling. As a reduced form of *men* it is what one expects; but if it has no synchronic connection with *men*, why do we not find regular Plurals (*policemans*, etc.) beginning to develop? One hears such forms from children (along with *singed* for *sang* and other hyper-regularities), but they do not become

[1] Cf. F. Kluge, *Etymologisches Wörterbuch der deutschen Sprache*, 17th ed., revised by W. Mitzka (Berlin, 1957), s.v. *-heit*.

established. The second and more important objection lies in the opposition between POLICEMAN and POLICEWOMAN. In meaning one is to the other as MAN is to WOMAN, and of course the latter is a more recent form which takes the former as its model. Nor would POSTWOMAN be unexpected, provided that 'postwomen' existed. The form in *-woman* would suggest that those in *-man* retain their quality as compounds too.

Another important boundary is between a lexeme which is synchronically derived (such as GENERATION) and one which is only etymologically 'derived' (such as, let us say, NATION). This too is often difficult for the synchronic linguist to determine. For example, is WEALTH a simple lexeme, or does it have a derived stem in *-th*? The *-th* formation has long ceased to be productive: for example '*coolth*', despite a long succession of literary examples (see *OED*), has still failed to become established. However, the intelligibility of '*coolth*' confirms that at least *warmth* is a lexical derivate of *warm*. In that case, we will argue, *length* and *strength* are likewise synchronically as well as diachronically derived from *long* and *strong*. The semantic relationship is regular, and at least some forms in *-th* (*length*, *breadth*, *depth* and *width*) fall naturally together as a class. The only complication is the change of vowel: [ɔ] in *long* being converted to [e] in *length*, and so on. If we then turn to *wealth* we can argue that it also ends in *-th*, and indeed it pointedly rhymes with *health* in the phrase *health and wealth*. The problem, of course, is that there is effectively no element to serve as base. For no speaker of English is there still a connection with WELL, and for most speakers WEAL scarcely exists even in idioms. If one wanted to pursue this analysis one would have to say that *weal-* [wel] was a 'partially independent' element (see Ch. I) which can only appear with *-th* following.

Similar problems arise repeatedly from the historical borrowing of learned formations. The Noun formation in *-ion* is at least semi-productive (as we remarked above). But does NATION, which we have just cited, in fact belong to it? Its source (via Old French) is the Latin NATIO 'race, nation', which was related synchronically to NATIVUS 'native', NATURA 'nature', and others on the base of the Verb NASCOR 'be born' (Past Participle *natus*). Many English speakers know this perfectly well, and in English itself there is at least a semantic connection between NATIVE and NATION, at least a morphological connection between NATIVE and NATIVITY (in *The Nativity*), and at least a semantic connection again between the latter and NATAL. In that case are they simply *nat-ion*, *nat-ive*, *nat-iv-ity*, *nat-al* – all being derived from the 'partially independent' base *nat*(*e*)-? The author does not find this helpful. But the case is at least a great deal stronger than for CYNIC and DOG (see Ch. I).

The most awkward cases are when languages borrow from their own earlier stages. French, like English, has a pattern by which Adjectives are formed in *-al* (or *-el*); thus *national* from *nation* 'nation', *original* from *origine* 'origin', or *personnel* 'personal' from *personne*. In both languages this began as a Latinising formation, the forms being either borrowed as wholes from Latin Adjectives in *-alis* (for example, Late Latin *originalis* from the stem of ORIGO 'origin') or formed from Noun stems, such as that of NATION, which were themselves of a sufficiently learned shape. But in French the Latin Noun will often have a natural reflex also. For example, alongside the Adjective-form *mensuel* 'monthly' (which is a nineteenth-century adaptation of Latin *mensualis*) we also have the Noun-form *mois* 'month', which has developed from the Latin stem *mense-* by the normal processes of sound-change.[1] Similarly *paternel* 'paternal' and *maternel* 'maternal' exist alongside *père* 'father' and *mère* 'mother', *monacal* 'monastic' and *clérical* 'clerical' alongside *moine* 'monk' and *clerc* 'clerk, cleric', and so on. Do these Adjectives all belong to the same synchronic formation? Are *moine* [mwan] and *mois* [mwa] in some sense the same root as *monac-* [mɔnak] and *mensu-* [mãsɥ]? Without retracing the history, it would be hard to account for their phonetic differences. Moreover, there are also doublets among the Adjectives themselves: from *matin* 'morning' there is the regular *matinal* '[taking place] in the morning', but we are also faced with the Latinate *matutinal* (from the stem of Latin MATUTINUS). Is *matutin-*, at least, a 'partially independent' base whose derivate bears only a semantic relationship to MATIN?

In extreme cases the Adjectives seem clearly independent. *Mental* 'mental' is ultimately from a Latin stem (that of MENS 'mind') which, on its own, has no French reflex either learned or popular; nor can *vernal* 'vernal, of the spring' be matched with anything but the Latin VER 'spring' and the derived Adjective VERNALIS. Again, in the case of *radical* 'radical' the etymologically related Noun (*racine* 'root') is too far removed in both form and meaning. At this extreme one can say with confidence that there is no synchronic connection, just as at

[1] The date, and other factual statements, are from E. Gamillscheg, *Etymologisches Wörterbuch der französischen Sprache* (Heidelberg, 1928).

the other extreme (that of *national* or *matinal*) one can be quite sure that there is. But between the extremes there is no firm criterion by which one can draw the line. Are *clerc* and *clérical* morphologically related or not – compare English *clerk* and *clerical*? There is no certain answer, and given the historical circumstances it is hardly to be expected that there should be. The decision is a matter of analytic convenience – and, as we hinted in Ch. I, it is often hard to decide when the morphological analyst should pack it in.

RELATED READING

In defining 'lexical' v. 'inflectional' I would rely on the prior notions of 'lexeme' v. 'word': this corresponds to the traditional formulation (e.g. in MARCHAND, p. 2). But the distinction may also be drawn between types of formation (e.g. ROBINS, p. 257) or word-construction (BLOOMFIELD, p. 222) or, most commonly, between types of morpheme (see Chs. I and V); for the last approach see especially BOLINGER, pp. 56ff. ('source' and 'system' morphemes), HILL, pp. 119ff. (English 'postbases' v. 'suffixes'). Whatever the scheme of definition, the same problems of criteria arise (see below).

For 'root' and 'stem' see first the *OED*: one of the 'ultimate elements of a language, that cannot be further analysed . . .' (s.v. *root*, sb[1], §15) versus '. . . the theme of a word . . . to which the flexional suffixes are attached' (s.v. *stem*, sb[1], §5. b). For a similar distinction in modern introductions see ROBINS, pp. 206f., 230; HOCKETT, *Course*, p. 240; also BLOOMFIELD, pp. 225, 240. Note, pace the *OED*, that there is no reason why inflections should be suffixes (see Ch. VII) in particular. For 'theme', in the definition just cited, see *OED*, s.v., §5; it is now unusual in English, although, for example, 'thème' is normal in French: compare 'synthème' (which has its own classical ancestry) in MARTINET, §4.35. 'Base' is another relevant term, which has been used both for 'theme' or 'stem' (see *OED*, s.v. *base*, sb[1], §14) and for 'root' (see HILL, p. 119); I would reserve it, informally at least, for the immediate 'base' of any particular formation (thus *unsightliness* on base *unsightly*, and so on). For the general notion of formations compare again ROBINS, p. 257; also *Inflectional Morphology*, p. 186.

For lexical morphology as the derivation of 'new words' see BOLINGER, 56ff. in particular; also references for productivity in Ch. XII.

The criteria for 'inflection' v. 'derivation' have been discussed by many writers, though few mention the whole range. For the part of speech of derived forms compare ROBINS, pp. 258f. (class-maintaining v. class-changing derivations); also HOCKETT, *Course*, pp. 243f., and, from another angle, HILL, Ch. 10. For the syntactic criterion for inflections see in general ROBINS, p. 257; HILL, pp. 122f.; BLOOMFIELD, p. 224; also Hockett's account of an inflection as 'much the same as' what he calls a 'marker' (HOCKETT,

Course, p. 209 and earlier pp. 153f.). The discussion of Italian Gender and Number should be compared with SAPIR, pp. 95f. (including an example from Latin) and with Martinet on French: cf. A. Martinet, *A Functional View of Language* (Oxford, 1962), pp. 15ff. For the most straightforward criterion for derivation (substitutability by a simple form) see MARTINET, §4.35; SAPIR, pp. 84f. (on *farmer* and *duckling*); BLOCH & TRAGER, p. 54; again ROBINS, p. 257. The difficulties with syntactic criteria are less commonly discussed, but for Grade as a marginal case see HILL, pp. 168ff. (who argues for English *-er* and *-est* as derivational); ROBINS, p. 260.

For the 'rigid parallelism' of inflectional paradigms see BLOOMFIELD, pp. 223f. For the relative freedom and unpredictability of derivations see HILL, pp. 121f. (also pp. 136f.); ROBINS, pp. 260f.; briefly, with the criterion of meaning, in my contribution to *New Horizons*, p. 113. For a lexicographer's discussion see L. Zgusta's interesting though ill-written *Manual of Lexicography* (Prague, 1971), pp. 127ff.; for semantic unpredictability *gaol/gaoler* and *prison/prisoner* are a nice example (p. 128). On meaning, in particular, it must be stressed that a CRITERION FOR derivation is not a DEFINITION OF it; compare HOCKETT, *Course*, p. 308, apropos of his concept of 'idioms'.

For a summary discussion of English Participles and Participial Adjectives see QUIRK *et al.*, pp. 242–6. For the boundary of composition and derivation see WARTBURG, §2.4; MARTINET, §4.36 (and *A Functional View*..., pp. 94f.); *policeman* is mentioned by QUIRK *et al.*, p. 978. For learned derivatives in French and English see ULLMANN, pp. 108ff. (also 145ff.).

IV
Traditional treatments of inflection

Preamble.
The classical framework: parts of speech and 'accidents'; differences in classical and modern treatment; formal and substantive categories; 'categories' of words and 'categories' of lexemes; morphosyntactic category, inflectional class.
Proportions and inflectional rules: the Word and Paradigm model; exemplary paradigms; analogy; rules for analogical formation; objections to classical rules; roots, inflectional stems and terminations, inflectional formations and formatives; continuing importance of traditional model.

In the next five chapters we will be concerned in the first instance with the problems of inflectional morphology. The techniques of analysis which we shall examine have sometimes been extended to the lexical field, and we will give illustrations of this where appropriate. But they were largely developed in response to inflectional problems (see Reading for Ch. v in particular), and in some cases the boundary between inflections and the lexicon is very sharp. Furthermore, some of these techniques are controversial. Two different linguists will sometimes describe the same language in quite different ways. In each chapter we will try to consider each of these separate models (see Ch. I) in its best light. But when we compare them as a whole we will find that there is ground for argument if (as is often suggested) the same techniques and terminology should be applied to the analysis of all languages (see the first part of Ch. VII in particular).

* * *

It is fitting that we should begin with the traditional background. For the classical grammarians of the Greek and Roman world the problem of the word was, above all, a problem of classification. At the highest level the forms which made up any particular sentence were classified into the eight parts of speech: Noun, Pronoun, Verb, and so on. The term 'part of speech' is here the continuation of a Latin phrase 'pars orationis' (itself a calque or loan-translation from the Greek μέρος τοῦ λόγου) which might perhaps be more aptly rendered 'part of the utterance' or 'element of the sentence'. At this level, therefore, the Latin sentence *nihil enim semper floret* 'For nothing flowers for ever' would be 'parsed' or analysed as consisting of a Noun *nihil* 'nothing', a Conjunction *enim* 'for', an Adverb *semper* 'always, for ever', and a Verb *floret* '[it] flowers'. The schoolroom term 'parse' (meaning, in the first instance, to assign to one part of speech or another) itself derives from the use of 'pars' ('part') in the Latin terminology.

At a more detailed level, each part of speech was then subclassified with respect to one or more variable characteristics. In Latin these are referred to as its 'accidentia' (its 'accidents'); it is this which gives rise to the older term 'accidence' for the study of words as opposed to the study of syntax. From the modern viewpoint, however, it is very hard to find a single translation which will cover all the 'classes' or 'categories' which an ancient writer brought under this heading. According to the fourth-century grammarian Donatus, the characteristics of the Latin 'Noun' (a class including both the modern Noun and the modern Adjective) included not only the apparently familiar categories of Case, Number, Gender and Grade of Comparison, but two further sets of distinctions which today are usually thought of rather differently. One of these is the general distinction between 'simple' Nouns and 'compound' Nouns (in a sense somewhat wider than our own in Chs. II and III). Thus, for Donatus, *indoctus* 'not learned, uneducated' was a compound as against the simple *doctus* 'learned, clever'. In Latin this characteristic was referred to as the 'Figura' (the 'Shape' – 'figure' would be a less apt translation). The other included the whole complex of distinctions between Proper and Common Nouns, between different types of Personal Name, between the various subclasses of Common Nouns, and so on. The Latin term for this was 'Qualitas' (the characteristic of 'being of a certain sort' – etymologically the source of English 'quality'). It will be seen that this last characteristic itself subsumes a considerable amount of hierarchical subclassification.

A similar treatment was adopted for the Verbs. Still according to Donatus, the variable characteristics of the Verb included those of Tense, Number and Person in approximately their modern sense. But that of Voice (Active versus Passive) formed part of a larger set of distinctions covering the so-called 'Deponent' Verbs (a class in Latin which can only appear with Passive terminations) amongst others. The term for this characteristic as a whole, 'Genus', is the same as for the Gender of Nouns. The category of Mood, again, was taken as one aspect of another set of wider distinctions; its counterpart included, among others, the category of derived 'Inchoative' Verbs (e.g. *calesco* 'I am becoming hot') which we mentioned briefly in Ch. III. This wider characteristic was referred to by the same term 'Qualitas' which covered the various subdivisions of Proper and Common Nouns. To sum up by means of an example, the Verb *floret* '[it] flowers' would be subclassified in terms of its characteristics as follows:

> 'QUALITAS': Indicative Mood, non-Inchoative, etc.
> CONJUGATION: Second
> 'GENUS': 'Neuter' (= Active incapable of having a Passive termination)
> NUMBER: Singular
> 'FIGURA' or 'SHAPE': Simple
> TENSE: Present (contrasting with Past and Future)
> PERSON: Third

where the further characteristic of 'Figura' (simple versus compound) is the same as for Nouns, and that of Conjugation refers to the particular forms which are taken by the Verbal endings.

Examples have been given from Donatus in view of his major influence on the later tradition. Other analyses, notably those of the equally influential sixth-century grammarian Priscian, gave slightly varying sets of characteristics or gave the values of individual characteristics differently. But it is the divergence between ancient and modern technique that is more important for our present purpose. To a modern writer the distinction between simple and compound is a different SORT of distinction from those of Singular and Plural Number or Present, Past and Future Tense. For most writers too the four traditional Conjugations (e.g. 2nd Conjugation in the case of *floret*) are another type again. One sets out paradigms FOR one Conjugation or FOR another; one does not envisage a single paradigm in which a distinction such as this (e.g. 1st Conjugation *amat* '[he] loves' versus 2nd Conjugation *floret*) intersects with those between Singular and Plural (*amat* versus *amant* 'they love'; *floret* versus *florent* 'they flower'), 3rd Person versus 1st and 2nd, and so on. Possibly the reasons will be intuitively obvious to many readers. Nevertheless it will be instructive to spell them out in greater detail.

For 'simple' and 'compound' ('Figura') one point is that such distinctions never enter into rules of syntax. In the phrase *homo indoctus* 'an uneducated man' the word *indoctus* 'uneducated' is Nominative (compare the corresponding Accusative *indoctum*), Singular (compare Plural *indocti*), and Masculine (compare Feminine *indocta*, Neuter again *indoctum*); all these characteristics enter into rules of agreement – *homo* 'man' being also Singular, Nominative and inherently Masculine – which are very similar to those for Italian which we illustrated in Ch. III. *Indoctus* is also in the Positive Grade of Comparison, and as such is again excluded (like English *hot* in Ch. III) from certain grammatical constructions. But there is no syntactic rule which must invoke its status as a 'compound'. In detailing the construction of phrases and sentences, the fact that *indoctus* is *doctus* plus *in-* (whereas *doctus* is 'simple' *doctus*) is entirely irrelevant.

We will conclude (still following Ch. III) that the opposition of *indoctus* and *doctus* is LEXICAL, whereas those of *indoctus* and *indoctum*, *indoctus* and *indocti*, etc., are INFLECTIONAL. But the terms 'simple' and 'compound' are more general than the category of 'Negative formations with *in-*' in particular. Within Latin they also apply to the unrelated case of *liquefacio* 'I make liquid' versus *facio* 'I make' (note that we are still contrasting the individual members of the paradigms), and indeed they apply to English *ice-cream* versus *cream*, French *pot à lait* 'milk jug' versus *pot* 'jug' (examples at the end of Ch. VI), and generally to words in any language which meet appropriate conditions. They form part, that is, of our general set of concepts for 'talking about language' or 'talking about languages'. Just as the general concept of 'inflection' stands to the particular inflections of *indoctus*, *indocta*, *indocti*, etc., or the general concept of a 'phoneme' to the particular Latin phonemes distinguished (up to a point) by the letters 'i', 'n', and so on, so also the general concept of a 'compound' (or, we would now prefer, of a 'lexical formation') can be applied to *indoctus* and *liquefacio* among many others.

To use a philosophical term, the concepts of a 'compound', 'phoneme' or 'inflection' belong to the **metalanguage** of linguistic description – the 'higher level language' ('meta-' is here used on the analogy of 'metaphysics' versus 'physics') with the aid of which we describe, as the objects of our study, the **object languages** Latin, English, or whatever. But at once there is a further point (and conceivably an objection) which will have occurred to some readers. If terms such as 'simple' and 'compound' can be applied to any language, so, for example, can 'Singular' and 'Plural'. In English *men* is Plural as compared with *man*, and in Latin *indocti* is Plural as compared with *indoctus*: we would not dream of inventing arbitrary terms in each particular grammar. Likewise Latin *amabat* 'was in love with' and Italian *cantava* 'was singing' are both 'Imperfect', Latin *homo* and English *he* both 'Masculine', and so on. Now it is true that a language might not have a Plural versus Singular inflection, and certainly there are many without the European system of Gender. But it would also be possible, in theory, to envisage a language without compounds – i.e. with a lexicon to which our terms 'compound' and 'simple' would be inapplicable. So have they indeed a different status?

To make the issue plain we must bring out two further points. Firstly, a term such as 'Plural' is used for something more specific than a simple classificatory label. Given that a Latin Noun is Plural, Nominative, 2nd Declension, Masculine and Positive Grade then (with the aid of rules whose form we will discuss below) it follows that its word-form will end in *-i*: thus *indoct-i*. But given that it is (in the classical sense) a 'compound', this merely tells us that SOME lexical formation is involved: it might be one in *in-*, or it might be in *con-* (e.g. *conscii* 'conscious [of]' with the root for 'know'), and so on, and naturally two or more different stems (in the sense of Ch. III) may be formed on the same base. There can be no rules which predict, from the 'compound' status of a word along with its other characteristics, precisely what the corresponding word-form looks like. In this sense 'compound' and 'Plural' have dissimilar rôles within the actual grammar of Latin (or, as they are used, for any other language).

Secondly, the conditions under which we apply these terms are fundamentally different. If we say that 'word' *A* is a compound, we mean that it has some structure of the general type *BC*, where *B* and *C* can each be related (for example, as stems) to other words which exist independently. This is all that is involved: the CONTENT of *A*, *B* and *C* (what they mean or what phonetic form they have) is quite irrelevant. In this sense the term 'compound' belongs more precisely to the **formal metalanguage** of linguistic description. The conditions under which it is applied refer to FORMAL interrelationships only. But the conditions for 'Plural' and 'Singular' are entirely different: they refer precisely to the content or (to use a widespread term) the **substance** of the relevant oppositions. English *men* and Latin *indocti* are labelled

'Plural' because, in their respective grammars, both belong to a category meaning broadly 'more than one' as opposed to 'one alone'. The conditions under which this term is applied refer not to the formal structure of the paradigm ('Number' *X* being merely opposed to 'Number' *Y* on one dimension, just as 'Case' *A* is opposed to 'Case' *B* on another), but to the SUBSTANTIVE RÔLES which its members, or the categories of its members, play. In this sense, 'Singular' and 'Plural' belong not to a formal, but rather to a **substantive metalanguage** (which, of course, is another important subject of general linguistic theory).

The distinctions which we have drawn can be a matter of argument in individual instances. But for the examples given the case seems clear, and indeed is not a matter of dispute in modern grammatical practice. That, then, is one improvement since the classical period. The others flow from the different senses of the 'word' which we have sought to elucidate in Ch. II. For the classical grammarians language had a single hierarchy of units. The letters were built up into syllables (e.g. *f*, *l* and *o* into *flo-*), the syllables in turn into words (e.g. *flo-* and *-ret* into *floret*), and finally the words as wholes into the total utterance or sentence. It was therefore the individual word, again as a whole, which had to bear the burden of grammatical classification. The Verb, as we have said, was a class of 'parts of sentences' which comprised *floret*, *amo* 'I love', and so on. In the same way, *floret* as such belonged to the more specific classes of 3rd Person or 2nd Conjugation, and *amo* as such to those of 1st Person or 1st Conjugation.

In this there is nothing, it will be seen, of the modern distinction between word and lexeme. For an ancient writer the forms of the 'same word' were, of course, related within the framework of categories. *Florent* 'they flower' was the Plural 'of' or corresponding to *floret*, and likewise *amabo* 'I will love' the Future corresponding to *amo*. Certain words could therefore be taken as diagnostic for a set of variable words in general. The Active Verbs, still citing Donatus, are 'those which end in *o* and turn themselves into Passives by adding *r*' ('quae o littera terminantur et accepta r littera faciunt ex se passiva');[1] here the 1st Singulars of the Present Indicative (e.g. Active *amo* 'I love' and Passive *amor* 'I am loved') are assumed to be diagnostic for the whole array of forms *amas* 'you love' versus *amaris* 'you are loved', *amat* '[he] loves' versus *amatur* 'is loved', and so forth. Similarly, the 1st Con-

[1] Ed. H. Keil, *Grammatici Latini*, Vol. 4 (Leipzig, 1864), p. 383.

jugation is 'the one which has a long *a*' ('quae . . . a productam habet') before, among others, the final *s* of the 2nd Singular Active of the Present Indicative.[1] Here a form such as *amas* (with long open vowel [ama:s]) is taken as diagnostic for the set comprising 1st Conjugation *amo* versus 2nd Conjugation *floreo* 'I flower' (compare *flores* [flo:re:s] 'you flower'), and so on. But it is the individual words which form the membership of these classes. Active, for example, is a class with the members *amo*, *amas*, *lego* 'I read, am reading', *legebat* '[he] was reading', etc. The term does not apply just to the words that are used as diagnostic (*amo*, *lego* and the like).

In its own terms this is arguably coherent. But if we talk of 'words' in different senses then there are naturally 'categories of words' in different senses too. In the case of the Active we are still concerned with individual words or word-forms. '*Amo*', for example, must be taken as diagnostic for the class *amo*, *amas*, *amat*, etc.; it cannot be diagnostic for the lexeme (AMO) since, of course, the paradigm of AMO has Passive members too. But there is no need to define a Conjugation as the class of individual members *amas* versus *flores*, *amat* versus *floret* – what would be the point, when the whole paradigm belongs to the class throughout? Here it is precisely the lexeme which is in question; '1st Conjugation' is a class with members such as AMO 'love' or PUTO 'think', and '2nd Conjugation' another with the members FLOREO 'flower', MONEO 'advise', and so on. For this reason, the classification is usually given in dictionaries, as part of an entry covering the forms of a lexeme as a whole. A similar distinction can be made for some of the other classes which we referred to earlier. In the sentence *O Brute, ubi es?* 'Brutus, where are you?' *Brute* 'Brutus' is in the Vocative Case and is also a Proper Noun. But whereas it is Vocative qua WORD (*Brute* contrasting with the Nominative *Brutus*, the Plural *Bruti*, etc.), it is 'Proper' qua LEXEME – as one form, that is, of the dictionary word BRUTUS. This information about BRUTUS again belongs to the dictionary and not to 'accidence' in modern practice.

It will be seen that this is not essentially a new distinction. According to the formula which we mentioned in Ch. II, we are used to saying that '*Brute* is the Vocative Singular of the Proper Noun BRUTUS'. One would never say that it was the 'Vocative Singular Proper' of BRUTUS instead. Similarly, *floret* is the '3rd Singular Present Indicative Active' of the '2nd Conjugation Verb FLOREO', not the '3rd Singular

[1] *Ibid.*, p. 382.

of the 2nd Conjugation' etc. 'of' FLOREO. In these statements only the method of writing FLOREO or BRUTUS (and the associated terminology of word and lexeme) is entirely new. However, it is as well to realise that the tradition began, at least, with a less satisfactory treatment of these points. It is the practice of later grammarians and schoolmasters, building on the statements of their ancient predecessors, that has brought us to our present stage of clarification.

By these means, the classical 'accidentia' or 'accidents' may be reduced to the more familiar set of dimensions (Tense, Voice, Number, etc.) which form the traditional framework of word-inflection. In the preceding discussion we have often referred to these as **categories**; of the various grammatical uses of this term this is perhaps the one which sits most appropriately. But since it can also be used more generally (Proper Nouns, for example, are another 'category' in conventional usage), it will be helpful to have a qualifying term for this type in particular. We will therefore refer to the intersecting categories of the WORD, in the strict sense of Ch. II (sense 3), as **morphosyntactic categories** specifically. The motive for this term should be obvious. As categories of the word, they play a rôle both in the rules of syntax (it is a syntactic statement, for instance, that certain Prepositions govern certain Cases) and in the morphological rules (e.g. rules for Case inflections) to which we will turn our attention directly. In many contexts, however, the unqualified term 'category' will be perfectly clear.

Of the remaining 'accidentia', some are purely matters of syntax or semantics. Thus the distinction of Proper and Common Nouns is never relevant to the inflections: a lexeme such as BRUTUS inflects in the same way, all else being equal, as a Common Noun such as DOMINUS 'master'. Others are purely formal distinctions: e.g. simple and compound for the reasons which we have given. But the traditional Conjugations are established specifically for the description of Latin, and naturally they ARE relevant to the morphology. If we want a specific term for 'categories' such as these, it seems most convenient to describe them as **inflectional classes**. They are classes, that is to say, which determine the form which an inflection will take from one paradigm to another. Whatever their precise applicability they are regarded as classes of lexemes (as above) in most cases at least.

* * *

The framework of intersecting morphosyntactic categories is the main contribution of what may reasonably be called the traditional MODEL of description. Although our illustrations have all been taken from Latin, it will be obvious that the formal terms which are exemplified (lexeme, word, morphosyntactic category, and so on) can be applied to any other language for which these techniques are felt to be appropriate. Only the substantive or descriptive terms will vary. For fairly obvious reasons, this is most usually referred to as the **Word and Paradigm** model. The word is its central unit, and the grammatical words (the Vocative Singular of BRUTUS, for example) are the minimal elements in the study of syntax. At the same time, the intersecting categories form a framework or matrix within which the paradigm of a lexeme may be set out. If a schoolboy is asked to recite the paradigm of MENSA or the paradigm of AMO he will deliver the sets of word-forms (*mensa*, *mensa*, *mensam*,...; *amo*, *amas*, *amat*,...) in an order which explicitly or implicitly expresses their assignment to the individual Cases, Persons, and so on. The term 'paradigm', in this modern usage, can be defined as a further term within our formal metalanguage.

So far, however, we have said nothing about the way in which particular inflections are to be stated. The 1st Conjugation endings differ, in part at least, from those of the 2nd Conjugation; otherwise it would be unnecessary for the inflectional classes to be distinguished. Likewise we saw in Ch. 1 that there are various different forms for the English Past Participle: *beget/begotten*, *sail/sailed*, *catch/caught*, and so on. In learning a new language we are often obliged to learn these various differences by rote. Since we usually succeed it may not greatly matter, from the practical viewpoint, WHAT precisely a theoretician of language will say that we have learned. But there are obviously descriptive generalisations to be made. For example, all 3rd Singular Active forms of Latin Verbs (whether regular like *amat* '[he] loves' or irregular like *est* '[he] is', whether Present – as here – or Perfect, Future, Imperfect or whatever) always end with the letter *t*. Where there are corresponding Passives the same *-t* appears before a following formative *-ur*: for example, *ama-t-ur* '[he] is loved'. Statements quite like these cannot be found in Donatus or in any other classical grammarian. But even for the learner they appear to be useful rules. To capture them we need a model by which we can study the parts of word-forms, in addition to (or instead of, some theorists would say) a model by which we classify words as wholes.

Again it will be helpful if we take the tradition from the beginning. In the work of the ancient grammarians, the techniques for specifying word-forms are of two main types: both may be illustrated from the works of Donatus (the *Ars Grammatica* or '*Manual of Grammar*' and the *Ars Minor* or '*Shorter Manual*') which we cited earlier. The first may be referred to as the technique of exemplary paradigms – the use of the paradigms of particular lexemes as exemplars or specimens (as παραδείγματα, literally 'patterns' in the original Greek sense) for sets of lexemes in general. In the *Ars Minor*, which is a catechism or series of questions and answers for master and pupil, the pupil recites the forms of MAGISTER 'schoolmaster' as an example of a Masculine Noun, MUSA 'Muse' as a Feminine, and so on, and in the sections on Verbs and Participles he is asked for the entire set of forms for LEGO 'read'. In a modern grammar we would expect a specimen paradigm of Nouns for each of the five 'Declensions' (inflectional classes similar to the Conjugations of Verbs), and further exemplars for a 1st Conjugation Verb (AMO) and each of the remainder. Certain additional paradigms would then be so irregular that they would have to be memorised separately: that of SUM 'be' in particular. Likewise, Donatus's pupil was made to rehearse the entire paradigms of several Pronouns in order to familiarise himself with the forms and their respective categories.

What precisely is implicit in this first technique? One learns, in effect, to predict any new form – any form whatever for any other lexeme one is concerned with – by ANALOGY with one specimen or another. Given *puto* as the 1st Singular Present Indicative 'I think', and given too that this lexeme belongs to the 1st Conjugation rather than the 3rd, it is possible to predict *putas* 'you think', *putat* 'he thinks', *putamus* 'we think', and so on, on the pattern of *amo*:*amas*:*amat*:*amamus*... Given *canet* '[he] will sing' as one word in a text, and given too that *cano* 'I sing' belongs to the pattern of the 3rd Conjugation, one can predict its grammatical analysis (3rd Singular of the Future Indicative Active) by analogy with the grammar-book specimen *rego*:*regit* ('I rule':'[he] rules'), *regam*:*reget* ('I will rule':'[he] will rule'). Analogies of this kind are normally left implicit. But if we followed the methodologists of 'programmed learning' they could easily be made explicit in the form of 'structural drills'. The pupil would be given exercises of the following form:

	'I *x*'	'you *x*'	'he *x*es'
'love'	amo	amas	amat
'think'	puto	——?	——?
'cut'	seco	——?	——?

and so on, and instructed to fill in the blanks until the 'structural pattern' was mastered. It is the same process made mechanical in a different way.

Analogy is an important concept in general linguistic theory, which has been emphasised in varying degrees by Paul, Bloomfield, and others. On the one hand it forms part, at least, of the process by which a child learns its native language. One of the most banal observations of children's speech concerns the extension of regular inflectional patterns (English *-ed*, *-s*, etc.) as an analogical replacement for irregular Noun and Verb forms: so *He oughted to do it*, *he bringed it* for *he brought*, and the like. By the same token it is also advanced as one important factor in the explanation of language change. Indeed the historical development of morphological systems (specifically as it affects the framework and the internal structure of the paradigms) provides important evidence for proportions of forms within what we have called the Word and Paradigm model. It is therefore natural that the classroom teaching of languages should seek to trade on the same instinct for regularity.

In the tradition, however, the learning of explicit rules has also played a considerable part. In the exercise table which we have given the pupil is asked, in effect, to apply a pair of OPERATIONS to each of the word-forms given in the left-hand column. Thus an operation for 2nd Singular is applied to the form *puto* to yield *putas*, and is then applied again to *seco* in order to obtain the corresponding form *secas*. The pupil will learn that for the 1st Conjugation in general, the 2nd Singular of the Present Indicative Active (*amas*, *putas*, *secas*,...) is formed from the 1st Singular (*amo*, *puto*, *seco*,...) by replacing the final *o* with *as*. By a second operation, 3rd Singulars are formed by replacing *o* with *at* – or, alternatively, we may say that 3rd Singulars are formed in general by replacing the *s* of the corresponding 2nd Singulars with *t*. In each case, the rule is at best implicit in the drill as such. Moreover, there are other ways (see Ch. V) in which the proportions might be analysed. Quite possibly this is not what many practitioners of 'applied linguistics' would like to feel their pupils are learning! But it is one obvious way of stating in general the relationships between the word-forms.

It is this kind of rule which forms the second of the two techniques referred to earlier. In Donatus's works they are made explicit only once or twice; it should be explained that the two *Manuals* together amount to only forty-eight pages in the standard edition.[1] But the treatment of the Genitive and Dative/Ablative Plurals of Nouns is one particularly appropriate instance. In the Ablative Singular, Donatus begins, all Nouns end with one of the five vowels: *a*, *e*, *i*, *o* or *u*. He then takes each possibility in turn, and states a rule for the formation of the Plurals in question. If the Ablative Singular ends in *a*, for example, a Noun forms its Genitive Plural with the syllable *-rum* and its Dative/ Ablative Plural with the syllable (sic) *-is*. He cites the example [*ab hac*] *Musa* '[by this] Muse' (Ablative Singular), with the Plurals [*harum*] *Musarum* '[of these] Muses' (*Musa* with added *-rum*), [*his*] *Musis* '[to these] Muses' and [*ab his*] *Musis* '[by these] Muses' (*Musa* with *-is* replacing *-a*). If the Ablative Singular ends in *e*, the rule depends on whether this *e* is short or long. If it is short, the Genitive Plural ends in *-um*; if long, it again ends in *-rum*. By these and other rules, a pupil is given instructions for predicting three different Genitive Plural endings (*-rum*, *-um*, *-ium*), and two different endings for the Dative/Ablative Plural (*-is* and *-bus*), which appear in varying combinations in the different Nominal Declensions. At each point Donatus gives exceptions to the rule, where necessary.

In Priscian's far longer grammar (two volumes in the standard edition),[2] rules of this kind are given in a thorough and systematic way. Book 7, for example, begins with the Nominative Singulars of Nouns in general, and points out that they can end in any of fourteen different letters. These are additionally broken down by Genders. He then takes each of the five traditional Declensions, and discusses the Case endings of each in turn. In the 1st Declension the Nominative can end in *-a*, *-as* or *-es* (the last two only in Greek loan-words), and the Genitive and Dative Singular are generally in *-ae*. In native forms the Accusative Singular then 'changes the diphthong of the Genitive and Dative into *-am*' ('"æ" diphthongum genetivi sive dativi mutat in "am"'): for example, [*hanc*] *Musam* '[this] Muse' from *Musae* 'to/of the Muse'. Of the remaining Singulars the Vocative ends in short *-ă* and the Ablative in long *-ā* ('in *a* productam desinit'). Turning to the Plurals, the Nominative and Vocative are identical to the Genitive/Dative

[1] Keil, *Op. cit.*, pp. 355–402.

[2] Ed. Keil, *Grammatici Latini*, Vol. 2 (1855), Vol. 3 (1859).

Singular (e.g. *Musae* 'Muses'), but the remainder are formed from the Ablative Singular (compare Donatus's treatment) by adding *-rum* for the Genitive, changing *-a* to *-is* for the Dative/Ablative, and adding *-s* for the Accusative (e.g. [*has*] *Musas* '[these] Muses'). In the case of the Genitive and Accusative Priscian brings out in particular the point that the vowel *ā* is long, as in the Ablative Singular rather than the Nominative/Vocative. In this way rules are given for all endings in all Declensions – exceptions and qualifications being stated thoroughly at every turn.

Many of the rules in Priscian's grammar have not been used traditionally for teaching purposes. It is a work of scholarship, as compared with the practical manuals of Donatus particularly. To take a further illustration, Priscian gives a full set of rules (Book 10) by which the 1st Singular Perfect Indicative of the 3rd Conjugation may be derived from the corresponding Present. So, for instance, Verbs 'ending in *-bo* with a long vowel preceding' ('in "bo" desinentia...vocali longa antecedente') 'form the Past Perfect by converting *b* to *ps*' ('"b" in "ps" convertentia faciunt praeteritum perfectum'): hence Present *scribo* [skriːboː] 'I write' but [Past] Perfect *scripsi* 'I wrote, have written'. The reason for the change to *p*, he remarks, is that a *b* never appears followed by an *s* beginning a syllable ('numquam enim b ante s in principio syllabae potest inveniri').[1] In practice, however, one usually learns these forms by rehearsing lists of 'principal parts'. For '*scribo*', a schoolboy will have by heart the entry which is traditionally set out as follows:

scribo 'write', scribere scripsi scriptum

comprising the 1st Singular Present Indicative (*scribo*) as an identification of the lexeme, the Infinitive (*scribere*) as a guide to the main inflectional class or Conjugation, and then a pair of forms – the 1st Singular Perfect (*scripsi*) and 'Supine' (*scriptum*) – which exemplify the two main points of irregularity. The entry for another Verb in *-bo* will then be learned separately – thus:

nubo 'marry', nubere nupsi nuptum

– although, as Priscian points out, there is a general rule which can cover both.

In teaching, the balance between techniques is bound to be a matter

[1] Keil, *Op. cit.*, Vol. 2, p. 506.

of practical decision. Any language is learned by a mixture of rote-learning, rules and practice, and it is the job of the language teacher to work out what combination is the most efficient. For our own purposes, however, it is the explicit rules which are obviously of the greatest interest. As we have seen, the wording of these statements will vary slightly from one case to another. Sometimes a grammarian talks of a set of forms 'ending in *x*'; at other times one set is formed from another by 'adding *x*' or 'substituting *x*' for something else. Doubtless, also, one may feel that certain particular rules are undergeneralised. But the general object of the technique is sufficiently clear. Given that one knows one member of a paradigm, and given other information about Conjugations, Declensions, etc., it is possible by rule to predict the remainder. The form that one must know is, of course, the **leading form** (in Latin the Nominative Singular of Nouns or the 1st Singular Present Indicative of Verbs) which also serves to identify the lexeme in general. It is worth asking, therefore, whether this is a technique which we ourselves can follow. And if not, why not?

In fact, its applications in pure linguistics are now very rare. The main objection, as the reader will readily appreciate, is that there is bound to be some inconsistency or loss in generalisation. It is possible, as we have seen, to state a single rule for all 3rd Singulars: in writing, simply replace the *s* of the 2nd Singular with *t*. Similar rules could be written for the *-mus* of the 1st Plural (e.g. *amamus* 'we love'), the *-tis* of the 2nd Plural (e.g. *amatis*), or any other individual termination. But in each set of Tense forms there must be some point at which the process begins: for example, if *amabam* 'I was in love with' is the source from which we predict *amabas* (2nd Singular), *amabat* (3rd Singular), and so on, by what rule is the *-m* of *amabam* itself predicted? In addition, it is not only the terminations which we would like to handle by general rule: for example, it will be clear that the Imperfects (e.g. *amabam*, *amabas*, *amabat*, etc.) always contain – as an ancient grammarian would call it – the syllable *-ba-*. Again, how can this rule be stated independently of the particular terminations? The answer (if we stay strictly within this system) is that it cannot. In Priscian's treatment, the form *amabam* 'I was in love with' is predicted as a whole from the 2nd Singular Present *amas*: the operation involves the deletion of final *-s* and the addition, again AS A WHOLE, of final *-bam* ('ablata s finali et addita "bam"').[1] But this allows us to say nothing about *-ba-* and *-m*

[1] *Ibid.*, p. 457.

individually. Nor, in particular, does it allow us to relate the *-m* of *amabam* to the corresponding *-m* of, for example, the Imperfect Subjunctive *amarem* '[if, etc.] I were in love with' or the Present Subjunctive *amem*. Again, *amarem* must be predicted AS A WHOLE, by means of a rule which adds the total 'ending' *-rem*, and *amem* by another (e.g. replacing *-as* of *amas* by *-em*).

These problems cannot be resolved if rules are simply to predict one word-form from another word-form. We must in some way split the realisation into parts (e.g. *amabam* into the parts *ama-*, *-ba-*, and *-m*) and make generalisations about these instead. In the modern philological tradition (derived ultimately from the Indian grammarians), the technique adopted is to build up word-forms by successive stages. Instead of taking the leading form as given, and then predicting the rest of the paradigm from that, one begins with what we have already called the lexical stem (see Ch. III): a 'common stock' which is neutral with respect to any individual member. This is effectively the 'root' (i.e. the ultimately irreducible form) insofar as the inflectional branch of morphology is concerned; it will therefore be convenient to label it the **root** quite simply – or, if we want to be more precise, the **inflectional root** (or root considered from the inflectional rather than the lexical standpoint). In the case of our lexeme AMO it might take the form *ama-* or possibly just *am-*. Assuming this as the form which is given, the inflectional rules will then go on to predict a set of **stems** (**inflectional stems** as opposed to lexical stems or roots), each of which is common to a particular section of the paradigm. For example, in the paradigm of AMO a stem *amaba-* (built from *ama-* by adding *-ba-*) will be taken as common to the whole Imperfect Indicative: *amaba-m*, *amaba-s*, *amaba-t*, and so on. Another is common to all forms which are Imperfect Subjunctive (*amare-m*, *amare-s*, etc.). To predict the word-form as a whole one must finally add a termination (e.g. *-m*, *-s*, etc., as above) to whichever stem is appropriate. For example, *amarem* and *amabam* are formed by adding *-m* (which is the most regular 1st Singular Active termination) to the stems which we have cited. To form the corresponding 2nd Singulars one has to add *-s* (*amaba-s*, *amare-s*) instead.

The form of the inflectional root is naturally a matter for the dictionary. *Am*(*a*)- for AMO or *leg-* for LEGO 'choose, read' must be given individually along with their meanings, syntactic uses, and so on. Of course, in many cases lexemes will have 'roots' which can themselves be analysed further from a lexical standpoint (Ch. III). But from an inflectional standpoint these too may be regarded simply as the 'given' basis for the relevant sets of word-forms. In certain cases, too, a lexeme might have two or more alternative 'roots': this is one way of handling what is traditionally called 'suppletion' (Ch. VII), for example the suppletion of *fer-* in Latin *fer-o* 'I carry' with the quite unrelated *tul-* of *tul-i* 'I carried'. In that case, once again, the generalised predictive rules will simply take the fact for granted.

In the tradition, the term 'inflection' is often restricted to the terminations – or the rules which specify the terminations – alone. But given the normal sense of 'inflectional morphology' (the sense which we have followed in Ch. III), it seems more natural to apply its base term in a correspondingly wider sense. By the 'inflection' of a word, category, or whatever we will therefore refer to the entire process, or to any part of the process, by which a word-form is derived. For example, we will say that *amabam* shows a 'Tense inflection' *-ba-*, or that Verbs in general are 'inflected for Tense', just as it also shows a 'Person/Number inflection *-m*' or is one of a set of forms 'inflected for Person/Number'. In the same spirit, we will also speak of **inflectional formations** (compare the lexical formations of Ch. III), which may be formations of stems in one case or of total word-forms in another. For example, the stem *amaba-* shows an inflectional formation in which the formative element *-ba-* is added to the base *ama-*. In such a model there is then no reason, of course, why we should not distinguish two or more successive stages of stem-formation. If *am-* were taken as the root of AMO (the second of the possibilities which we mentioned) then *amaba-* may be derived first by the addition of *-a-* to yield *ama-*, and then by the addition of *-ba-* to that. Indeed in many cases it is normal to recognise more rudimentary or intermediate stems, which serve as the common stocks for larger sections of the paradigm. For example, *amaveram* 'I had loved' may be derived via a stem *amav-* (common to all forms that are grammatically 'Perfective'), from which in turn is derived a further stem *amavera-* (characteristic of the 'Pluperfect' or Perfective Past Indicative in particular). The addition of the termination may be seen merely as the last inflectional stage of all.

In the same spirit, we will also generalise the term **inflectional formative** (compare again the lexical formatives of Ch. III) to refer to elements at any stage throughout the derivation. In *amabam*, for example, there is an inflectional formative *-m*, preceded by another inflectional formative *-ba-*, preceded (on one of our analyses) by yet another, *-a-*. Likewise, *amaveram* has a root *am*(*a*)- which is followed by an inflectional formative *-v-*, the formative of the stem for the 'Perfective', followed in turn by additional formatives of the Past Perfective Indicative and the 1st Singular. If we compare this with the ancient treatment, it will be clear that every 'paradigm-forming' element can now be treated individually. Just as *-t* in *amabat* can be isolated, and its distribution generalised in terms of the '3rd Singular', so also can the *-m* of *amabam* be isolated and related, on its own, to the '1st Singular'. By the same token, the *-ba-* of *amabam* may also be taken on its own; in itself, it forms the stem for any regular word-form classified as 'Imperfect Indicative'. By deriving the form in stages, and establishing separate formatives at one stage after another, each element of the word-form can be examined without the others interfering.

Here, then, we have the gist of one alternative model, whose attractions we will return to later (Chs. VII and VIII). Its terms will be broadly familiar to any reader trained within the European philological tradition. Another model will be discussed in Ch. V – although this brings with it, as we shall see, a rejection of the basic Word and Paradigm framework. For the pure description of Latin (and of many other languages) either of these alternatives is superior to the technique of the classical grammarians or of the teaching traditions developed from them. The main argument is rather between these later models themselves. However, it does not follow (we must stress) that the older methods are inferior for teaching purposes also. When the author was at Prep school the traditional rules and paradigms served him pretty well.

It is easy to make jokes about the Western grammatical tradition. It is particularly so for linguists who have not read the sources, and who come across what are merely bad or selective misapplications (paradigms of Case in English are a hackneyed instance). Another temptation is to ignore it, to feel that all this has passed under the bridge. Now the older grammarians undoubtedly made mistakes. But it is possible to learn from them, as perhaps this chapter has shown. In the author's view it is also possible to learn from their virtues. We will therefore return to the fundamental concept of a 'Word and Paradigm' model (Ch. VIII).

RELATED READING

For the background to the ancient grammarians see R. H. Robins, *Ancient and Mediaeval Grammatical Theory in Europe* (London, 1951); also *A Short History of Linguistics* (London, 1967), Chs. 2 and 3. For the parts of speech and accidents in individual grammarians see I. Michael, *English Grammatical Categories and the Tradition to* 1800 (Cambridge, 1970), Part 1. For technical formulations of the Word and Paradigm model see Reading for Ch. VIII.

For 'metalanguage' see C. Cherry, *On Human Communication: a Review, a Survey, and a Criticism* (New York, 1957), pp. 79ff. and passim. Although the term is very common in linguistics, introductions to the subject rarely explain it. 'Formal' and 'substantive' are here used in Chomsky's sense: see CHOMSKY, *Aspects*, pp. 27ff.; for the different uses of 'formal', in particular, see LYONS, pp. 135ff. For a more elaborate treatment of what I have here called the 'substantive metalanguage' see my contribution to *Word Classes* (= *Lingua*, **17** (1967)), pp. 153–81 (apropos of the terms for parts of speech).

Ancient treatments of inflection are rarely discussed: for a technical reinterpretation of Priscian's rules for Verb-forms, and a wider criticism, see *Inflectional Morphology*, pp. 10ff., 27ff. For a detailed technical discussion of the root-based system see *Inflectional Morphology*, §9.3, but inevitably much of the formulation is my own.

For analogy see PAUL, especially Ch. 5; BLOOMFIELD, pp. 275ff. For its rôle in language change see BLOOMFIELD, Ch. 23; also the works mentioned for Ch. I, especially Kuryłowicz, *Esquisses linguistiques*, pp. 66–86 (also in *RiL* II, pp. 158–74). Recent studies of the child's learning of morphology are surveyed by D. McNeill, *The Acquisition of Language* (New York, 1970), pp. 84–6.

Most readers will have experienced the effectiveness of paradigms in learning languages, but I have been told of no study which satisfactorily explains it.

V
Morpheme and allomorph

Morphemes as the functioning parts of words; as basic units of grammar; as units of distribution; as 'sames of form and meaning'; as classes of morphs or allomorphs; continuing importance of morphemic model.
Illustration (structure of Nouns in Turkish): alternation and alternants; vowel harmony; consonant alternations.
Types of alternation: alternations between parts of allomorphs; recurrent v. non-recurrent alternation; grammatical v. phonological conditioning; lexically restricted v. automatic alternations; mixture of types for individual morphemes (Past Participle in English).

A word is a unit which is assigned to a specific class and which can have a number of specific grammatical functions. In a couplet from Yeats which we cited in Ch. I:

> And therefore I have sailed the seas and come
> To the holy city of Byzantium.

holy, for example, is an Adjective which functions as the grammatical Modifier of *city*. Classes and functions may similarly be established for larger units. Thus the first line of the couplet, *the seas*, is a member of the class Noun-phrase which functions as the grammatical Object of *have sailed*. But in that case can we not extend the analysis to smaller units also? The word *sailed* (let us not distinguish between words and word-forms for the moment) consists of a Verbal formative *-ed* functioning as the 'Qualifier', let us say, of the Verbal root *sail-*. Likewise *seas* consists of a Nominal formative *-s* functioning as Qualifier of the Noun root *sea-*. In these examples particular units (*sail-*, *-ed*, *sea-*, *-s*) again have specific functions (Root or Qualifier) in relation to other units. The method of analysis is the same whether it is phrases, words or parts of words that are in question.

As the reader will recall from Ch. I, the smaller units (the 'parts of words') are generally referred to as morphemes. One such morpheme is accordingly identified by the *-s* of *seas* and another by the *-ed* of *sailed*. However, for reasons which the reader will again recall, the grammatical units in question cannot be equated with the formatives

(*-s* or *-ed*) as such. We will therefore distinguish them by abstract labels, writing PLURAL (for the *-s* of *seas*) or PAST PARTICIPLE (for the *-ed* of *sailed*) with the same conventional use of small capitals that we have already introduced in the case of lexemes. But since *-s* and *-ed* represent morphemes, then, for consistency, their partners in construction must be morphemes too. To be precise, the grammatical units are not the FORMS *sail-* and *sea-* as such, but again a pair of abstract units which they identify: following the same convention we may label them as SAIL and SEA. In stricter terms the grammatical analysis of *sailed* and *seas* may thus be displayed as follows:

Root	Qualifier
SAIL	PAST PARTICIPLE

Root	Qualifier
SEA	PLURAL

– all four participating units (SAIL, PAST PARTICIPLE, SEA and PLURAL) being now of the same theoretical type.

In this way the morpheme is established as the single minimal or primitive unit of grammar, the ultimate basis for our entire description of the primary articulation of language (see Ch. I). Words, phrases, etc., are all seen as larger, complex or non-primitive units which are built up from morphemes in successive stages. Just as the word *sailed* has the analysis shown above, so the analysis of the phrase *have sailed* (still following a fairly traditional account of functions) may be set out as follows:

Auxiliary	Main Verb
HAVE	SAIL + PAST PARTICIPLE

that of the Predicate or partial clause *have sailed the seas* as follows:

Predicator	Object
HAVE + SAIL + PAST PARTICIPLE	THE + SEA + PLURAL

and so on. The description of a word in terms of morphemes (e.g. *sailed* in terms of SAIL and PAST PARTICIPLE) is thus of precisely the same formal type as that of a phrase in terms of words (e.g. *have sailed* in terms of the words HAVE and SAIL + PAST PARTICIPLE) or that of a clause in terms of words and phrases. This insight (whether good or bad) is fundamental to many of the theories of grammar developed in the 1960s. In particular, it is common ground between the 'tagmemic' and 'scale and category' theories of Pike and Halliday (referred to in Ch. I); it is also fundamental to most transformationalist concepts of 'surface structure', though the functions, as we have seen, are analysed quite differently at the 'deep' level. Naturally, all these theories have been modified in subsequent development. But this is one point which many theorists of grammar would regard as incontrovertible: namely, that the formal make-up of words is essentially the same as that of phrases, sentences, or any other larger unit.

Looking further back, the same insight was also fundamental to the American theories of grammar in the immediate post-war period. At that time, many scholars even spoke of 'suprasegmental' morphemes – morphemes identified not by 'segmental' sound units such as [s], [iː], etc., but by the simultaneous features of stress, intonation, and the like. A sentence such as *Hád he arrived?*, with emphasis on *had* and an intonational rise on *-rived*, could thus be represented as a sequence of morphemes:

HAVE + PAST TENSE + EMPHASIS   HE   ARRIVE + PAST PARTICIPLE   ?

where '?' symbolises a morpheme which is identified by the generally rising sentence-contour, and EMPHASIS is another morpheme identified by features of stress, duration and pitch on *had*. Since the morpheme is an abstract concept (not to be identified with anything at the phonological level), naturally that of 'sequence' between morphemes is an abstract concept too. There is therefore no reason, in principle, why analyses of this kind should not be adopted. Even the simplest utterance such as *Please* or *No*! would then 'consist', grammatically, of two morphemes in a syntactic construction: the segmental units (PLEASE or NO) and another 'suprasegmental' unit to account for the intonation. Many other scholars (Halliday among them) have tried to handle the grammar of intonation in a different way. Without doubt the 'suprasegmental' morpheme – more strictly the morpheme identified 'suprasegmentally' – is far less popular than it was. But it is perfectly consistent with the syntactic approach to the morpheme which we have been trying to outline so far in this chapter.

In the American school of the 1940s it was common, however, to approach the unit from a phonological rather than a syntactic angle. In describing a language one states the possible distribution of each of its elements. (Of course one does other things as well, but this was seen as at least the central problem.) One such element is the phoneme: the linguist establishes, for example, that English has a phoneme which would normally be written /v/ and that its distribution includes the possibility of occurrence initially (as in /voulz/ *voles*), but excludes, among others, that of occurrence after initial /k/ (see Ch. I on *quab* and [kvɔb]). The evidence is the character and distribution of the phonetic features themselves: labiodental articulation, varying degrees of voicing plus relatively short duration, distributional contrast with the longer and voiceless [f] of *foals*, and so on. But then one finds that larger fragments of an utterance also seem to recur as distributional units. In the phonemic transcriptions of *I have been sailing*, *I sailed the Channel*, *He sails his own yacht*, etc., we find a single piece /seil/ which can contrast with other pieces such as /swim/ in *I have been swimming*, /rou/ in *I rowed the Channel*, or /stiə/ in *He steers his own yacht*. We must therefore set up a second unit, the morpheme, to account for these recurrences in turn. Thus the morpheme SAIL has a distribution which allows /seil/ to appear in each of these environments but not, for example, to substitute for /strɔŋ/ *strong-* in *He is stronger than me*. Naturally SAIL is not identical with /seil/ as such, any more than the phoneme /v/ is identical with the phonetic fragment [v]. But again it is the recurrence of /seil/, and its contrasts with other fragments such as /swim/, which form the essential evidence.

In many theoretical discussions only the utterance as a whole (e.g. the phonemically written /aivbiːnseiliŋ/) was taken for granted. Furthermore, the units were to be established on strictly distributional evidence – i.e. without using evidence of meaning or syntactic function. This is particularly true of Harris's important *Methods in Structural Linguistics* (HARRIS). But a similar analysis may be based on the study of proportions within paradigms (Ch. IV). In the following array of Verb-forms:

sail	sailing	sails [seilz]	sailed [seild]
row	rowing	rows [rouz]	rowed [roud]
fish	fishing	fishes [fiʃiz]	fished [fiʃt]
cross	crossing	crosses [krɔsiz]	crossed [krɔst]

the words in each column have an equivalent range of grammatical functions, and those in each row have a common range of lexical meaning. We may therefore establish proportions by which *sail* is to *sailing* as *row* to *rowing*, *sail* to *row* as *sailing* to *rowing*, and so on. At the same time, each form in the second, third and fourth columns consists of the form in the first (*R*, let us say) with another fragment following. The second has the structure $R+ing$; we may accordingly say that the presence or absence of *-ing* is parallel to the grammatical difference between each of the pairs *sailing*:*sail*, *rowing*:*row*, etc. The third has the structure $R+$[z] or $R+$[iz]; the presence of [z] or [iz] accordingly parallels whatever is grammatically in common here. Likewise in the fourth column the presence of [d] or [t] matches the grammatical or semantic feature which is common to *sailed*, *rowed*, *fished* and *crossed*.

By the same token, the value of R is constant for any of the four individual rows. We may accordingly say that the value R = *sail* or [seil] is parallel to the semantic features which are in common to the first row, R = *row* or [rou] parallel to those for the second, and so on. To sum up, the array as a whole may be said to display an abstract structure as follows:

A	A X	A Y	A Z
B	B X	B Y	B Z
C	C X	C Y	C Z
D	D X	D Y	D Z

in which A, B, X, etc., may be understood to refer EITHER to the features of meaning or grammatical function on the one hand, OR to the forms [seil], [rou], [iŋ], etc., on the other. Thus Y is indifferently interpretable either as the form in the third column which varies between [z] and [iz], or as the features of meaning and grammar which all of *sails*, *rows*, etc., have in common. In this sense each of A, B, X, Y, etc., stands for a corresponding 'same of form and meaning'. Furthermore they are MINIMAL 'sames of form and meaning'; we cannot group the words into other proportions in such a way that even smaller forms will be seen to parallel more detailed features of grammar and semantics.

In Bloomfield's theory the morpheme is defined in just such a sense. The fundamental assumption of linguistics (if we may briefly summarise his argument) is that form and meaning are in some way in correspondence. If a sentence is uttered on Tuesday and then uttered again on Wednesday, it has the same form and is employed with a meaning which we take to be the same also. This then is one 'same of form and meaning' which, as such, is either minimal or non-minimal as the case may be. If minimal, the whole utterance is itself one morpheme. If non-minimal, it is composed of smaller fragments which themselves are morphemes. But there is an obvious difficulty if the morpheme in this sense is to be reconciled with the morpheme qua minimal syntactic unit which we considered earlier. As we pointed out in Ch. I, the proportions:

catch [kætʃ] caught [kɔːt]
beget [biget] begotten [bigɔtn]
sail [seil] sailed [seild]

and so on, are impeccable on grounds of meaning and syntactic function, but whereas we may perhaps say that the same feature of form (alveolar plosive varying between voiced and voiceless) recurs as the second fragment of *caught* and *sailed*, we certainly cannot say that it recurs in *begotten* also. Nor can the notion of the 'same form' be stretched to cover [kætʃ] and [kɔː] (*caugh-*). At the same time, the [n̩] of *begotten* can reasonably be identified with the [ən] of [swoulən] in the further pair *swell*:*swollen*. Features of form vary while features of syntax and semantics remain constant.

In Bloomfield's formulation [d]/[t] would be one 'morpheme' (one phonetic form being a 'phonetic modification' of the other), and [n̩]/[ən] would be a different 'morpheme'; they are related only in that both could be associated with the same 'sememe' or unit of meaning. But the notion of a 'sememe' is decidedly problematic (particularly for a concept such as that of the 'Past Participle'). Moreover, Bloomfield's successors were concerned (as we have said) with a basically distributional problem. For this reason, they proceeded to establish a single distributional unit also. In phonology, they pointed out, a single phoneme can subsume a set of quite distinct phonetic fragments. In many Spanish dialects, for example, the 'phones' [s] and [h] (in ['kasah] 'houses') might be grouped as variants or 'allophones' of the same phoneme /s/: thus /'kasas/, as in the spelling *casas*. A necessary test – though not in itself sufficient – was to determine whether the 'phones' or fragments concerned are in CONTRASTIVE or in COMPLEMENTARY distribution. If Spanish had a word-form with [s] such that, by substituting [h], one would obtain a different word-form (either actual or possible), then there would have to be two different phonemes /s/ and /h/. But in fact this is not so: [s] appears only in positions or environments where [h] does not appear, and vice versa. On this and other evidence we proceed to establish the single phoneme /s/, which in the American phonologies of the period would be considered a CLASS of allophones [s], [h], etc., in complementary distribution. A similar distributional test was then applied for the morpheme also. Within our proportions the forms [t] and [d], [n̩] and [ən] are likewise in complementary distribution: the dental appears in environments where the nasal cannot appear (e.g. after the [kɔː] of *caught*), and again vice versa. On this basis we may establish a single distributional unit (the one which we have labelled 'PAST PARTICIPLE') which, again, may be considered as a class of complementary variants: namely, [t], [d], [ən], [n̩], and so on. It is to this more abstract unit that the term 'morpheme' was then applied.

In its purest form, this approach is characteristic (as we have remarked) of the Post-Bloomfieldian linguistics of the 1940s. In application it was always problematic: in what sense, for example, is the *-ed* of *sailed* a 'same of form and meaning' (or an independent distributional fragment) while the *-th* of *North* and the *-(u)mp* of *bump* are not (see Ch. I)? The general theory has also been heavily criticised, in particular for the parallel between the morpheme and the phoneme or between morphology and phonology generally. Nevertheless, it is an approach which has had considerable success, and whose terminology has become very widespread. In the most usual formulation, the phonetic or phonological fragments ([t], [seil] in *sailed*, and so on) are referred to as **morphs**. *Caught*, for example, would be analysed into the successive morphs [kɔː] and [t] and *sailed* into the morphs [seil] plus [d]. At this level, therefore, [t] and [d] are simply two different fragments, just as [n̩] and [ən] are further fragments different from both [t] and [d] and one another. Each such morph is then said to be an **allomorph** of the appropriate abstract unit. So, for example, all of [t], [d], [ən], [n̩], etc., are allomorphs of the morpheme PAST PARTICIPLE. Likewise CATCH is a morpheme with the allomorphs [kætʃ] and [kɔː] and BEGET, in turn, subsumes both the allomorphs [biˈget] and [biˈgɔt]. The last morpheme SAIL has, we would say, the single allomorph [seil]. By abstraction from the individual morphs or phonological fragments, our proportion may thus be represented morphemically as follows:

CATCH	CATCH + PAST PARTICIPLE
BEGET	BEGET + PAST PARTICIPLE
SAIL	SAIL + PAST PARTICIPLE

and so on – precisely as we would want to analyse it in terms of the syntactic approach to the morpheme which we adopted earlier.

Throughout this book we will continue to talk of 'morphs' and 'allomorphs' whenever we are concerned with a similar morpheme-based model. It is therefore important that the readers should know the background to this terminology and should be aware, in particular, of the parallel with contemporary theories of phonology. But this does not mean that we will accept the system of definitions of which these terms form part. From a more modern standpoint, the morpheme is not 'a class of allomorphs in complementary distribution'. It is simply a unit in various theories of syntax, theories in which morphemes such as SAIL precede or follow other morphemes, such as PAST PARTICIPLE, as basic elements in our representation of the primary articulation of language. However, the student of morphology still has the task of describing and relating the various forms by which the morphemes of a language are identified. It is because these are so often DESCRIBABLE AS 'morphs' (SAIL being identified by the separable segment [seil], PAST PARTICIPLE by its 'allomorphs' [t], [d] and so on) that such insights have a genuine and permanent value.

* * *

Before we take the theoretical discussion of allomorphs further (see the last section of this chapter), it will be helpful to look at an illustration which will bring out many of the points which have to be captured. For this purpose, Turkish is of all the languages of Europe easily the clearest and best suited; we may add that Lewis's *Turkish Grammar*, which we will refer to (LEWIS), is a well organised work which the reader can enjoyably study further. Let us begin with the single lexical unit meaning 'village', part of whose paradigm runs as follows (LEWIS, p. 29):

	Singular	*Plural*
Absolute	köy	köyler
Accusative	köyü	köyleri
Genitive	köyün	köylerin
Dative	köye	köylere
Locative	köyde	köylerde
Ablative	köyden	köylerden

From the viewpoint of syntax and semantics this introduces two of the relevant categories, that of Number (Singular and Plural) and that of Case, whose different terms Absolute (for a Subject or an Indefinite Object), Accusative (for a Definite Object 'the village'), and so on serve here to distinguish the various syntactic and semantic functions of the Nominal phrase. At the same time, the forms themselves may be analysed into a minimal word-form *köy* (classified in itself as Absolute Singular) which may be followed either by one or by two further formatives. Throughout the second column it is followed immediately by *-ler*; we may therefore posit a PLURAL morpheme with this as (so far) its only allomorph. In the first column there is no morph – nothing that we might posit as a 'SINGULAR' allomorph – corresponding. Turning to the rows, there is again no further morpheme which we may posit in the first row *köy* and *köyler*. But in the remainder each of these forms is followed by a further morph which may be assigned to a Case morpheme ACCUSATIVE, GENITIVE, and so on. In the fourth, fifth and sixth rows the morphemes DATIVE, LOCATIVE and ABLATIVE each have one allomorph only: respectively, *-e*, *-de* and *-den*. In the second and third, however, the form can be seen to vary between an allomorph with an *ü* vowel in the first column (ACCUSATIVE *-ü*, GENITIVE *-ün*) and one with an *i* in the second (ACCUSATIVE *-i*, GENITIVE *-in*). When the forms identifying a morpheme vary, a normal usage is to talk of an **alternation** between them; for example, the allomorphs of the English morpheme CATCH **alternate** between [kætʃ] and [kɔː], as above. In Turkish, therefore, there is an alternation between two different allomorphs – we will also say two different **alternants** – of the ACCUSATIVE morpheme, namely *-ü* and *-i*. Similarly, there is an alternation between *-ün* and *-in* as allomorphs of GENITIVE.

On the basis of this analysis the general structure of these dozen forms may be summed up by the following formula:

KÖY (PLURAL) (Case)

meaning that the morpheme which we will represent as KÖY 'village' may be followed by the morpheme PLURAL alone, by PLURAL followed in turn by a Case morpheme, by a Case morpheme alone, or by neither. The brackets round 'PLURAL' and 'Case' in the formula mean that these elements may be independently present or absent depending on the particular instance. If we then turn to the corresponding forms for a further lexical unit meaning 'end' (LEWIS, p. 30), we will find that the same general structure is maintained:

	Singular	*Plural*
Absolute	son	sonlar
Accusative	sonu	sonları
Genitive	sonun	sonların
Dative	sona	sonlara
Locative	sonda	sonlarda
Ablative	sondan	sonlardan

and indeed it will be maintained for any other lexical unit we examine.

At the same time, the forms for 'end' introduce a fresh set of allomorphs for each of the morphemes which we have posited. In *köyler* PLURAL had the allomorph *-ler*; in *sonlar* etc. the corresponding morph is *-lar*. In *köye*, *köyde* and *köyden* DATIVE, LOCATIVE and ABLATIVE were represented by the morphs *-e*, *-de* and *-den*; in *sona*, *sonda* and *sondan* they are represented by *-a*, *-da* and *-dan*. For all four morphemes we can accordingly posit a further variation or alternation between a set of morphs with *e* in one paradigm (*-ler*, *-e*, *-de* and *-den*) and a set with *a* in the other (*-lar*, *-a*, *-da* and *-dan*). Finally, the paradigm for 'end' establishes two further allomorphs both for the ACCUSATIVE and for the GENITIVE. In the forms for 'village' the alternations lay between a morph in *ü* and a morph in *i*; here they lie between morphs in *u* (*-u* or *-un*) and in *ı* (*-ı* or *-ın*). Each of these morphemes will accordingly subsume at least four phonologically distinct variants.

If we were trying to discover the structure of Turkish from scratch (an unnecessary task, but in learning linguistics it is helpful to put oneself in this kind of position), we would rapidly suspect that the alternations of allomorphs which we have posited have some fairly general rationale. They seem to form a regular feature of the system – not, as it were, a set of isolated peculiarities of individual morphemes. Otherwise why do the same vowel variations keep recurring, in our present exposition for up to four units already? In fact the general rules are well known, and are of a type which is found in many other languages. Vowels, first of all, may be classified as phonologically Front or Back. Those which appear in the 'village' paradigm (broadly [ɛ] *e*, [œ] *ö*, [i] *i* and [y] *ü*) form the Front class, and those in the 'end' paradigm (broadly [ɑ̟] *a*, [ɔ] *o*, [ɯ̟] *ı* and [u] *u*)[1] are the corresponding members of the Back class. In any native phonological word (see Ch. II) all the vowels must belong either to one class or to the other. This is a rule of phonology, quite regardless of morphological structure (LEWIS, pp. 15f.), but since the PLURAL and Case morphs both form part of the phonological word it follows that they must conform to it also. In the first paradigm *köy* has a Front vowel; accordingly, all the following allomorphs *-ler*, *-ü*, *-ün*, *-e*, etc., have Front vowels to match. In the second *son* has a Back vowel; accordingly, *-lar*, *-u*, etc., are also Back.

[1] But I do not wish to give the impression that the phonetics of vowels in Turkish is dead easy. In practical classes, students often have difficulty both in transcription and in working the system out.

In addition to the Front/Back oppositions, vowels may also be divided into Close (*i*, *ü*, *ı*, *u*) versus Open (*e*, *ö*, *a*, *o*) and on another dimension into Unrounded (*i*, *ı*, *e*, *a*) and Rounded (*ü*, *u*, *ö*, *o*). The total system may accordingly be displayed as follows:

	Front		Back	
	Unrounded	Rounded	Unrounded	Rounded
Close	i	ü	ı	u
Open	e	ö	a	o

(compare Lewis, p. 13), where the two-way alternations for one set of morphemes (ABLATIVE *-den/-dan*, PLURAL *-ler/-lar*, etc.) can be seen to involve the two vowels that are both Open and Unrounded, and the four-way alternations in the ACCUSATIVE and GENITIVE (e.g. ACCUSATIVE *-i/-ü/-ı/-u*) to involve the entire set of Close vowels, both Front and Back (as explained already) and also Rounded and Unrounded. Again, this can be explained by purely phonological restrictions (Lewis, pp. 15–16, 18) on Rounded and Unrounded Close syllables. In *köyün* or *sonun* the allomorph of GENITIVE is Rounded (*-ün* or *-un*) because the preceding syllable has the Rounded *ö* or *o*; in *köylerin* or *sonların* it is Unrounded (*-in* or *-ın*) because in these forms the preceding syllable has an Unrounded *e* or *a* instead. It follows that a Noun morpheme whose own allomorph has an Unrounded vowel will be followed by Unrounded allomorphs of ACCUSATIVE and GENITIVE in the Singular paradigm also. Thus for the Absolute *el* 'hand' (with Front vowel *e*) we may predict the Accusative *eli* and Genitive *elin* (Note: with Front vowels in the Case allomorph, following the first rule), and for the Absolute *akşam* [ɑkʃɑm] 'evening' (with Back vowel *a*) we may predict the corresponding forms *akşamı* and *akşamın* (Lewis, pp. 29, 30).

These rules for vowel or syllable sequences (rules of **vowel harmony**, as they are generally called) are confirmed for morpheme after morpheme in the remainder of the paradigms. One way of marking personal 'possession' ('my village', 'our village', and so on) is by a Person morpheme coming between the PLURAL and Case morphemes if any. With the 1st Singular 'my' the paradigm for 'village' may be illustrated as follows:

	Singular	*Plural*
Absolute	köyüm	köylerim
Accusative	köyümü	köylerimi
Dative	köyüme	köylerime

(Compare Lewis, pp. 39–41), where the intervening morpheme – 1ST SG, let us call it – has allomorphs alternating between the Front Rounded *-üm* after *köy* in the first column and the Front Unrounded *-im* after *-ler* in the second. Likewise the corresponding forms for 1st Plural 'our' show an alternation between *-ümüz* and *-imiz*:

	Singular	*Plural*
Absolute	köyümüz	köylerimiz
Accusative	köyümüzü	köylerimizi
Dative	köyümüze	köylerimize

– and so on for other Person morphemes. If we turn to a Noun with Close Back harmony instead we find, as we would expect, that the 1ST SG morpheme alternates between *-um* and *-ım* and the 1ST PL 'our' morpheme between *-umuz* and *-ımız*. Examples are the Absolute Singular and Plural *çocuğum* 'my child' and *çocuklarım* 'my children', and the corresponding forms *çocuğumuz* 'our child' *çocuklarımız* 'our children'. Note that the allomorphs of the Noun morpheme, ÇOCUK 'child', alternate between *çocuk* (phonetically [tʃɔdʒuk]) in some contexts and *çocuğ-* (see below) in others.

Nor are the effects confined to the inflectional or grammatical morphemes alone. The Noun *dişçi* 'dentist' is formed from *diş* [diʃ] 'tooth' by the addition of a formative which in this context takes the form *-çi* [tʃi] (Lewis, p. 59). But in *sütçü* 'milkman' (from the Front Rounded *süt* 'milk') it has an *ü* vowel, and in other cases it will have an *u* or an *ı*. In such forms we would recognise a further morpheme – let us call it the AGENTIVE – whose allomorphs behave according to the same rules as the Case and other morphemes which we have considered earlier. So, for example, we would predict that the form for 'of my dentists' could be represented as a sequence of morphemes as follows:

DIŞ AGENTIVE PLURAL 1ST SG GENITIVE

where the last four elements will all be subject to rules of vowel harmony dictated, ultimately, by the first. The resulting form will be analysable into the sequence of morphs *diş-çi-ler-im-in*.

We need hardly add that similar two-fold and four-fold alternations (morphs in *e* alternating with morphs in *a*, allomorphs with Close vowels varying between *i*, *ü*, *ı* and *u*) are also shown by the majority of morphemes which accompany Verbs (Lewis, pp. 96ff.). But in the course of the grammar we will also find a number of other systematic variations.

The morpheme ÇOCUK 'child' enters into one such pattern. As we have seen, it ends in *k* in some contexts: namely, when it is final (*çocuk*) or before a consonant (*çocuklar* 'children'). But when it is followed by a vowel there is phonetically no velar consonant; instead the preceding *u* lengthens and 'swallows up' (LEWIS, p. 5) the vowel in question. It is this effect which is marked in writing by the letter *ğ* (the 'soft *g*') in *çocuğum* [tʃɔdʒuːm] or *çocuğumuz* [tʃɔdʒuːmuz]. A similar alternation is found in the forms of other morphemes: for example, Absolute *ekmek* 'bread' but Accusative *ekmeği* [ɛkmɛː]. More widely, it may also be related to variations of other consonants in the same environments. For example, the morphemes KITAP 'book' (from Arabic) and TAÇ 'crown' (from Persian) have the allomorphs *kitap* and *taç* [tɑtʃ] in one case but in the other *kitab* and *tac* [tɑdʒ] (e.g. Accusative *kitabı*, *tacı*). It must be noted, however, that a pattern of this kind does not hold for all morphemes with allomorphs ending in one or other of these consonants. In part, at least, it is necessary for individual cases to be distinguished (examples later in this chapter).

There are other consonant variations which do hold regularly. In Nouns such as *yolcu* 'traveller' from *yol* 'road', *eskici* 'old-clothes man' from *eski* 'old', *toptancı* 'wholesaler' from *toptan* 'wholesale', and *tütüncü* 'tobacconist' from *tütün* 'tobacco', we may establish the same morpheme AGENTIVE that accounted for *-çi* in *dişçi* 'dentist' (LEWIS, p. 59). But the allomorphs that appear in these forms begin with a voiced consonant (*-cu* [dʒu], *-ci* [dʒi], *-cı* [dʒɯ] and *-cü* [dʒy]) whereas those in our earlier examples began with a voiceless *ç* [tʃ]. In this case we are concerned with a general pattern (LEWIS, p. 12) by which any morpheme whose alternant begins with *c*, *d* or *g* in one set of contexts (e.g. after the *l* of *yol* in *yolcu* or the vowel of *eski* in *eskici*) will have as its alternant a corresponding morph in *ç*, *t* or *k* whenever it is preceded, within a word, by a morph whose final consonant is itself voiceless (e.g. the *diş* or *süt* of the forms *dişçi* and *sütçü* which we cited above). This one morpheme AGENTIVE has, accordingly, a set of allomorphs with two quite independent patterns of phonological variation (the four-fold vowel harmony on the one hand and the voiced/voiceless consonant variation on the other): it may therefore be identified by any one of eight different morphs.

* * *

The reader may feel, perhaps, that this has been something of a digression on Turkish. But it is important to become familiar with this very widespread style of morphological description. It is also important to have some conception of a markedly agglutinating language (see Ch. I). This is a type which is common in the world at large – and which particularly lends itself to this kind of treatment – but, as we shall see, it is not that of the European languages with which the reader is most likely to be familiar. For both these purposes a more extended illustration seems appropriate. Returning to the theory, however, it will be clear that throughout our exposition the concept of an 'alternation' (or a set of 'alternants') has played a crucial rôle. How then is this concept to be integrated into the morphemic model? What, more precisely, are the techniques by which alternations are to be handled?

We have said, first of all, that alternations hold between the allomorphs of a morpheme. The Turkish PLURAL, for example, exhibits an alternation between the morphs *-ler* and *-lar*, ABLATIVE between *-den* and *-dan*, and so on. In this sense we have added little, perhaps, to the theoretical picture already given in the first part of this chapter. But the reader will have noticed that the alternants of a morpheme regularly have much of their phonological make-up in common. For instance, *-ler* and *-lar* have in common the consonants *l* and *r*; in addition the vowel is in each case Open and Unrounded, the only difference being that in one form it is Front and in the other Back. Even in English CATCH the two alternants [kætʃ] and [kɔː] have in common at least the initial [k], and for the Turkish AGENTIVE the eight allomorphs *-ci*, *-cü*, *-cı*, *-cu*, *-çi*, *-çü*, *-çı* and *-çu* share a consonant which is in general a Palatal Occlusive (Voiced [dʒ] in the first four, Voiceless [tʃ] in the last) and a vowel which is throughout Close as opposed to Open. For this reason it is helpful to speak of alternation not only between allomorphs as wholes (*-ler* alternating with *-lar*, [kætʃ] with [kɔː]), but also between the PARTS of these allomorphs which actually differ. Accordingly, within the morphs which identify the Turkish PLURAL we will isolate a specific alternation between a Front vowel in *-ler* and a Back vowel in *-lar*. Similarly, the allomorphs of CATCH show an alternation between, specifically, the [ætʃ] and the [ɔː], and those of the Turkish AGENTIVE morpheme show (for the moment, let us say) an eight-way alternation between Voiced consonant with Front Unrounded vowel, Voiced consonant with Front Rounded vowel, and so on.

On this basis, the SAME alternation may then be said to recur in two or more different sets of allomorphs. In the case of English CATCH this is not so: there is no other morpheme which we could establish whose alternants would display an identical variation between [ætʃ] and [ɔː]. That, therefore, is a **non-recurrent** alternation – one which is instanced in one morpheme only. But in the Turkish PLURAL the variation is precisely the same as in the ABLATIVE: *e* in *-ler* alternates with *a* in *-lar* and likewise *e* in *-den* alternates with *a* in *-dan*. It also takes place under conditions which can be stated identically: the Front alternants *-ler* and *-den* are found with a Front vowel in the preceding syllable, and the Back *-lar* and *-dan* whenever it is Back instead. We will therefore say that there is a **recurrent** alternation between the Open Unrounded vowels – recurring, in fact, not only in the PLURAL and ABLATIVE, but also in the LOCATIVE (*-de* alternating with *-da*, as we have seen), DATIVE (*-e* alternating with *-a*), and in many other Turkish morphemes. Similarly, our description has pointed to a recurrent alternation between the Close vowels *i*, *ü*, *ı* and *u* (as parts of the allomorphs of ACCUSATIVE, GENITIVE, and so on), and to yet another which is exemplified by the final consonants of *kitap* and *kitab* (Voiceless versus Voiced Bilabial) or *taç* and *tac* (Voiceless versus Voiced Palatal). Finally, in the case of the Turkish AGENTIVE morpheme, we can now make explicit two distinct recurrent alternations (Voiced *c* versus Voiceless *ç*; Front Unrounded *i* versus Back Rounded *u*, and so on), each of which recurs independently throughout the language. For the vowel variation compare again the allomorphs of the ACCUSATIVE or GENITIVE; for the consonants see the additional illustration at the beginning of Ch. VI.

In addition to classifying alternations as recurrent or non-recurrent, we may also classify them according to the different types of conditions in which they take place. In some cases, the presence of one variant or another depends entirely on the particular morphemes which form their context or environment. To return to English, the nasal alternants of the PAST PARTICIPLE morpheme (the *-en* of *begotten* or *swollen*) simply appear when certain individual Verbal morphemes, such as SWELL or BEGET, precede them. There is nothing in the phonology of modern English (in the sense that we spoke of a phonological rationale for Turkish vowel harmony) which explains why *swollen* should have an *-en* whereas *holed*, for example, has a regular alternant with a dental. The alternation between written *-en* ([n̩] or [ən]) on the one hand and written *-ed* ([d], etc.) on the other is accordingly said to be **grammatically** (or **morphemically** or **morphologically**) **conditioned**. The same is also true of the vowel variations in preceding morphemes such as SWELL: the alternant [swoul] appears before PAST PARTICIPLE specifically, and its counterpart [swel] elsewhere (*swells*, *swelled*, *swelling*, *swell*). It is worth remarking that a grammatically conditioned alternation may, naturally, be either recurrent or non-recurrent. There is no other morpheme in English with a variation identical to that of the PAST PARTICIPLE. But the alternation in *tell* and *told* is identical to that of *sell* and *sold* both in the nature of the difference ([e] versus [ou]), and in the conditions under which the alternants appear: *tol-* and *sol-* before PAST TENSE and PAST PARTICIPLE (more widely than the *swoll-* of *swollen*), but *tell* and *sell* in the remainder of the paradigm.

In other cases an alternation is **phonologically** (or **phonemically**) conditioned. In all our Turkish examples, as we have seen, the conditions may be stated in terms of the vowel in the preceding syllable (whether Rounded or Unrounded, Front or Back), of the nature of the immediately following phoneme (whether vowel, in *kitab-ı*, or otherwise, in *kitap-lar*), and so on. It is not necessary to refer to the particular morphemes (e.g. the particular Nouns KÖY, SON, etc.) which form the environment in a grammatical or lexical sense. But one may also recognise a subsidiary distinction within the phonologically conditioned type. In the case of the Noun morphemes *kitap/kitab-*, *çocuk/çocuğ-*, etc., we mentioned that the pattern was not entirely regular. Among monosyllables, Absolute *çok* 'much' has a corresponding Accusative *çoğu*, and Absolute *gök* 'sky' has as one possibility the Accusative *göğü*. But the normal pattern for monosyllables is that of *kök* 'root', Accusative *kökü*, and with the morpheme for 'sky' the Accusative may also be *gökü* instead (LEWIS, p. 10). Now we might define the **domain** of an alternation as the set of morphemes which actually exhibit it: so, for example, the English alternation between [ætʃ] and [ɔː] has as its domain the single morpheme CATCH, and (less trivially) the alternation now under discussion has a domain including ÇOK 'much' and ÇOCUK 'child', but excluding KÖK and others. In this case, therefore, we may go on to say that the domain is **lexically** (or, more generally, **morphemically**) **restricted**. Although the alternation itself is conditioned solely by phonological factors (position before a vowel, before a consonant, at the end of a word), we have to indicate specifically which morphemes enter into it and which do not.

For our remaining Turkish alternations the domain is unrestricted.

Any non-initial morpheme with an allomorph in *e* in one set of paradigms will have an *a* in others, and vice versa. Any Close vowel in the allomorphs of such a morpheme will alternate between *i*, *ü*, *ı* and *u* under identical conditions. Any such allomorph beginning with *c*, *d* or *g* will alternate with another beginning with *ç*, *t* or *k*, and again vice versa. In such circumstances the alternation may be said to be **automatic**. The same rule holds automatically for any morpheme meeting the appropriate conditions (namely, those with allomorphs containing Close vowels, Open Unrounded vowels, and so on), in addition to applying automatically in any appropriate environment. A further point, for these examples at least, is that the variation is in some way forced by the phonological structure of words in general. 'Villages' must be *köyler* and 'ends' must be *sonlar* because, as we remarked, the alternatives *köylar* or *sonler* are not of a native Turkish shape. Priscian made a similar point about the *p* in Latin *scripsi* 'I wrote' as opposed to the *b* of *scribo* 'I write' (see Ch. IV). This is important, and we will return to it later (Ch. XI).

When a morpheme exhibits several different alternations we will naturally expect that some may be of one type and others of another. Among the English Past Participles, phonological factors alone determine that *swollen* is [swoulən] not [swoulņ]: in the author's speech, final syllabic nasals are normal after an alveolar plosive (e.g. *garden* [gɑːdņ) provided no other consonant precedes (e.g. *Eastern* [iːstən]), but not after the lateral [l] amongst others. The same rules in reverse determine that *begotten* is [bigɔtņ] and not, in normal speech, [bigɔtən]. But the nasal as such is selected by the grammatical items specifically. Both types of alternation must therefore be stated in order to account for the allomorphs of PAST PARTICIPLE in general.

The same point can also be made for the alveolar alternants in *sailed*, *fished*, etc. But here the facts are a little more complex. Let us begin (the reason will appear directly) with the regular alternants of three other morphemes: PLURAL and POSSESSIVE as accompaniments of Nouns and 3RD SINGULAR PRESENT as a further accompaniment of Verbs. As we can see from the following examples, each of these has three varying forms, which are phonetically [iz], [z] and [s]:

PLURAL	POSSESSIVE	3RD SINGULAR PRESENT
classes [klɑːsiz]	Chris's [krisiz]	pushes [puʃiz]
masts [mɑːsts]	Pat's [pæts]	rips [rips]
arms [ɑːmz]	John's [dʒɔnz]	cries [kraiz]

The alternation is also phonologically conditioned. If the preceding Noun morph ends in a sibilant (as in the first row) the allomorph of each morpheme takes the form [iz]: examples with other sibilants are *batches* [bætʃiz], *badges* [bædʒiz] or *buzzes* [bʌziz]. If it ends with a voiceless consonant (other than a sibilant), the allomorph is [s]: other examples are *cliffs* [klifs], *Jack's* [dʒæks] or *deaths* [deθs]. Finally, if it ends with anything else (voiced non-sibilant or vowel) the allomorph is [z]. We may sum up by saying that all three alternants have an alveolar sibilant in common; if it is preceded by a sibilant in the Noun or Verb then it is voiced and separated by an intervening [i], but when anything else precedes it is simply voiced ([z]) or voiceless ([s]) as required.

If we now return to the PAST PARTICIPLE morpheme, we will find a very similar alternation among its *-ed* forms. In *waited* [weitid] the alveolar plosive is voiced ([d]) and is separated from a preceding alveolar plosive by the same vowel [i]: so also in *faded* [feidid], where the preceding alveolar is [d] instead of [t]. After any other voiceless consonant it too is voiceless ([t]): for example, in *pushed* [puʃt] or *ripped* [ript]. Likewise it too is voiced ([d]) in contexts such as those of *cried* [kraid], *hugged* [hʌgd], and so on. Apparently the same general pattern may be recognised in all four morphemes: PLURAL, POSSESSIVE and 3RD SINGULAR with a constant alveolar sibilant and PAST PARTICIPLE with constant alveolar plosive. The same pattern with the plosive also appears in the regular PAST TENSE allomorphs: *I waited*, *I pushed*, *I cried*. So far, then, everything appears very neat. But what of the [t] in *I caught* and *I have caught*, in *I burned* and *I have burned* (which are both [bəːnt] in the author's normal speech), in *learned* [ləːnt], and so on? We cannot say that this is a further detail of phonological conditioning; if it was, then why is *turned* phonetically [təːnd] (to the best of my knowledge, no English speaker says [təːnt]), or *cawed* phonetically [kɔːd] and not a homonym of *caught*?

The normal way of resolving this difficulty is to say that the [t] of *caught* or [bəːnt] is an irregularity distinct from the [t] of *pushed* or *ripped*. The grammatically conditioned alternations of PAST PARTICIPLE will accordingly lie between a nasal [n̩] or [ən] in one group of cases, an inherently voiceless alveolar plosive [t] in another, and another alveolar plosive which is inherently neither voiced nor voiceless, but which alternates between [id], [t] and [d] depending on circumstances. The advantage of this analysis is that within this third group strict phonological conditioning may again be maintained.

In handling this one morpheme, we are compelled to recognise a number of typologically different alternations among its allomorphs. But at the grammatical level it remains an identical unit throughout ('PAST PARTICIPLE'). And at a more detailed level the same notions of 'morphs', 'alternants', etc., are employed at every turn of the description. It is the striking homogeneity of this approach which has been claimed as its greatest attraction.

RELATED READING

For Halliday's (earlier) theory of grammar see his 'Categories ...' (in fn. to Ch. 1); more accessibly in M. A. K. Halliday, A. McIntosh & P. D. Strevens, *The Linguistic Sciences and Language Teaching* (London, 1964), Ch. 2. For Pike's the most accessible accounts are those of R. E. Longacre, e.g. *Grammar Discovery Procedures* (The Hague, 1964), Introduction.

For suprasegmental morphemes see HILL, pp. 102–14 on 'stress' and 'pitch' morphemes; HOCKETT, *Course*, pp. 167, 177. The notion was developed by G. L. Trager & H. L. Smith, *An Outline of English Structure* (Norman, 1951), pp. 55ff.; see also HARRIS, pp. 281ff. The underlying theory of 'suprasegmental phonemes' is surveyed by D. Crystal, *Prosodic Systems and Intonation in English* (Cambridge, 1969), §2.7. For other approaches to intonation and grammar see the section with this title in D. L. Bolinger (ed.), *Intonation: Selected Readings* (Harmondsworth, 1972), and M. A. K. Halliday, *Intonation and Grammar in British English* (The Hague, 1967); these remove it, quite properly, from the morphological field.

For Bloomfield's theory of morphology see BLOOMFIELD, Chs. 10, 13; the notion of a minimal same of form and meaning ('a linguistic form which bears no partial phonetic-semantic resemblance to any other form') is on p. 161. For the analysis of proportions compare LYONS, pp. 182ff. For the background to the Post-Bloomfieldian school see LEPSCHY, Ch. 7 (though I do not agree that Bloomfield's theory was inexplicit (p. 113)); also *Inflectional Morphology*, §7.2; C. F. Hockett, *The State of the Art* (The Hague, 1968), Ch. 1. Their theory of the morpheme is most fully developed by HARRIS, Chs. 12ff. (but note that Harris's 'morphology' = our 'morphology'+syntax); it is also usual in American textbooks (e.g. the excellent account of GLEASON, Chs. 5 and following). For the original articles see Joos's anthology (*RiL*); the earliest by Harris ('Morpheme alternants in linguistic analysis') and the 1947 article by Hockett ('Problems of morphemic analysis') are the most important for this chapter. The work of E. A. Nida (NIDA and 'The identification of morphemes' (in *RiL*)) stands slightly apart. For a summing up see HOCKETT, *Models*, and later C. F. Hockett, 'Linguistic elements and their relations', *Lg*, **37** (1961), pp. 29–53; important later work is summarised in my contribution to *New Horizons*, pp. 100–3. For a thorough discussion of the entire trend in North American linguistics see R. D. Huddleston, 'The development of a non-process model in American structural linguistics', *Lingua*, **30** (1972), pp. 333–84.

For specific criticisms of Post-Bloomfieldian morphology see Reading for later chapters. For general criticisms of the school see fnn. to *Inflectional Morphology*, §7.2. Those of Haas (on analytic procedures) and of Bazell (on false parallels between morphology and phonology) are particularly relevant: W. Haas, 'On defining linguistic units', *TPhS*, 1954, pp. 54–84, and 'Linguistic structures', *Word*, **16** (1960), pp. 251–76 (review of HILL); C. E. Bazell, 'Phonemic and morphemic analysis', *Word*, **8** (1952), pp. 33–8. For the sememe see more generally Bazell in *RiL* II, pp. 329–40.

For alternations an article by R. S. Wells, 'Automatic alternation', *Lg*, **25** (1949), pp. 99–116, is of capital importance. For different typologies see also BLOOMFIELD, pp. 210f. (in the context of 'phonetic modification'); HARRIS, pp. 208–12, 220ff.; HOCKETT, *Course*, pp. 277ff. The reader will find that these differ among themselves (both substantively and in terminology), and that I have borrowed features from all. Much of the Reading for Chs. VI and XI is also relevant.

For the homogeneity of the morphemic model see HOCKETT, *Models* (*RiL*, p. 397), and compare Joos in *RiL*, p. 115. The simplicity of the approach is spelled out in *Inflectional Morphology*, pp. 117ff., but we must add the advantage (if it is an advantage) of bringing both inflectional formatives (e.g. Turkish *-ler/-lar*) and derivational formatives (e.g. those of Turkish AGENTIVE) under the same heading.

For the morphology of the English Past Participle see PALMER, Ch. 3.

VI
Sandhi

Basic forms and modifications (Greek velar/labial + *s*); basic forms distinct from actual alternants; 'euphony'; assimilation, regressive and progressive; dissimilation; sandhi as 'joining'.
Fusion: dynamic v. static model; examples of fusion (Greek dental + *s*, Attic contracted Adjectives).
Sandhi across word-boundaries: external v. internal sandhi; fusion across word-boundaries (Modern Greek vowels).

One way of handling a phonologically conditioned alternation is to set up a **basic form** which undergoes a **modification** where necessary. In Turkish *eski-ci* 'old-clothes man' (see Ch. v) the lexical formative begins with a voiced [dʒ], but in *diş-çi* 'dentist' it is unvoiced under the influence of the preceding *ş*. This is the normal statement (compare LEWIS, p. 12), and may be spelled out in detail by establishing a form with *c* [dʒ] as basic, and formulating a rule by which it is modified to *ç* [tʃ] whenever a voiceless consonant ends the morph immediately before it. The same general rule would also apply, for example, to two of the possible alternants of the ABLATIVE morpheme. The basic form would be established with an initial *d* [d], as suggested by forms such as *köy-den* 'from [the] village'. But this would be modified to voiceless *t* [t] in the same range of environments: for example Ablative *damat-tan* for the Absolute *damat* 'son-in-law' or *kitap-tan* for our earlier *kitap* 'book'.

In many cases the basic form of a morpheme (sc. the basic form set up to account for all or some of its allomorphs) would be the same as one of its actual alternants. For illustration, let us go back twenty-four centuries to look at a very similar process in Ancient Greek. The paradigms for the lexemes meaning 'sentry', 'goat', 'vulture' and 'vein' have Nominative and Genitive Singulars as follows:

	'sentry' (φύλαξ)	'goat' (αἴξ)
Nominative	pʰýlaks	aíks
Genitive	pʰýlakos	aigós

	'vulture' (γύψ)	'vein' (φλέψ)
Nominative	gy:ps	p^hléps
Genitive	gy:pós	p^hlebós

where the Case formatives, accents apart, are simply *-s* and *-os*.[1] But whereas the preceding morph is constant for 'sentry' and 'vulture' (*p^{h}ylak-*, *gy:p-*), in the other two paradigms it varies between a form ending in a voiceless consonant before *s* (*aik-*, *p^{h}lep-*) and another ending in the corresponding voiced consonant before a vowel (*aig-*, *p^{h}leb-*). The same partial alternation is found before other Case formatives (e.g. Dative Plural *p^{h}lepsí* but Accusative Singular *p^{h}léba*), and also for other lexemes (e.g. Nominative *másti:ks* 'whip' (μάστιξ), Genitive *másti:gos*). We may accordingly establish *aig-*, *p^{h}leb-*, *masti:g-*, etc., as the basic forms, and posit a rule by which the *g* or *b* is modified to voiceless *k* or *p* whenever *s* (itself a voiceless consonant) follows. One practical reason for taking these alternants as basic – why we do not, instead, establish basic *aik-* or *p^{h}lep-* with voicing of *k* or *p* before vowels – is that the rule of alternation can then be stated as automatic (compare automatic alternations in Ch. v); if there was voicing, then why not *p^{h}ýlagos* and *gy:bós* also?

In other cases the basic form may be different from any of the actual alternants. In the rules for Turkish vowel harmony, the Front vowel of PLURAL *-ler* or ABLATIVE *-den* was specified on the same level as the corresponding Back vowel of *-lar* or *-dan*. The two alternants are opposite sides of a single coin. Similarly, the four vowels of the Turkish ACCUSATIVE or AGENTIVE morphemes (*i*, *ü*, *ı*, *u*) would be specified equally by rules for Front Unrounded, Front Rounded, Back Unrounded and Back Rounded environments. Now, for practical purposes, it may be convenient to use a single alternant as the citation-form for the whole. For example, we might speak of the ACCUSATIVE formative '*-i*' or the PLURAL formative '*-ler*' (compare LEWIS, p. 18), meaning, in general, 'that form which consists of a Close vowel' (whichever it may be in particular circumstances) or 'that form which consists of an *l* plus an Open Unrounded vowel (whichever it may be) plus *r*'. This is similar to using particular members of a paradigm as the citation-forms for

[1] The romanised forms are an attempt at a phonemic spelling, and it is these that will form the basis of our discussion. But I will also give at least the leading forms in the normal Greek alphabet, in order that readers who do understand Greek will be able to identify them. For the phonetics of Attic Greek see W. S. Allen, *Vox Graeca* (Cambridge, 1968).

lexemes (see Ch. II). But '*-i*' and '*-ler*' would not refer to the alternants *-i* and *-ler* with the vowels *i* and *e* specifically. Nor would it be implied that these are in any sense basic to the remainder.

For these formatives a clearer alternative is to write the basic forms as *-I* and *-lEr*, where the capital letters stand not for an actual phoneme but for the SET OF PHONOLOGICAL FEATURES which two or more phonemes have in common. '*I*' would accordingly mean the feature 'Close' (which is all that is in common to *i*, *ü*, *ı* and *u*), '*E*' the features 'Open' and 'Unrounded' (which are common to both *e* and *a*), and the 'modification', as it were, would involve the 'filling in' of the remaining features as necessary. Similarly, we can establish *-dEn* as the basic form of the ABLATIVE morpheme and *-cI* as that of the AGENTIVE, where of the two alternations affecting each one would be stated in terms of the filling in of features (*E* filled in as *e* or *a*, *I* as *i*, etc.) and the other in terms of a change of features (change of Voiced to Voiceless) in the specific phonemes *d* and *c*. It will be obvious that either technique could, strictly speaking, be employed for either alternation. It would be possible to state the rules for vowel harmony as modifications of basic *i* and *e* (or basic *ü* and *e*, *ı* and *a*, or *u* and *a* for that matter). Conversely, it would be possible to set up basic '*D*' (meaning the features 'Dental' and 'Plosive' which are in common to both *d* and *t*) and basic '*C*' (meaning those which are in common to *c* and *ç*). Which alternative we choose depends on our phonological analysis, and, in part, on the way in which we regard the relationship between phonology and morphology (see Ch. XI).

But even when a basic form consists entirely of a complex of phonemes (as in the case of Greek *aig-*, *pʰleb-*, etc.) it can still undergo modification in every context in which it is posited. An illustration is provided by the corresponding Ancient Greek forms for 'hair':

	'hair' (θρίξ)
Nominative	tʰríks
Genitive	trikʰós

in which it will be seen that there are two quite different alternations involving aspirated and unaspirated consonants. The second of these, between a *k* in the Nominative and a *kʰ* in the Genitive, is part of the same pattern as the voiced/voiceless alternation in *aig-/aik-* or *pʰleb-/pʰlep-*. Although each consonant series has distinct aspirated, voiced, and voiceless unaspirated plosives (e.g. *kʰ*, *g*, *k* in the velar series), the distinctions are not maintained – are 'neutralised' (see Ch. XI) – when another consonant follows. Before *s*, specifically, there can be no distinction between a plosive with immediate sibilant release ('unaspirated' [ks]) and another with the sibilant delayed ('aspirated' [k^hs]). This alternation might therefore be handled by establishing a basic form with final aspirated k^h, with a rule by which it is modified to *k* where necessary.

However, the other (initial) alternation is also phonologically conditioned: unaspirated *tr* [tr] when the velar is aspirated, but aspirated t^hr [tr̥] when it is not. Compare Dative Plural $t^hriksí$, but Accusative Singular $trík^ha$. In the development of Ancient Greek from Indo-European, this is explained by a sound-change ('Grassmann's law') in which an earlier aspirate was unaspirated when the following vowel was succeeded by another aspirate: hence, in the Genitive, etc., $*t^hrik^h$- > $trik^h$- whereas t^hrik-, in the Nominative and Dative Plural, remains. But a similar process can be stated as the modification of our own basic form. Although the alternation is not automatic it is true that in general 'the Greeks...avoided two rough [i.e. aspirated] consonants in successive syllables' (to give a traditional formulation).[1] We could accordingly establish a basic form t^hrik^h- with aspirates at both the beginning and the end. The k^h at the end is unaspirated in one set of environments (e.g. $t^hrík$-*s*), and the t^hr at the beginning in all the remainder (e.g. $trik^h$-*ós*). In no actual alternant is the basic form as a whole preserved.

All this may be advanced simply as a method of handling alternations within morphemes, as we said. But there is another more general and more fruitful way of looking at it. In such cases, however precisely each one is to be handled, we are concerned with a phonological process by which the basic forms adapt themselves to the other forms which surround them. The basic form t^hrik^h, for example, is said to end in an aspirated consonant. In $trik^hós$ this means, phonetically, that the onset of voicing for the following *o* is perceptibly later than the release of the velar closure: it is the intervening period of noise or turbulence that gave rise to the traditional term 'rough' (Greek δασύς) for consonants of this kind. But what could this mean in the Nominative, when a turbulent fricative immediately follows? The basically aspirated k^h and the inherently noisy *s* combine to form a complex [ks] which is identical with the [ks] of $p^hýlaks$ (basic $p^hýlak$-*s*) and the like.

In the older grammars processes of this kind were commonly re-

[1] GOODWIN, p. 23.

ferred to under the heading of 'euphony' (e.g. GOODWIN, pp. 13ff.). Although they are most certainly NOT the product of absolute phonetic laws (the phonological distinction between *k^hs* and *ks* could easily be maintained by other means), and although they most certainly DO depend on the phonological structure of the particular language (e.g. Turkish has vowel harmony but Ancient Greek did not), nevertheless for the phenomena which we encounter we expect to find some form of general phonetic explanation. We expect them to make sense in articulatory terms. In many cases, the explanations fall into a number of familiar categories. In Greek *aíks* or *p^hléps* we have what is normally called a process of **assimilation**. The basic *g* or *b* is adapted or assimilated in respect of voicing to the inherently voiceless *s*. More precisely, it is a case of **regressive assimilation** – the voicelessness of the *s* having an effect backwards, as it were, on the preceding element. In Turkish *dişçi* we have, by contrast, a case of **progressive assimilation**. The voicelessness of the *ş* extends forwards to unvoice the [dʒ] of the following basic *-cI*. Turkish vowel harmony also has an effect of progressive assimilation (see again LEWIS, p. 16), the vowels in each formative adapting to the vowels preceding.

In the case of Greek *trik^hós*, we have what is normally called a process of **dissimilation**. When the velar aspirate joins with *-ós* to form a following syllable *k^hós* then, as a secondary effect, the repetition of successive aspirates is destroyed. Assimilation, in brief, is a process by which two elements are made more alike and dissimilation one in which they are made more different. In all these cases, we must repeat, there is no phonetic compulsion by which the modifications or adaptations must take place. Certainly it is possible to utter aspirated consonants in successive syllables, in the author's pronunciation of *pepper* for example. Equally it is possible to have clusters which we would transcribe as [ʃdʒ], [gs], etc.; it merely happens that they are not permissible in Turkish and Greek specifically. Nor is there any phonetic reason why assimilation should be regressive in some languages and progressive in others. This is patently a feature of the particular system. Nevertheless we still expect the adaptations to have some phonetic rationale. We would be puzzled if, in some language, a uvular [q] appeared to dissimilate to [c] between back vowels, and, at the same time, a palatal [c] appeared to dissimilate to [q] before front vowels. For a start, we would suspect that something was seriously wrong with our analysis into morphemes.

The traditional notion of 'euphony' can thus be said to capture one important aspect of the phenomena. Moreover, it is an aspect which is often stressed by specialists in a particular language. In Lewis's *Turkish Grammar*, for example, the principle of vowel harmony is said to be 'due to the natural human tendency towards economy of muscular effort' (LEWIS, p. 15) – again, the general linguist must insist, a tendency which plays a great rôle in the vowel system of Turkish but none whatever for the phonetically similar rounded and unrounded vowels of French or German. In the past decades, however, it has become more normal to refer to processes of this kind as processes of **sandhi** (a Sanskrit term meaning 'joining'). We will accordingly speak of the modification of forms in sandhi, of **sandhi forms** which have undergone such modifications in specific circumstances, of general **rules of sandhi** or **sandhi rules**, and so on. Thus, for example, the Greek word-form *aíks* is derived from a sequence of basic forms *aíg-s* (since this does not represent an occurring form let us mark it with an asterisk to remind us: **aíg-s*) by a process of sandhi modification (let us show this with an arrow: **aíg-s → aíks*) which may be handled by the general sandhi rule: 'Any voiced consonant is unvoiced when an *s* (or other voiceless consonant) follows'. Likewise Turkish *kitap-tan* (← basic **kitap-dEn*) contains a sandhi form of the ABLATIVE formative which is derived by two separate sandhi rules, one concerned with consonant assimilation and the other with vowel harmony. The reader will see that all our statements can be recast elegantly within this formulation.

The motive for speaking of sandhi or 'joining' should be as clear as the motives for speaking of euphony. In each of our examples (again, however precisely the sandhi rules are expressed), an actual form *F* is derived by the putting together of basic forms *A* and *B* – schematically:

$$A + B \rightarrow F$$

– in such a way that *F*, as a whole, will meet the rules for the phonological or secondary articulation of the language (see Ch. I). Typically, at least, the form *AB* itself will not meet them. So, for example:

$$\text{t}^{\text{h}}\text{rík}^{\text{h}} + \text{s} \rightarrow \text{t}^{\text{h}}\text{ríks}$$

where the actual form [tr̥iks] is permitted by the general rules for consonant clusters, but the unmodified **t^{h}rík^{h}s* (as a form hypothetically distinct from *t^{h}ríks*) is by the same rules excluded. The details, as we have said, are a matter of joining the inherent properties of k^h and *s* into a single phonetic complex. Assimilation or dissimilation are other types of sandhi falling within the same overall schema.

* * *

This way of looking at the phenomena is more fruitful and also more general, as we remarked. In Ch. V we spoke of word-forms being divided into morphs, of morphs being classed together into morphemes, of variations between one allomorph and another, and so on – an essentially STATIC model for the analysis of words and word-forms. But the model of sandhi is essentially DYNAMIC. The word-form emerges by the interaction and influence of one basic form on another. In almost all the instances which we have discussed so far, it is possible to argue that either model could be applied appropriately. Greek *t^hríks* may be profitably analysed, as we have seen, within the schema of sandhi modification. But it can also be divided into separate morphological segments (first *t^hrík*, then *-s*), and these morphs may be assigned as allomorphs or alternants to successive lexical and grammatical elements: first T^hRIK^h 'hair', then NOMINATIVE SINGULAR. In this respect the phonemic spelling is morphologically more perspicuous than the written form, θρίξ, in which *ks* as a whole is represented by the single letter ξ. However, the sandhi model allows for real cases in which this perspicuity would be lost – cases (as appears only at first sight in the spelling θρίξ) in which it is no longer appropriate for a segmentation into morphs to be carried out.

It is in this sense that the sandhi model is more general. 'Joining' (if we may follow the metaphor) can be accomplished in more than one way. Sometimes units are joined or stuck together like bricks, so that each still occupies its separate space. It is this case that allows us to speak of allomorphs or of alternations among classes of separate segments. Sometimes they are slotted together or dovetailed: the analogy here is with a phoneme, perhaps, which might yet be analysed into features assigned to different morphemes. But they can also be welded or woven into a continuous piece. In Turkish [tʃɔdʒuːm] 'my child' (written *çocuğum* – see Ch. V) one cannot legitimately say at what point the ÇOCUK morpheme (basically *çocuk-*) ends and the 1ST SG morpheme (basically *-Im*) begins. Nor does there seem any point in trying to do so. Within the schema of sandhi modification:

çocuk + Im → [tʃɔdʒuːm]

one can say everything that needs to be said about its phonetic realisation. Only in talking about the basic form **çocuk-Im* does a concept of separate 'morphs' appear to be helpful.

Sandhi phenomena of this more drastic type can best be considered under the special heading of **fusion**. In the realisation of written Turkish *ğ*, the preceding and following phonemes **fuse** into a single long vowel in which the quality of the former (again, by the overall progressive pattern) will prevail. Thus, to give a more striking example, the written *alacağız* 'we will take' is simply [ɑlɑdʒɑːz] (compare LEWIS, p. 5), with the Open Unrounded quality over the whole final syllable. In Turkish, fusion is relatively rare. Phonetically, let alone in writing, the word-forms have a structure in which the patterning of morphemes is largely transparent.[1] But in many other languages, Ancient Greek among them, it is very widespread. For a simple example, let us return to the same pattern of Noun inflection (that of the traditional 3rd Declension) but with basic forms in dentals instead of labials or velars. The following are the forms for lexemes meaning 'bird', 'hope' and 'hired worker' which correspond to those for 'goat', 'sentry', etc., given earlier:

	'bird' (ὄρνις)	'hope' (ἐλπίς)	'hired worker' (θής)
Nominative	órniːs	elpís	tʰɛ́ːs
Genitive	órniːtʰos	elpídos	tʰɛːtós

By a similar argument the Genitives point to basic forms *orniːtʰ-*, *elpid-* and *tʰɛːt-* followed by the same formatives *-s* and *-os*. But whereas the velars and labials merely lose their voiced or aspirated features before *s* (so **aíg-s* → *aíks* or **tʰríkʰ-s* → *tʰríks* beside *pʰýlak-s*), the dentals lose their identity entirely. Any dental plosive (whether aspirated *tʰ*, voiced *d* or voiceless unaspirated *t*) is simply run together with the following fricative: **órniːtʰ-s* → *órniːs*, **elpíd-s* → *elpís*, **tʰɛ́ːt-s* → *tʰɛ́ːs*.

In these examples we could, of course, maintain the segmentation into allomorphs if we liked. The form *elpís*, for example, would consist of an allomorph *elpí-* of the morpheme ELPID- 'hope' followed, again, by the same allomorph *-s* of NOMINATIVE SINGULAR. In *elpíd-os*, ELPID- merely has the different allomorph *elpíd*. If we wanted to speak of

[1] I MEAN 'phonetically'. In practical analysis a student will often be sure of the morphemes BEFORE he knows how many phonemes (or even syllables) to put in his phonemic transcription.

basic forms and modifications, we could do so by establishing the form with *d* as basic and positing a rule by which a dental is deleted in the appropriate environments. Hence **elpíd-s* → *elpí-s* (likewise **órniːtʰ-s* → *órniː-s*, **tʰɛ́ːt-s* → *tʰɛ́ː-s*), where the hyphen in the sandhi form shows that the integrity of the morphs *elpí-* etc. has been technically preserved. However, the notion of *tʰ*, *d* or *t* being 'deleted' is phonetically unilluminating. What is truly involved is a process in which an occlusive (a consonant with closure) and a fricative (without closure) are no longer distinguished as separate articulations. In *tʰríks* (if we may use a metaphor which was cited for Turkish in Ch. v), the fricative hypothetically 'swallows up' the aspiration of the velar. The result, in effect, is a velar occlusive with a sibilant release. In *órniːs* etc. (so far as we can judge from the spelling) the fricative 'swallows up' not only the release of the occlusion but the occlusion itself. The result is an indivisible sibilant in which the articulation of what would otherwise be a plosive and what would otherwise be an [s] are run together. The reason why this happens with dentals but not with velars or labials is that the *s* itself has a dental place of articulation. It is this type of account which the dynamic concept of fusion is intended to capture.

In other cases two successive consonants may lose their identity by sandhi processes. The following are the corresponding Masculine forms of an Adjective meaning 'black' and another Adjective meaning 'all':

	'black' (μέλας)	'all' (πᾶς)
Nominative	mélaːs	pâːs
Genitive	mélanos	pantós

Taking the 'black' case first, we may establish a basic form *mélan-* and a sandhi rule by which *-an+s* is combined to *-aːs*. In Ancient Greek no word-form could, in fact, end with the cluster *ns*. Turning to the 'all' case, we may then establish a basic *pant-*, which in the Nominative will undergo not only the process by which *t* fuses with *s* but this second process for the nasal also. Again the basic form **pánt-s* would be excluded by the general rules of Greek phonology.

In these forms the basic structure is still comparatively transparent. But elsewhere (in particular where vowels and accents are involved) it can become considerably obscured. In the following, for example, we contrast (a) the paradigm of a Masculine Noun meaning 'gold', (b) the corresponding Masculine forms of a regular Adjective meaning 'clever', and (c) the same forms (specifically in the Attic or Athenian dialect) for the Adjective meaning 'golden':

	(a) 'gold'	(b) 'clever'	(c) 'golden'
Nom. Sg.	kʰryːsós (χρυσός)	sopʰós (σοφός)	kʰryːsûːs (χρυσοῦς)
Acc. Sg.	kʰryːsón (χρυσόν)	sopʰón (σοφόν)	kʰryːsûːn (χρυσοῦν)
Gen. Sg.	kʰryːsûː (χρυσοῦ)	sopʰûː (σοφοῦ)	kʰryːsûː (χρυσοῦ)
Dat. Sg.	kʰryːsɔ̂ːi (χρυσῷ)	sopʰɔ̂ːi (σοφῷ)	kʰryːsɔ̂ːi (χρυσῷ)
Nom. Pl.		sopʰoí (σοφοί)	kʰryːsôi (χρυσοῖ)
Acc. Pl.		sopʰuːʹs (σοφούς)	kʰryːsûːs (χρυσοῦς)
Gen. Pl.		sopʰɔ̂ːn (σοφῶν)	kʰryːsɔ̂ːn (χρυσῶν)
Dat. Pl.		sopʰôis (σοφοῖς)	kʰryːsôis (χρυσοῖς)

(All sequences of vowels, please note, are diphthongs; of the accents the acute represents a high tone and the circumflex, marked here on the first mora of a long vowel or diphthong, represents a high plus low (presumably falling) tone on the whole syllable.)[1] Now in these paradigms we observe, first of all, that the endings are identical in columns (a) and (b): Nom. Sg. *-os*, Gen. Sg. *-uː*, and so on. This observation would be confirmed by many other Masculine Nouns and Adjectives. We would therefore expect, at least, that the same formatives should be valid as basic forms in column (c). So *kʰryːsûːs*, for instance, should have a form before sandhi which in some way ends in *-os*. It also seems clear that the Noun 'gold' and the Adjective 'golden' are systematically related. This too is confirmed by other lexemes: e.g. Nom. Sg. *árgyros* 'silver' (Noun), but *argyrûːs* 'made of silver, silvery'. We would hope, therefore, to establish some further basic form which makes the difference between columns (a) and (c). For example the Nom. Sg. *kʰryːsûːs* must, as it were, be **kʰryːs-X-os* with something else (*X*) before the ending. But what precisely?

A reader who has learnt Greek at school can supply an answer, of course. But even he will appreciate that it is by no means transparent in the forms themselves. If we look at the apparent endings for 'golden' and 'clever' we find that in two cases there is a difference of vowel accompanied by an accentual difference: Nom. Sg. *-ós* versus *-ûːs*, Acc. Sg. *-ón* versus *-ûːn*. In two others we then find the accentual difference on its own: Nom. Pl. *-oí* versus *-ôi*, Acc. Pl. *-uːʹs* versus *-ûːs*. Elsewhere (i.e. in half the paradigm) the endings are the same for both. Faced with this data in the field (if we can imagine for a moment that

[1] For the Greek accentual system see Allen, *Vox Graeca*, Ch. 6.

we are working with a fourth-century informant) we might well guess that the consistent accentuation of column (c) is the most important feature. Let *X* as a hypothesis be simply a high plus low accent: thus **kʰryːs-^-* plus the endings, as it were. In the Genitives and Datives these endings (as exemplified by *sopʰûː* etc.) would have such an accent anyway: hence no difference is made. In the Nom. and Acc. Pl. the high plus low tone overrides the high tone: thus **kʰryːs-^-oí → kʰryːsôi*, **kʰryːs-^-uːś → kʰryːsûːs*. For the Nom. and Acc. Sg. we would then go on to establish basic **kʰryːs-^-ós* and **kʰryːs-^-ón*. Here the sandhi is more complicated, but as a first step the high plus low accent will again override the high: so far as that is concerned we would therefore expect *kʰryːsôs* and *kʰryːsôn*. However, in Greek phonology the high plus low can only be carried by a long vowel or diphthong; as a second step it will therefore seem reasonable to suppose that the vowels are lengthened in order that they may carry it here. As a third and final factor we will then find that the language has no long *oː* [oː], but only the short *o*, the long *ɔː* [ɔː] of *sopʰɔ̂ːn* etc., and the long *uː* [uː] which in fact appears in the word-forms now under consideration (*kʰryːsûːs*, *kʰryːsûːn*).[1] Is the *uː* anything more, we will surmise, than a secondary effect of the vowel lengthening – an adjustment which is merely necessitated by the non-existence of an '*oː*' as distinct from *uː*?

This hypothesis is not disconfirmed by the remainder of the Adjectival paradigm. The following are the corresponding Feminines for the same Adjectives 'clever' and 'golden':

	(b) 'clever'	(c) 'golden'
Nom. Sg.	sopʰɛː́ (σοφή)	kʰryːsɛ̂ː (χρυσῆ)
Acc. Sg.	sopʰɛː́n (σοφήν)	kʰryːsɛ̂ːn (χρυσῆν)
Gen. Sg.	sopʰɛ̂ːs (σοφῆς)	kʰryːsɛ̂ːs (χρυσῆς)
Dat. Sg.	sopʰɛ̂ːi (σοφῇ)	kʰryːsɛ̂ːi (χρυσῇ)
Nom. Pl.	sopʰaí (σοφαί)	kʰryːsâi (χρυσαῖ)
Acc. Pl.	sopʰaː́s (σοφάς)	kʰryːsâːs (χρυσᾶς)
Gen. Pl.	sopʰɔ̂ːn (σοφῶν)	kʰryːsɔ̂ːn (χρυσῶν)
Dat. Pl.	sopʰâis (σοφαῖς)	kʰryːsâis (χρυσαῖς)

where, it will be seen, there is not even a secondary problem of vowel-qualities. The only differences are precisely those of accentuation: Nom. Sg. *-ɛː́* versus *-ɛ̂ː*, Acc. Sg. *-ɛː́n* versus *ɛ̂-ːn*, Nom. Pl. *-aí* versus

[1] I am assuming that written ου was [uː] (or at least [ʊː]) by the date of our imaginary informant (see Allen, *Op. cit.*, p. 73).

-âi, Acc. Pl. *-aːʹs* versus *-âːs*. Compare also the only other distinct form in the Singular and Plural paradigms: Neuter Nom. and Acc. Pl. *sop^há* versus *k^hryːsâː* (←, on this hypothesis, **k^hryːs-^-á* with the ending again long to carry the high plus low tone). In the remainder of the Feminine paradigms there is again no difference in ending between the (b) and (c) columns.

These conclusions are very reasonable, and (whether right or wrong) may serve to illustrate the tonal and accentual phenomena that are possible. It is phonetically very plausible that one tone should override another, and that a vowel should be lengthened to receive a complex (high plus low) unit. The proposed changes of *o* to *uː* (**k^hryːs-^-ós* → *k^hryːsûːs*) are also plausible – given, in particular, that the maintenance of the half close quality is phonologically excluded. We could happily proceed with our analysis of the language on this basis. But in fact any classicist will argue that we have grasped the wrong end of the stick. The true basic forms, he would say, should be established with *X* (the 'unknown' Adjectival formative) = *e*: thus **k^hryːs-e-os*, **k^hryːs-e-on*, *k^hryːs-e-uː*, etc. His most crucial evidence – crucial for the quality of the vowel especially – is that trisyllabic forms such as these are indeed attested by the spelling of other dialects: *k^hryːʹseos* (χρύσεος), Genitive *k^hryːséuː* (χρυσέου), and so on. The falling accent, which seems at first to be the basic feature of column (c), is in fact a special secondary effect which accompanies fusions in this class of Adjective in the Attic dialect.

Nor is this the end of the vowel sandhi which may be posited for these examples. If we examine the endings as such it is obvious that at least some can be segmented into separate Gender and Case/Number formatives. Thus in the following forms for 'clever':

	Masculine	*Feminine*
Acc. Sg.	sop^{h}-ó-n	sop^{h}-έː-n
Nom. Pl.	sop^{h}-o-í	sop^{h}-a-í
Dat. Pl.	sop^{h}-ô-is	sop^{h}-â-is

the endings *-ón*, *-oí*, *-ôis* (as we originally discussed them) are divided into Masculine *-o-* followed by the separate formatives *-n*, *-i* and *-is*,[1] and likewise *-εːʹn*, *-aí* and *-âis* are divided into the same formatives preceded by Feminine *-εː-* or *-a-*. In general, as may be seen from the paradigm as a whole, an *-εː-* is found throughout the Feminine Singulars,

[1] The accents are not relevant to this particular part of the discussion.

an *-a-* in all but one of the Feminine Plurals, and some form of back quality, by contrast, throughout the Masculines. Although two of the remaining Case/Number formatives appear to vary under morphological conditions (final *-s* in the Nom. Sg. Masculine but not in the Feminine; conversely, final *-s* in the Gen. Sg. Feminine but not in the Masculine) one can argue that at least the Gender affixes should be generalised.

In brief, we might posit basic forms as follows. In the Acc. Pl., the Feminine has a final *s* with the preceding Gender formative lengthened: basic **-a-ːs*, as it were. The Masculine would accordingly have basic **-o-ːs* → *oːs* except, as we remarked earlier, that there is no distinct '*oː*' in the language. In this case *o* lengthened to *uː* is certainly justified, and we may posit:

Acc. Pl. *soph-o-ːs → sophuːs *soph-a-ːs → sophaːs

The same Back Close quality is also found in the Masculine Gen. Sg.; although other basic forms might be suggested (**-o-ː* or **-o-uː* in particular), the following is certainly possible:

Gen. Sg. *soph-o-o → sophuː soph-ɛː-s

– **o-o* → *uː* being securely established by another class of Attic versus dialect differences. The alternation between *-o* and *-s* seems irregular, as we said.

If we then take the Nom. Sg. to contain an irregularity also:

Nom. Sg. soph-o-s soph-ɛː

(with apparently no Case/Number formative in the Feminine), this leaves the Gen. Pl. and Dat. Sg. In the latter the Feminine is at first straightforward: basic **-ɛː-i* → *-ɛːi* by the mere formation of a diphthong. But why is the Masculine then *-ɔːi* instead of *-oi*, which is the ending we would expect on the evidence of the Dat. Pl.? So far as the length is concerned, the best answer is to say that the Feminine is basically **-ɛː-ːi*, where the affix *-ːi* would have a lengthening effect (compare the Acc. Pl.) except that the preceding *-ɛː* is long already. As for the quality, we note again that *oː* would be contrary to the phonology. So also would the long diphthong *uːi*, the only back vowel which can come in this environment being in fact the half open *ɔː*. We may therefore posit:

Dat. Sg. *soph-o-ːi → sophɔːi *soph-ɛː-ːi → sophɛːi

Finally, in the Gen. Pl. the modifications could simply be as follows:

Gen. Pl.   *soph-o-ɔːn → sophɔːn   *soph-a-ɔːn → sophɔːn

with the distinction between the Gender formatives obliterated entirely.

This is not the place to discuss the Ancient Greek vowel sandhi in detail. The reader will sense that we have glossed over certain problems with the accent. Other complications would confront us as we turned to other classes of lexemes, among them the many Verbs whose forms show similar fusions (traditionally 'contractions'). But enough has been said to illustrate its far-reaching effect on the basic structures of the word-form. In the forms for 'golden' the endings may be regularly analysed into three basic formatives. Thus in summary:

	Masculine		*Feminine*	
Nom. Sg.	*′-e-o-s	→ -ûːs	*′-e-ɛː	→ -ɛ̂ː
Acc. Sg.	*′-e-o-n	→ -ûːn	*′-e-ɛː-n	→ -ɛ̂ːn
Gen. Sg.	*′-e-o-o	→ -ûː	*′-e-ɛː-s	→ -ɛ̂ːs
Dat. Sg.	*′-e-o-ːi	→ -ɔ̂ːi	*′-e-ɛː-ːi	→ -ɛ̂ːi
Nom. Pl.	*′-e-o-i	→ -ôi	*′-e-a-i	→ -âi
Acc. Pl.	*′-e-o-ːs	→ -ûːs	*′-e-a-ːs	→ -âːs
Gen. Pl.	*′-e-o-ɔːn	→ -ɔ̂ːn	*′-e-a-ɔːn	→ -ɔ̂ːn
Dat. Pl.	*′-e-o-is	→ -ôis	*′-e-a-is	→ -âis

– assuming, as it were, a basic **k^{h}ryːs-* with accent (′) following. The modifications so set out would be described in terms of three general sandhi processes: first, the fusions for the last two formatives as such (these or similar processes hold for all Greek dialects); secondly, the further fusions or contractions for the endings as wholes; thirdly, the special reorganisation of the accent. The result is that in some forms both the Adjectival formative (*-e-*) and the Gender formatives (*-o-*, *-ɛː-*, *-a-*) lose their basic identity. The former loses it throughout.

Once again it must be stressed, as earlier in this chapter, that there is no absolute rule of 'euphony' by which such fusions take place. Disyllabic vowel + vowel is phonetically possible and indeed natural. Even if the phonology of a language excluded it, another form of sandhi could involve the insertion of a 'buffer' or 'epenthetic' consonant instead. Compare the example of English *murderer* (← *[məːdə] + [ə]) below. Nevertheless fusions do play an extensive rôle in many languages. Faced with drastic sandhi on the one hand, and with unfamiliar semantic and syntactic categories on the other, it can often be very hard to work out what the basic forms should be. Bloomfield's descriptive analysis of the Central Algonquian languages (and his comparative work on the family in general) is one major achievement which deserves to be mentioned in this context.[1]

* * *

Sandhi processes are commonly found across as well as within word-boundaries. English word-forms such as *hair* or *murder* end with their final vowel or diphthong when they are followed by a consonant, but with an added [r] (the so-called 'linking *r*') when the next form begins with a vowel: thus [hɛədu:] *hair-do* and [mə:dəkeis] *murder case*, but [hɛərɔil] *hair oil* and [mə:dərinvestigeiʃn] *murder investigation*. The extent of this phenomenon varies for different speakers, different speaking styles and different grammatical or other contexts. But after [ə] it is certainly not restricted to words which happen to have an *r* in the spelling: according to Gimson, 'spelling consciousness remains an inhibiting factor, but the present general tendency among RP speakers is to use intrusive /r/ links after final /ə/ (e.g. in words such as *drama* or *India*], even – unconsciously – among those who object most strongly'.[2] At the same time a more regular alternation is also found within word boundaries. In 'derived' forms such as *rainy* or *speaker* the roots [rein] and [spi:k] are followed directly by the vowel formatives [i:] and [ə]; but in other forms such as *hairy* or *murderer* the roots would in isolation end in vowels ([hɛə] and [mə:də]) and again a linking *r* intervenes to form [hɛəri] or [mə:dərə]. It is the same phenomenon, but within words it is regular whereas across word boundaries it is subject to at least some restrictions for at least the majority of speakers.

In many languages where the word structure is less simple than in English, it is convenient to make a distinction between **external sandhi** (sandhi 'external' to the phonological word or operating across word boundaries) and **internal sandhi** (sandhi operating within them). The rules might then be stated separately, though naturally we expect some congruence or similarity between them. But in other cases the 'word' (at least in its orthographic sense) will not in itself supply sufficiently precise conditioning factors. In French there is a widespread alternation by which a form ending normally in a vowel (e.g.

[1] See his summary: L. Bloomfield, 'Algonquian', in H. Hoijer *et al.*, *Linguistic Structures of Native America* (New York, 1946), pp. 85–129.

[2] A. C. Gimson, *An Introduction to the Pronunciation of English*, 2nd ed. (London, 1970), p. 209.

[po], orthographically *pot*, 'jug' or 'pot') appears in a consonantal form ([pɔt]) in certain cases where another vowel comes afterwards. Within word-forms this can be seen in derivational formations: for example, *potée* 'potful, jugful' is phonetically [pɔt] plus the formative [e]. Across word-forms it is normally referred to as the phenomenon of 'liaison' – the forms being 'bound together', that is, when they stand in certain constructions. For example, the Plural Definite Article has a vocalic form [le] in *les chapeaux* 'the hats', but a consonantal form [lɛz] in *les amis* 'the friends'. But the conditions under which liaison takes place are very complex. Under the entry for '*pot*', MANSION gives [poaflœːr] for *pot à fleurs* 'flower pot' and [poabjɛːr] for *pot à bière* 'beer mug'; on the other hand it gives [pɔtalɛ] for *pot à lait* 'milk jug' and, under its own entry, [pɔtofø] for *pot-au-feu* 'dish of boiled beef and vegetables'. Unless the 'word' in French is redefined precisely by this criterion (*pot à lait* being a compound 'word' because it shows liaison and *pot à fleurs* two 'words' because it does not) the conditions must be qualified by numerous individual instances.

Just as sandhi in general is found across as well as within word boundaries, so also is fusion in particular. In Modern Greek the word is a clearly defined linguistic unit, both by phonological and by grammatical criteria; nevertheless within the phrase or sentence it may often be modified both segmentally and with respect to its accent. The phenomena of vowel 'elision' and 'prodelision' are of particular interest here. If we take the form for 'I heard', *ákusa* (ἄκουσα), and combine it with a preceding object *to* (τὸ) 'it', the resulting form for 'I heard it' is not *to ákusa* but *tákusa*, with the *o* 'elided' (to use the traditional term) before the *a*.[1] Again, if we take the form *évlepa* 'I saw' (ἔβλεπα) and combine it with the Neuter Plural *ta* 'them' (τὰ), the result is the sandhi form *távlepa* 'I saw them', with what is traditionally called a 'prodelision' of the *e* after the *a*. The rule is that if two successive vowels are the same, they will simply collapse into a single vowel of the same quality: hence, for example, *ta* (τὰ) 'the' [Neuter Plural] + *arxéa* (ἀρχαῖα) → *tarxéa*. If, however, they are different then the choice between 'elision' and 'prodelision' is determined by their position on a scale of phonological strength or dominance. According to this scale, the single open vowel *a* is 'stronger' than any of the

[1] Examples are taken from A. Mirambel, *La langue grecque moderne: description et analyse* (Paris, 1959), pp. 43f. See also F. W. Householder, K. Kazazis & K. Koutsoudas, *A Reference Grammar of Literary Dhimotiki* (Bloomington, 1964), pp. 12ff.

others: hence the *a* of *ákusa* 'wins' over the *o* of preceding *to*, but conversely the *a* of *ta* also 'wins' over the *e* of following *évlepa*. By the general rule it is dominance and not position that is decisive.

Of the other combinations of vowels that are possible, a back vowel (*o* or *u*) is stronger or more dominant than a front (*e* or *i*). Hence, for example, *to* and *éleγa* 'I was saying' (ἔλεγα) combine or fuse to *tóleγa*, and likewise *tu* (τοῦ) + *éleγa* ('I was saying to him') → *túleγa*. We may also generalise by saying that mid vowels are stronger than close, although the order of *i* and *e* is not so certain (see examples in Householder *et al.*, *Op. cit.*, p. 12). To sum up, therefore, the scale of dominance might be shown by a diagram of the following form:

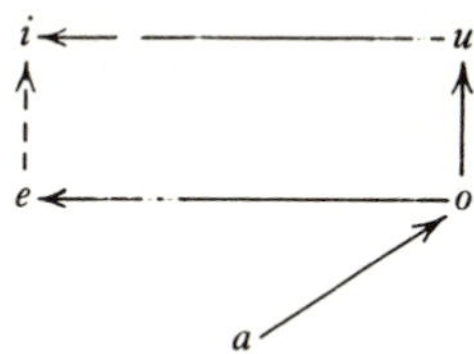

(dotted line for the less certain case), in which vowel *x* is weaker than vowel *y* if there are one or more arrows (one, e.g., for *o* and *e*; two e.g., for *a* and *u*) leading from *y* to *x*. In phonetic terms, the more sonorous open and back vowels 'win' over the less sonorous mid/close and front.

These are all quite systematic examples. But if readers listen carefully to their own speech they will find numerous detailed phonetic effects of a fusional or sandhi-like nature. They are strongly urged to do so.

RELATED READING

For 'basic forms' of morphemes compare BLOOMFIELD, p. 164 (but Bloomfield's 'phonetic modification' is again a wider category); HOCKETT, *Course* apropos of alternation (Ch. 33); NIDA, p. 45; also *Inflectional Morphology*, pp. 53ff. Greek **t^hrik^h-* is an example of what Hockett calls a 'theoretical base form' (pp. 282f.).

For assimilation etc. the most usable accounts are still diachronic: see, for example, BLOOMFIELD, Ch. 21; more recently M. L. Samuels, *Linguistic Evolution* (Cambridge, 1972), §2.3. The classic work is by M. Grammont, *Traité de phonétique* (Paris, 1933); may we hope for a new synthesis, now that the study of sound change is again fashionable? For Grassmann's law see BLOOMFIELD, pp. 349ff.

For sandhi in Sanskrit and in general the best exposition is that of W. S. Allen, *Sandhi* (The Hague, 1962). For a traditional Sanskritist's account see

A. MacDonnell, *A Sanskrit Grammar for Students*, 3rd ed. (Oxford, 1927), Ch. 2 ('Rules of sandhi or euphonic combinations of letters'); for a convenient example of Sanskrit external sandhi see M. Mayrhofer, *A Sanskrit Grammar*, tr. G. B. Ford (University, Ala., 1972), pp. 35f. Outside Sanskrit, the term has been used by specialists since the nineteenth century (see *OED*, Supplement) and generally at least since BLOOMFIELD, pp. 186ff. Nevertheless it may still be confusing, in that (a) not all scholars use it, and (b) for those who do use it its precise import is apt to vary. The student must look for a similarity of ideas rather than terminology.

(a) Among contributions which do not speak of sandhi, two reprinted in *RiL* are important: M. Swadesh & C. F. Voegelin, 'A problem in phonological alternation' (before the development of Post-Bloomfieldian morphemics), and the introduction to F. G. Lounsbury's *Oneida Verb Morphology* (New Haven, 1953), 'The method of descriptive morphology' (which compares the 'method of morpheme alternants' with what Lounsbury calls 'the method of internal reconstruction'). The article by Swadesh & Voegelin may be compared with Bloomfield's contemporary 'Menomini morphophonemics', *TCLP*, **8**, pp. 105–15 ('morphophonemics' there = internal sandhi), and both in turn with the recent work of the generativists (see Reading for Ch. XI).

(b) In later books the best short definition I have found is that of Householder's index (HOUSEHOLDER, p. 349): 'phonological adjustments at boundaries'. On the terms of this definition (not discussed in his text), note first that ANY grammatical boundary may be in question. ROBINS (p. 201) appears to restrict it to word-boundaries, as also Mayrhofer for Sanskrit: 'the mutual influence of final sounds and initial sounds of words following one another in the flow of speech' (*Op. cit.*, p. 30). But our usage is more normal (see references for internal and external sandhi below). Secondly, Householder's 'adjustments AT boundaries' should not be understood too strictly. Sometimes it is not the 'final sounds and initial sounds' that are affected – most notably in the tonal sandhi of East Asian languages: see Y.-R. Chao, *A Grammar of Spoken Chinese* (Berkeley/Los Angeles, 1968), pp. 26ff.; P. Kratochvíl, *The Chinese Language Today* (London, 1968), pp. 35ff. (excerpted in FUDGE, pp. 345ff.); also the technical article by W. S.-Y. Wang discussed by HOUSEHOLDER, pp. 283ff. Thirdly, the notion of 'adjustment' is crucial: the phenomena must make sense for the phonological elements involved. Hence, pace ROBINS, *loc. cit.*, the Celtic mutations do not belong under this heading. Here and in earlier accounts (*Inflectional Morphology*, pp. 71f., 80f., *New Horizons*, p. 106) I have adopted a dynamic view of 'adjustment' (compare Allen, *Op. cit.*, pp. 19ff.) in which the 'mutual influence' of neighbouring sounds or sound-complexes (as in Mayrhofer's formulation) has a central rôle. But many scholars would not see a discrepancy between 'sandhi' and the statement of 'morpheme alternants'; for example, compare again HOCKETT, *Course*, Ch. 33.

For 'fusion' in my sense see *Inflectional Morphology*, §6.2: compare, e.g., Samuel's diachronic usage (*Op. cit.*, p. 39). Many general linguists use the term more widely: compare BOLINGER, p. 106; SAPIR, pp. 129ff. (followed by Lounsbury, *Op. cit.* (p. 379 in *RiL*)); PIKE, Ch. 14 (a most useful general discussion of dynamic v. static models). Again, many scholars who do not use the term describe the phenomena in substantially similar ways.

For external v. internal sandhi see again HOCKETT, *Course*, p. 277; also Allen, *Op. cit.*, p. 15, MacDonnell, *Loc. cit.* (for Sanskrit), Bloomfield, 'Menomini morphophonemics', p. 105.

VII
Morphological processes

Problems of morphemic analysis (Past Participle *come*, Plural *men*); zero morphs; objections to zeros; morphemic v. classical model; morphological processes; in root-based model; 'replacive morphs'; morphological processes and sandhi; further objections.
Types of morphological process: affixation; prefixation, suffixation, infixation; reduplication; modification; vowel change; directionality of processes; suppletion; 'discontinuous morphs', 'suprafixes', 'subphonemic affixes'; subtraction.

In Ch. I we drew attention to the semantic and grammatical proportionality of *sail*:*sailed*, *beget*:*begotten*, *catch*:*caught*, *come*:*come*, and so on. In terms of morphemes, the first member of each pair is a Verb and the second the same Verb followed by a further morpheme PAST PARTICIPLE. In terms of allomorphs (Ch. V), PAST PARTICIPLE is represented by [d] in *sailed*, [n] in *begotten* and [t] in *caught*. But how is it represented in *I have come*? COME and COME+PAST PARTICIPLE are homonymous, as we remarked in Ch. II. We also drew attention to the proportionality of *sea*:*seas*, *arm*:*arms*, *that*:*those*, and *man*:*men*. In terms of morphemes *sea* etc. are Nouns and *seas* etc. are Nouns followed by PLURAL. In terms of allomorphs PLURAL is represented, as we have seen in Ch. V, by a [z] in *seas* and *arms*. *That*:*those* we have not discussed, but one possible answer (if we compare the treatment of *begotten* and *caught*) is that *those* consists of the same [z] preceded by a grammatically conditioned alternant [ðou] of the first morpheme THAT. But how is PLURAL represented in *men*? The actual difference between *man* and *men* is obvious enough. But where are the PLURAL and PAST PARTICIPLE 'morphs' in these examples? Can these morphemes still be defined as classes of allomorphs (Ch. V)?

This problem gave rise to an important literature in the period after the Second World War. Of the solutions attempted, the best known or most notorious involved the hypothesis of a 'zero morph'. Between *sailed* and *sail* or between *seas* and *sea* the difference lies, as we have seen, in the presence or absence of an ending. *Sailed*, according to Ch. V, consists of a morph *sail* plus a further morph *-ed*, and *seas* of the morph *sea* plus *-s*. Turning then to *come*, the form which is grammatically COME + PAST PARTICIPLE is identical with the one which is grammatically COME; in other words, there is zero difference between them. Following the same format (so the argument runs) we may say that *come* in *I have come* consists of the morph *come* plus, quite simply, zero. Just as in arithmetic we use two digits to represent the number '10' (symbolising a one in the 'tens' position plus zero in the 'units' position) so this word-form may be represented as *come* + 0, symbolising a morph *come* in the Verb position plus zero in the position following. The second position, as such, is still established by the non-zero morphs in forms such as *sailed*. In the same way (it is then suggested) that the formative *-ed* is assigned as an allomorph of PAST PARTICIPLE, so this zero may be assigned as its allomorph also.

For other irregular forms, such as *caught* versus *catch* or *those* versus *that*, we have already established a morphologically conditioned alternant of the Noun or Verb morpheme ([kɔː] as an allomorph of CATCH, [ðou] as an allomorph of THAT) which is followed by a morph such as [t] or [z]. So why not say (to continue the argument) that *men* consists of a morphologically conditioned alternant of MAN in the Noun position plus, once again, a zero following? In other words, this is *men* + 0 just as *come* is *come* + 0. The zero of *men* may then be assigned as an allomorph of PLURAL just as the zero of *come* is an allomorph of PAST PARTICIPLE. Speaking generally, the case illustrated by *men* (irregular alternant of the Noun or Verb followed by zero morph) is to that illustrated by *caught* (irregular alternant followed by non-zero morph) as that illustrated by *come* (regular allomorph with zero morph) is to the regular case of *sailed* or *seas*. Nor is there any need (it would be said) for us to go beyond our existing model of morphemes, morphs and allomorphs as explained in Ch. V.

Most theorists would agree that this was a bad argument, and that these were not coherent solutions. Certainly they did not save the contemporary definition of the morpheme. The PLURAL morpheme of *men* and the PAST PARTICIPLE of *come* can no longer be defined as 'classes of allomorphs in complementary distribution' – the reason being, quite simply, that one cannot examine one's data and determine the 'distribution' of 'zero'. One cannot say that in some forms 'nothing' is 'there' but in others it is not 'there', that the 'presence' of 'nothing' in one form 'contrasts' with the 'absence' of 'nothing' in another, and so on. The only valid concepts are still those of proportionality within paradigms (Present *come* being opposed to Past Participle *come* as Present *sail* is to Past Participle *sailed*), and of ZERO DIFFERENCE or homonymy (Present and Past Participle *come* being homonymous, while Present *sail* and Past Participle *sailed* are distinct). Within the context of a Post-Bloomfieldian analysis of language – an analysis in which forms are divided on distributional evidence into phones and morphs, and these are classified, again on distributional evidence, into phonemes and morphemes (see Ch. V) – such treatments strictly did not make sense.

But let us return to a more modern conception of the morpheme. Syntactically, the *sailed* of *I have sailed* is SAIL + PAST PARTICIPLE; we are therefore justified in saying that the *come* of *I have come* is syntactically COME + PAST PARTICIPLE. Our problem is merely to specify the word-form, *come*, by which COME + PARTICIPLE is represented or realised. Can we not therefore say, taking it morpheme by morpheme, that COME is represented by its normal alternant *come* and PAST PARTICIPLE, quite simply, has no representation or realisation at all? This is surely quite coherent; there is all the difference in the world between saying that a grammatical element 'has zero realisation' and saying that a word-form 'contains a zero allomorph'. But then let us return to *men*. There is no doubt, again, that this is syntactically MAN + PLURAL just as *seas* is SEA + PLURAL. Our problem, again, is simply to specify the corresponding word-form *men*. Can we not do so, in an entirely parallel way, by saying first that MAN is represented by a morphologically conditioned alternant *men*, and then that PLURAL, like the PAST PARTICIPLE of *come*, has no representation of its own whatever? Again, we are not suggesting that the word-form *men* is in some sense 'analysed into' *men* + o, but merely that PLURAL itself is in no way realised within it. Surely, this too is quite coherent and meaningful?

The answer is that it is meaningful, indeed. But by the same token it is also wrong – or, at the very least, the ordinary meanings of 'represented by' or 'realised by' are flagrantly violated. How can one maintain that PLURAL has 'no representation' or 'no realisation' in *men*, when the vowel quality [e] is specifically distinct from that of the Singular or non-Plural *man*? In many other cases vowel-distinctions of this kind recur for two or more or several lexemes. The difference between Plural *teeth* and non-Plural *tooth* is the same as that between *geese* and *goose* and almost the same as that between *feet* and *foot*. The set of differences between *sink* (morphemically SINK), *sank* (morphemically SINK + PAST TENSE) and *sunk* (SINK + PAST PARTICIPLE), though irregular, is paralleled by various other paradigms in *-nk* or *-ng*: *sing*:*sang*:*sung*, *drink*:*drank*:*drunk*, and so on. If we return to the terms in which we first began to talk about English Nouns and Verbs (see Ch. I), the PLURAL morpheme is as clearly identified by the [iː] of *teeth* or the [e] of *men* as it is by the [z] of *seas* or the [s] of *masts*. Likewise, PAST TENSE and PAST PARTICIPLE are as clearly identified by the [æ] of *sank* and the [ʌ] of *sunk* as they are distinguished (from the rest of the paradigm, that is) by the [d] of *sailed* or the [t] of *fished*. If the distinctive endings are related directly to their respective morphemes, surely the distinctive vowel-qualities should be related directly too.

This objection is important and is worth underlining. The aim of morphological analysis, as of linguistic analysis in general, is to bring out the relationships which are systematic in the given language. It is not simply to specify the forms or to 'generate' the 'phonetic signals' (see Ch. XII) somehow. We must also distinguish the significant features of these 'signals', and generalise their relationship to the grammatical terms of the paradigm. In Ch. IV, as the reader will recall, we criticised Priscian's account of the Latin Verb for failing to do so in at least some forms. For example, if the 1st Singulars *legebam* 'I was reading', *legerem* '[if, etc.] I were reading', and so on were derived individually as wholes one would fail to generalise the relationship of final *-m* to the Person and Number category. An argument for preferring the model of morphemes and allomorphs is that this relationship can be brought out better. The final *-m* would be one of the alternants of a 1ST SINGULAR morpheme, just as the preceding morphs (*-ba* and *-re*, let us say) are allomorphs of the Mood and Tense, the contrasting *-t* of *legebat* etc. the only allomorph of 3RD SINGULAR, and so on. This is a standard argument for analysing the word-form into its separate formatives.

In the case of *men*, *teeth*, *sank*, etc., the classical treatment would, however, be better than the analysis with zeros that we have just described. The Plural *men* would be derived from *man* (sc. by altering the vowel) in the same sense that the regular *seas* can be predicted or derived from its Singular *sea* (sc. by adding *-s*). For a certain inflectional class (SINK, SING, etc.) the Past Tense and Past Participle are predictable according to a rule by which the *i* of the Present Tense is replaced by *a* or *u*. For the regular class they are likewise predictable according to a rule by which the Present has *-ed* added to it. It does not matter whether the resulting features of the word-form are a certain vowel-quality (as in *men*, *sank* or *sunk*) or the presence of a certain ending (as in *seas* and *sailed*). Each is specified by a rule which relates it directly to the grammatical terms Plural, Past Tense and Past Participle. But in the morphemic solution the two cases will be analysed in unequal ways. On the one hand an ending is assigned directly to the morpheme which it realises. No linguist would maintain, for example, that *sailed* was a grammatically conditioned alternant of SAIL with zero as the realisation of PAST TENSE or PAST PARTICIPLE. Yet it is precisely such a solution which has been suggested for *sank* or *sunk*. The vowel-qualities are parts of the alternants of SINK, and the only generalisation concerns a recurrent but lexically restricted alternation (see Ch. V) for which PAST TENSE etc. are merely the conditioning factors. Likewise the *s* in *seas* is the direct realisation of PLURAL, but *men* or *teeth* are merely alternants realising MAN and TOOTH when PLURAL follows.

Most linguists would broadly agree with these criticisms. In some way the oppositions of vowel-quality must be related to their grammatical elements, and the obvious way (as in the traditional model) is by the statement of a **morphological process** or operation: replace *a* in *man* with *e*, replace *i* in *sing*, *sink*, etc., with *a* or *u*, and so on. This has rarely been treated as a live issue in the past decade. But how wide a rôle should processes play in a description? How far do we have to abandon the concept of morphemes and allomorphs to accommodate them? There is little active controversy on these points, simply because morphological theory has in general been neglected in recent years (Ch. I). But there is much practical disagreement in describing individual languages.

The oldest view is that everything should be handled by processes deriving word-forms from other word-forms. This we have rejected for Latin (see again Ch. IV), but the same arguments do not apply to languages such as English, in which the relevant members of the paradigm would be derived in only a single step. *Sailed* and *sank*, for example, come by a single step from *sail* and *sink*, the generalisations concerning *-ed* and *-a-* being thus expressed perfectly, as we have seen. Moreover the leading forms *sail*, *sing*, etc., have in general no feature of their own in common; hence no generalisation is missed at that point even. If we reject this treatment for English it must be on grounds of non-universality (many linguists would require, a priori, that all languages should be described in the same general way), or for quite different reasons altogether.

An alternative model, which we introduced at the end of Ch. IV, is to build up the form by processes starting from a root. Thus *sailed* and *sank* would be derived not from the word-forms *sail* and *sink* themselves – the Past Tense of Verbs from the Present Tense specifically – but from the roots *sail* and *sink* which happen to be identical with them. Similarly, *men* or *teeth* would be derived from the root *man* or *tooth* and not from the Singular (also *man* or *tooth*) as such. This model has advantages, as we have seen, for any language with more complex word-structure. If all members of the paradigm have at least one formative requiring generalisation (as is the case in Latin, Italian, Ancient Greek, Modern Greek, and other languages of a familiar type), the general rules can all be stated in equal terms: see our discussion of the Latin Person/Number endings in Ch. IV. If certain members have two or more such formatives (as is true in the same group of languages), then each can be handled separately. For example, the *-ba-* of Latin *amabam* 'I was in love with' can be the subject of one rule and the *-m* of another (see again Ch. IV). Any language could strictly be brought within this model if it seemed appropriate.

A consequence for English, however, is that the word-forms *sail*, *sink*, *man*, *tooth*, etc., must be derived in a similar way. We must postulate a zero operation or **identity operation** – an operation whose output is identical with its input – by which the Present Tense of SAIL is derived from the appropriate root *sail*, the Singular of MAN from *man*, the Present Tense as well as the Past Participle of COME from *come*, and so on. This is perfectly consistent, once we have decided to adopt this model. Nor does an identity operation raise conceptual difficulties of the sort which we have discovered with zero allomorphs. There is no nonsense here of 'adding a zero ending' or of the resulting forms 'containing a zero formative'. But although it is consistent, many readers will feel that it is in a real sense otiose. Surely it is more economical to take the Present Tense and Singular forms as given. Indeed, do we need to talk of SAIL or SINK 'in the Present Tense' as opposed to the Past Tense, seeing that Past alone has an explicit identifying formative? Grammatically, why cannot these members of the paradigm just be SAIL and SINK full stop?

For these and other reasons, many linguists have tried to accommodate processes with as little disturbance as possible to the general theory of the morpheme. One suggestion in the post-war period was to present them as a special type of allomorph. *Men*, for example, would be said to consist of the regular allomorph *man* of the morpheme MAN plus a 'replacive morph' ('replace *a* with *e*' or '*a* → *e*') which was assigned as yet another allomorph of PLURAL. The PLURAL morpheme would thus be regarded as a class of morphs with [z] (in *seas*), [s] (in *masts*), zero (in *sheep*: compare the treatment of *come* above), and '*a* → *e*' among its members. Likewise, *sank* would 'consist' of a morph *sink* plus a further morph '*i* → *a*', where this '*i* → *a*' would be another allomorph of PAST TENSE.

This was nonsense, of course. A process of replacement is no more a 'morph' than zero is a 'morph'. The concept of the morpheme as a class of alternating allomorphs cannot be saved that way. But as in the case of zero something can perhaps be rescued from this proposal. Let us think, once again, of the relation between syntactic elements (morphemes as determined syntactically) and their representations in the word-form. In a regular form such as *seas* or *sailed* the morphemes PLURAL, PAST TENSE or PAST PARTICIPLE are realised by separate formatives, which can then be combined with their neighbours by processes of sandhi (Ch. VI) where necessary. But for irregularities such as *men* or *sank*, the lexical and grammatical morphemes combine at once by means of an operation sparked off in the former by the latter. Given the grammatical word SINK + PAST TENSE, where SINK is a morpheme which would be represented in isolation by its basic form *sink*, PAST TENSE loses its position in the sequence and is represented solely by the effects of vowel change (*sink* → *sank*). Given the word MAN + PLURAL, the two elements will similarly combine to form a unified basic *men*.

Again, we are no longer talking of alternants or allomorphs, but of the PROCESS by which two morphologically separate elements react with each other to form a single realisation. There is a parallel here with the theory of sandhi as we explained it in Ch. VI. In a form such as [*He*] *hit* [*me*] there are no separate alternants of HIT and PAST TENSE (this was indeed one of the stock examples of zero morphs). But one attractive solution is to say that *hit* results from the fusion of basic **hit-t*, the inherently voiceless *-t* which is found in *burned* [bəːnt], etc. (see the end of Ch. V) being run together with the *t* of the preceding *hit-* by a process which has an obvious phonetic and phonological rationale. In *men* there are likewise no separate alternants of MAN and PLURAL. The difference is that in this case there is no rationale (a form such as *mans* would be possible, and there would be nothing natural in **man-s* → *men*), and by the same token no basic segment for PLURAL can be posited.

Morphological processes and sandhi must obviously be distinguished (just as grammatically conditioned alternation must be distinguished from phonologically conditioned alternation). But both are part of a dynamic rather than a static concept of word-structure. In both the morpheme is only the syntactic input to processes which are in no way required to preserve it as a separable fragment of the word-form.

Some such treatment has been adopted or implied by many linguists, though perhaps not all would be willing to talk about it in precisely these terms. But a linguist trained in the classical and philogical tradition may be forgiven if he still has doubts. Why should the *-ed* of *sailed* be handled one way (namely, as an allomorph of PAST TENSE or PAST PARTICIPLE specifically), and the *a* of *sank* in another (namely, by a process with both SINK or *sink* and PAST TENSE as input)? What we wanted, surely, was a way to handle all identifying features equally. And how do we analyse forms such as *sold* and *told*, where there is both a following formative and a vowel variation? In terms of morphemes and allomorphs *-d* alone belongs to PAST TENSE, whereas *sol-* and *tol-* are special allomorphs of SELL and TELL (see Ch. V). Do we retain this analysis, relating PAST TENSE specifically to *-d*, and SELL/TELL specifically to *sol-/tol-*? It is not obvious that we can do otherwise. But BOTH the *-d* AND the vowel quality have an identifying rôle. Surely we want to handle both as realisations of the 'Past Tense', again on equal terms.

This is part of a wider argument (as we shall see in Ch. VIII). But one important issue is again that of universality. Of our various process models, the one which is based on the root seemed otiose in English *sail* → *sail*, *man* → *man*. We may add that it is even more pointless for a language such as Turkish, as the reader may easily check from the paradigms in Ch. V. Conversely, the model based on whole word-forms is inadequate for Latin (Ch. IV). Finally, the one based on the morpheme has just been questioned, for English at least. We should begin to ask whether it is right or necessary to apply the same theoretical model to every type of language.

* * *

The preceding argument has many theoretical ramifications. It has therefore seemed helpful to restrict it, for the sake of clarity, to the most familiar English examples. But these can give no impression of the rich variety of morphological processes to be found throughout the languages of the world. In English two main types have been illustrated: the addition of a basically separate ending (assuming, that is, that a form such as *sailed* is to be treated by process rules) and another which involves an internal vowel change. Other languages, however, have processes of types which are not found in English at all: the 'reduplications' of Ancient Greek or Latin (see below) are one case which will be familiar to many readers. A detailed typology would be too much, perhaps, for this kind of book. But it may be useful to consider the main distinctions which are logically possible.

The first major division is between addition or **affixation** (for example, the affixation of *-ed* in *sail* → *sailed*) and all the remainder. Affixation is defined by two characteristics. Firstly, the derivand (the form which results when a process or operation is applied) will consist of the operand (the form that it is applied to) plus a new formative which has been added or 'affixed' to it. Thus, for instance, the derivand *sailed* consists of the operand *sail* plus the formative written as *-ed*. Secondly, this additional formative (the **affix**) will be a constant; it will be the same whatever particular operand is in question. So, for example, the affixation of *-ed* in English may be represented as follows:

$$\mathrm{O} \rightarrow \mathrm{O}+\mathrm{ed}$$

where *O* stands for any of the possible operands *sail*, *fish*, *wait* and so on, and the single constant *-ed* is added to all. An affix may, of course, be modified in accordance with other rules: as we have seen, the *-ed* formative varies between [d], [t] and [id] (end of Ch. V). But as a basic form, in the sense of Ch. VI, it is the same throughout.

Processes of affixation may then be divided into **prefixation**, **suffixation** or **infixation**, depending on whether the affix is added before the operand, after it, or at some determined point within it. By the same token, the affix itself may be a **prefix**, a **suffix**, or an **infix**. In English the commonest processes are those of suffixation: they are involved in most lexical formations (*generate* → *generate* + *ion* = *generation* – see Ch. III; *happy* → *happy* + *ness* = *happiness*, and so on) and in all inflectional formations (*sail* → *sailed*, *sea* → *sea* + *s*, etc.). Examples of prefixation are found, however, in the negative formations of *happy* → *un* + *happy* – schematically:

$$\mathrm{O} \rightarrow \mathrm{un}+\mathrm{O}$$

– or of *order* → *dis* + *order*. The English tendency to suffixation continues a characteristic of Indo-European which has substantially resisted change through the millennia. But outside Europe there are other families where prefixation predominates. The following, for example, is a fragment of a paradigm of basic forms in Chipewyan:[1]

	Perfective	*Future*
2nd Sg.	*γɛ-n-tsaγ	*γwa-n-tsaγ
2nd Pl.	*γɛ-uh-tsaγ	*γwa-uh-tsaγ

(by sandhi becoming *γĩtsaγ* and *γwuhtsaγ* 'you (Sg.), you (Pl.) have cried', *γwũtsaγ* and *γwuhtsaγ* 'you (Sg.), you (Pl.) will cry'), in which the stem *-tsaγ* 'cry' is accompanied by the Subject prefixes *n-* and *uh-* (2nd Sg. and Pl.) and the Aspect prefixes *γɛ-* and *γwa-* (Perfective and Future). Inflection by prefixes is characteristic of the Athapaskan family, to which Chipewyan belongs.

An example of infixation is provided by the Imperfective stems in the following (for the Latin Verbs RUMPO 'break', with root *rup-*, and RELINQUO 'leave behind', with root *reliqu-*):

	Imperfective	*Past Participle*
'break'	rump-	rup-t-
'leave behind'	relinqu-	relic-t-

In the second column the Past Participle stems are derived by the addition of a suffix *-t-* to the roots (*relict-* being a sandhi form for, as it were, **reliqu-t-*). But the Imperfectives (traditionally the 'Present' stems) are instead derived by adding a nasal infix (sandhi forms [m] in *rump-*, [ŋ] in *relinqu-*) immediately before its final consonant. The boundary between infixation and prefixation or suffixation is not always as simple, however, as a neat typological definition may suggest. Firstly, the same formative may be introduced 'infixally' in some instances, but as an apparent 'suffix' or 'prefix' in others. In Latin, the same operations will also derive the corresponding stems for SINO 'allow':

'allow'	sin-	si-t-

where both the *-t-* and the nasal ([n] in this case) are added following the root *si-*. The reason is that the root *si-* has no final consonant; since the nasal is added before a consonant where there is one (thus *rup-* → *ru*+nasal+*p*), it follows that without one it will simply be added at the end (*si-* → *si*+nasal). To show this, the operation may be schematised in the following way:

$$\ldots \mathrm{V}\ (\mathrm{C}) \rightarrow \mathrm{V} + \text{nasal} + (\mathrm{C})$$

[1] From the sketch by Li Fang-Kuei, 'Chipewyan', in *Linguistic Structures of Native America*, pp. 398–423.

where *V* stands for vowel and *C* for consonant, and the brackets around the *C* indicate that in some cases it is present and in others not.

Another point of confusion might arise from the order in which successive processes are applied. To derive the Chipewyan form **γε-n-tsaγ* (see above), a proponent of this type of description would first prefix *n*- to the base *-tsaγ* to yield an inflectional stem *n-tsaγ*, and then taking this as the base he would prefix *γε*- in turn. He would not derive *γε-tsaγ* first and then, as it were, 'infix' *n*-. But in the Athapaskan Verb an Adverbial or other lexical prefix (lexical in the sense of Ch. III) regularly precedes either all or some of the inflectional prefixes: for example, in the corresponding Perfective forms for a derived Verb meaning 'eat':

2nd Sg.	*ʃέ-γε-n-tĩ
2nd Pl.	*ʃέ-γε-uh-tĩ

(→ *ʃέγĩtĩ*, *ʃέγwuhtĩ*; cf. Li, article cited), the *ʃέ*- and *-tĩ* together form a lexical 'theme' which must be associated as a whole with the lexical meaning. One might then say that the inflectional formatives *γε*-, *n*- and *uh*- are added not as 'prefixes' to *-tĩ*- (which is naturally what is normally said), but rather as 'infixes' to the theme *ʃέ...tĩ*. The issue is not of great importance, except that it may lead to typological disagreements between one investigator and another.

In all processes of affixation, as we have said, the derivand consists of the operand plus an added constant: in infixation the internal structure of the operand is also broken into, whereas in prefixation and suffixation it is left intact. However, there are other processes of 'addition' in which the formative is not a constant but has a basic form determined (either wholly or in part) by the form of the operand itself. The following, for example, is a set of regular Verb stems in Ancient Greek:

	Future	*Perfective Active*
'strike'	pai-s-	pe-pai-k-
'love'	pʰilɛː-s-	pe-pʰilɛː-k-
'order'	keleu-s-	ke-keleu-k-
'heap up'	kʰɔː-s-	ke-kʰɔː-k-

which may be abstracted from the 1st Singulars *paísɔː* 'I will strike' (παίσω) and *pépaika* 'I have struck' (πέπαικα), *pʰilɛ́ːsɔː* and *pepʰílɛːka* (φιλήσω, πεφίληκα), *keleúsɔː* and *kekéleuka* (κελεύσω, κεκέλευκα), *kʰɔ́ːsɔː* and *kékʰɔːka* (χώσω, κέχωκα). The Futures, it will be seen, are formed by the suffixation of *-s* and the Perfectives in part by the suffixation of *-k*, but the latter also have a 'prefixal' element – schematically *Ce* – in which the consonant (*C*) varies in harmony with the initial consonant of the root. If the latter is a labial then the 'prefixal' consonant is also a labial (*pepaik-*, *pep^{h}ilɛːk-*; also, e.g., *be-bíɔː-k-a* (βεβίωκα) 'I have lived'); if velar then it is also velar (*kekeleuk-*, *kek^{h}ɔːk-*; also, e.g., *ge-gámɛː-k-a* (γεγάμηκα) 'I [a man] have married [so-and-so]'). If the root consonant is a voiced plosive, then the prefixed consonant is also voiced (*bebiɔːk-*, *gegamɛːk-*); if a voiceless plosive (aspirated or unaspirated) then it is voiceless unaspirated. The same principle extends throughout the consonant inventory: thus if the root begins with *l*, the prefixed formative is likewise *le-* (e.g. *lé-ly-k-a* (λέλυκα) 'I have unfastened'), and so on. In the broadest terms the *e* of the prefix is constant, but the *C* simply 'repeats' the relevant features of the root initial.

Processes of 'repetition' are generally referred to under the heading of **reduplication**. In Ancient Greek, then, a process which may be represented in the most schematic form as follows:

$$C^1 \ldots \rightarrow C^2e + C^1$$

(C^2 in principle identical with C^1, but with qualifications for *pep^{h}ilɛːk-* not *p^{h}ep^{h}ilɛːk-* and others)[1] is a reduplicative operation forming part – but only part (see discussion from a different angle in Ch. VIII) – of the formation of Perfects. In this case the reduplication also includes a constant element (*e*); furthermore, it is **partial** (in the sense that only part of the operand is reduplicated), and it is prefixal and initial (in the sense that the reduplicative formative is added before the operand and it is the beginning of the operand which is repeated). But reduplication without constants is very common, as in some Latin examples (see below). It is also possible to have **complete reduplication** – schematically:

$$O \rightarrow O + O$$

Again, one can have suffixal formatives (formatives following the operand) which result from processes of final reduplication (repetition of the end of the operand). One can also have cases of infixal reduplication, in which the structure of the operand itself is again broken into,

[1] Historically, the first of the two expected aspirates was dissimilated by Grassmann's law (compare discussion of **t^{h}rik^h-ós* → *trik^{h}ós* in Ch. VI). So synchronically, if we like, **p^{h}e-p^{h}il-ɛːk-a* → *pep^{h}ilɛːka*.

and moreover in such cases the reduplicated material might conceivably originate initially, medially or finally. Even in cases of complete reduplication one could decide from the general pattern of the language that it was prefixal in one case and suffixal in another.

However, it would be unwise to insist too far on this kind of logic-chopping detail. In Latin there are a handful of Perfects which are also formed with reduplication: for example, *cu-curr-i* 'I ran', *mo-mord-i* 'I have bitten', or *fe-fell-i* 'I deceived' (← basic **fe-fall-i* by a separate morphologically restricted process). So far we have the same effect as in Ancient Greek, except that a back vowel in the root (*curr-*, *mord-*) is also reduplicated (*cu-curr-*, *mo-mord-*). But there are three other examples which might, in isolation, be assigned to different categories. The first is an effectively complete reduplication of the root of DO 'give': *d-* → *ded-* with *e* intervening (compare *dedi* 'I gave'). In fact this is the same process as in *fefelli*; however, just as the *-n* of *sin-* was 'suffixed' in the absence of a final consonant (see above), so the reduplication of one element appears 'complete' if, it so happens, it is the only element present. The other two examples concern the roots of SPONDEO 'pledge, pledge oneself' and STO 'stand', both of which begin with an *s*+plosive cluster. For the former one could strictly say that the reduplication is infixal and medial: *spond-* → *spo-po-nd-*, with repetition of the *-po-* (compare *spopondi* 'I pledged'). For the latter one might even say that it was suffixal: *st-* → *st-et-*, with repetition of *t* and again an intervening *e* (thus *steti* 'I stood'). But it seems better to treat them all as reflexes of a single operation – one which might perhaps be shown schematically as follows:

$$(s)\ C^1\ (V^1) \ldots \rightarrow (s)\ C^2\ V^2\ C^1\ (V^1) \ldots$$

where C^2 is identical with C^1, V^2 is variously either *e* or identical with V^1, and the dots stand for the remainder of the operand (if any). The unity of this process is not impugned by its apparently differing effects in differing types of instance.

The last major category of morphological processes are those which involve a **modification** (either total or partial) of the operand itself: in English the partial modification of *man* to *men* is an obvious example. The possible subdivisions of this type are very numerous, and can profitably be distinguished by phonetic as well as purely logical criteria. In addition, sundry particular terms – such as the German 'Ablaut' (see below) and 'Umlaut' (see the end of Ch. VIII) – are conventionally employed for particular classes of operation in particular languages or groups. To survey them all would be a tour through a curiosity shop. We will therefore restrict ourselves to a handful of theoretically interesting or problematic instances.

The case of **vowel change** may be illustrated with a plethora of processes in English, some of which have been mentioned already (those of *sink* → *sank*, *foot* → *feet*, and so on) and others not. So [uː] → [ɔ] (as in *shoot* → *shot*), [au] → [ai] (as in *mouse* → *mice*), conversely [ai] → [au] (as in *find* → *found*), and so on. It is important, however, that we should try to generalise such operations whenever they fit coherently within the phonological system. In examples such as *break* → *broke*, *bear* → *bore* and *get* → *got* we have, on the face of it, three separate changes: [ei] → [ou], [ɛə] → [ɔː], and [e] → [ɔ]. Each seems separate again from that of *find* → *found* or *grind* → *ground* ([ai] → [au]). But let us chart them on a table of vowels arranged according to their phonological features. In the system of short vowels:

	Front	Back
Close	i	u
Mid	e	ɔ
Open	æ	ʌ

the vowel of *got* is, it will be seen, the Back equivalent of the Front vowel in *get*. Likewise in the system of 'closing' long vowels and diphthongs (closing towards cardinal 1 if Front, towards cardinal 8 if Back), the diphthongs in *found* and *broke* are the Back equivalents of those in *find* and *break*:

	Front	Back
Close	iː	uː
Mid	ei	ou
Open	ai	au

For the remaining long vowels and diphthongs the RP system is unstable and is difficult to analyse; but again it seems certain that the vowel in *bore* ([ɔə] rather than [ɔː] for many speakers) is the Back equivalent of the Front [ɛə] in *bear*. All four instances may accordingly be referred to a single operation which we can represent as follows:

Front → Back

– i.e. a Front vowel at any point in the system is changed to the Back vowel corresponding.

Other generalisations can be made within the same schema of oppositions. For example, upwards of twenty Verbs show a change of [iː] to [e], accompanied either by a separate suffix *-t* (as in *fel-t* versus *feel*) or, we may suggest, by a *-t* which is fused by sandhi with the root (e.g. **met-t* → *met* – compare **hit-t* → *hit* in an earlier passage of this chapter). In terms of the vowel systems this is a change from Front Close in the 'Closing' set ([iː]) to Front Mid in the Short. However, *lose* → *los-t* and *shoot* → **shot-t* show an identical change with Back instead of Front: Close [uː] in the 'Closing' system → Mid [ɔ] in the Short. Again, therefore, it would be possible to establish a single operation – or two successive operations of 'shortening' and 'lowering' – which would cover both. Of course, one must not pursue this à outrance. At some point in these Verbal patterns even the most determined generaliser will begin to feel that his generalisations are capturing little of significance. But major groupings ought not to be overlooked.

In postulating vowel change or any other sort of 'change' one has to check that the direction of the process can be justified. Why, that is, do we derive *x* from *y* instead of *y* from *x*? In our English examples the main reason will be obvious. In cases of affixation, the Past Tense and Participle are regularly derived from the Present (or from a root identical with the Present – see earlier in this chapter); we therefore preserve the pattern by writing *get* → *got*, *break* → *broke* or *broken*, etc., and not *broke* → *break* and *breaks* or *got* → *get*. In one group, moreover, the pattern is also established by the forms themselves. For *caught*, *brought* or *taught* we can postulate a process by which the vowel and final consonant of the Present ([ætʃ] in *catch*, [iŋ] in *bring*, etc.) are replaced as a whole by [ɔːt] (or [ɔː] plus *-t*). This could be handled by a single operation:

. . . V (C) → [ɔːt]

(the brackets around the *C* allowing the rule to cover *buy* → *bought* as well). But if the Presents were derived from the Pasts we would need separate operations – [ɔːt] → [ætʃ], [ɔːt] → [iŋ], [ɔːt] → [iːtʃ] (in *teach*), and so on – for the individual instances. The process can be generalised in one direction, but not in the other.

Sometimes, however, it is not obvious that any direction can be justified. The processes in the Germanic 'strong Verb' (which we have just illustrated from English) are in part a reflex of a regular pattern in Indo-European, by which a root will have an *e* in some stems, an *o* in others, and in others no corresponding vowel at all. A transparent inflectional example is provided by the forms for 'leave' and for 'see' (in a poetic style) in Ancient Greek:

1st Sg. Present	*1st Sg. Perfect*	*1st Sg. Aorist*
leíp-ɔː (λείπω)	lé-loip-a (λέλοιπα)	é-lip-on (ἔλιπον)
dérk-o-mai (δέρκομαι)	dé-dork-a (δέδορκα)	é-drak-on (ἔδρακον)

in which the stems vary between *leip*, *loip-* and *lip-* in one case and *derk-*, *dork-* and *drk-* (> *drak-* by sound change) in the other. The same variation also played a rôle in the relationships of Noun stems and Verb stems: for example, Latin *fīdō* (< *feid-*) 'I put trust in', *foedus* (< *foid-*) 'treaty' and *fides* (< *fid-*) 'faith'.

In explaining this pattern in his *Introduction*, Meillet most happily compares it to another pattern in Semitic.[1] The following, for example, are the 3rd Singular Masculines of the Simple Perfective and Imperfective ('he *X*ed' versus 'he *X*es, will *X*') for three Verbs in Egyptian Colloquial Arabic:[2]

	Perfective	*Imperfective*
'write'	kátab	yí-ktib
'ask'	ṭálab	yú-ṭlub
'understand'	fíhim	yí-fham

from which it will be seen that the only elements in common to each pair are a skeleton of consonants (*C-C-C*) with the value *k-t-b* in the first, ṭ*-l-b* in the second, and *f-h-m* in the third. The grammatical difference is then made partly by a prefix in the Imperfective (basically *y-* with *i* or *u* following), but otherwise by a variation in the pattern of vowels and syllabification: *CaCaC* or *CiCiC* in the Perfective versus Imperfective *-CCiC*, *CCuC* or *-CCaC*. Further patterns of vowel variation also appear in the lexical morphology or in the Singulars and Plurals of Nouns. For example, with the same skeleton *k-t-b* (as for 'write') we have the forms *kitáab* 'book', *kútub* 'books', *káatib* 'clerk', *kátaba* 'clerks', the Passive Participle *ma-ktúub* 'written', and so on.

What would be the direction of the processes in these examples? The practice of specialists would certainly imply that there is none. An Indo-Europeanist will simply talk of the *e*-grade, the *o*-grade and the

[1] A. Meillet, *Introduction à l'étude comparative des langues indo-européennes*, 7th ed. (Paris, 1937), pp. 153f.

[2] Examples from T. F. Mitchell, *Colloquial Arabic* (Teach Yourself Books: London, 1962), pp. 36 and 72f. I have followed Mitchell's orthography but conflated the back and front variants of *a*.

zero, weak or reduced grade of a given root (e.g. the root *derk-/dork-/drk-*). In referring to the phenomenon in general he will talk of 'vowel alternations' (Meillet, *loc. cit.*) or of 'Ablaut' (the German term adopted by Grimm for the Germanic reflexes in particular).[1] A Semitist will say that our Arabic roots are simply the consonantal skeletons *k-t-b*, ṭ-*l-b* or *f-h-m* – not, for example, either *-ktib* ('becomes' *katab*, *kitaab*, etc.), or *katab*, or any other form with a specific vowel and syllable pattern. The triconsonantal *k-t-b* is the best base for all the variants. In this sense neither Indo-European nor Arabic would have directional 'vowel change' of the sort exemplified for English.

Directionality can also be a problem in the case of total modification (usually called **suppletion**). For English *go* → *went* it may seem obvious why we write it that way rather than as *went* (or *wen-*) → *go*; we have the regular pattern of suffixation, the further pattern of *teach* → *taught* and so on, and the only additional detail is that in this case *go* is changed completely. But is it so obvious why we should write either? In Ancient Greek the Verb for 'bear' or 'carry' had the Present stem *pʰer-* (*pʰérɔː* (φέρω) 'I carry'), the Future stem *ois-* (*oísɔː* (οἴσω) 'I will carry') and, for example, the Aorist *εːneŋk-* (*ɛ́ːneŋka* (ἤνεγκα)). Clearly there is suppletion, but nevertheless neither Future nor Aorist is morphologically simple: the former consists of *oi-* with a Future suffix *-s* which we have already seen in forms such as *paí-s-ɔː* 'I will strike' (παίσω), and the latter is a sandhi form for **e-eneŋk-* with a prefix *e-* whose rôle will appear in Ch. VIII). This leaves an 'alternation' between *pʰer-*, *oi-* and *-eneŋk-*; does it help to say anything more? Coming back to *went*, we might say that this is *wen-* plus the suffix *-t* which we have already established in forms such as *burnt* or *felt*. Do we then gain anything by talking of *go* being modified to *wen-*? Would it not be clearer to speak, IN THE DICTIONARY, of a **suppletive alternation** between two different roots?

Dictionary treatment will not do, of course, for our problems in Cairene Arabic or Indo-European. There are undoubtedly general processes to be stated. But do they necessarily belong to the category of modification with which we started? If the root is simply *k-t-b* then *katab*, for example, is that PLUS (as it were) a broken or two part infix *-a-a-*. According to many linguists the process would not be one of change or alteration of the operand, but rather a special instance of

[1] J. Grimm, *Deutsche Grammatik*, I (1819), p. 10 (p. 8 in the more accessible edition (Berlin, 1870)).

affixation, involving what has sometimes been called a ‘discontinuous morph’ (or morpheme realised ‘discontinuously’). Likewise in Greek *dérk-o-mai* and *dé-dork-a* we might say that the root is strictly *drk-*, the so-called ‘*e* grade’ and ‘*o* grade’ being derived by infixation of *-e-* and *-o-* respectively. Indo-Europeanists do not speak in these terms, but one can imagine some typologist insisting (on strictly logical grounds) that they should. There are other areas too in which the boundary between affixation and modification could be disputed. English Nouns of the type *tránsport* or *cónvict* are derived from the Verbs *transpórt* or *convíct* by, it would usually be said, a process of **stress change** or ‘shift of stress’ (e.g. Quirk *et al.*, p. 1018). But others have treated it differently, saying that the Nouns consist of *transport* etc. PLUS a stress pattern ‘_́ _’ (stress on first syllable), and the Verbs of the same roots plus another pattern ‘_ _́’ (stress on second). These patterns would then be assigned to yet another class of affixes, called ‘suprafixes’ (affixes imposed ‘on top of’ the operand). The same alternatives are possible in cases of **tonal modification** (or, more neutrally, of ‘tonal variation’). In many languages a morphological distinction may regularly be carried by tone alone: the ‘Near Past’ _ ¯ ¯ [aːβoːne] and ‘Perfect’ ¯_ [aːβoːne] for ‘he saw’ in Lumasaaba (a Bantu language of East Africa) is an example taken at random from the author's shelves.[1] In such a case some would speak of modification or ‘modulation’ of the word-form, while others would say that the forms ‘consist’ of the ‘segmental’ elements plus a ‘suprasegmental’ formative which is realised simultaneously. On the second analysis the Tenses would be clear examples of a ‘suprasegmental morpheme’ (see Ch. v).

Nor are the most straightforward processes immune to reanalysis. In English, again, there are Verbs derived from Nouns by – it is usually said – a voicing of the final consonant (e.g. Quirk *et al.*, *loc. cit.*). So *house* [haus] → *house* [hauz], *relief* → *relieve*, and so on, by a process which we might schematise as follows:

. . . Voiceless → Voiced

(compare Front → Back in *get* → *got*, etc.). But at a phonological level [z], in a sense, is [s] plus ‘voicing’ (or ‘plus’ the phonological feature ‘Voiced’), and [v] is likewise ‘Voiced’ + [f]. Hence, some scholars might say, this too is not a CHANGE of features (a shift, within the system, from Voiceless Fricative to the Voiced Fricative corresponding),

[1] Cf. G. Brown, *Phonological Rules and Dialect Variation* (Cambridge, 1972), p. 9.

but rather the ADDITION of a feature – this feature (Voiced) amounting to what may be called a 'subphonemic affix'. In the author's view this reanalysis adds little, but it has the effect of transferring the facts from one terminological category to another.

In all typological work the most elementary error is to forget that different linguists will inexorably describe things differently. For a final subtype of modification we may turn to the Adjectives in French, where the Masculines are normally said to be derived from the Feminines by a process of **subtraction**. Thus Feminine *blanche* [blɑ̃:ʃ] → Masculine *blanc* [blɑ̃] by the removal of final [ʃ], *bonne* [bɔn] → [bɔ̃] by removal of [n] (with accompanying nasalisation of [ɔ]), *longue* [lɔ̃:g] → *long* [lɔ̃], and so forth. The reason for this treatment is similar to the one which we gave for English *teach* → *taught* or *bring* → *brought*. If the Masculines are derived from the Feminines, then we can postulate a single operation: subtract the final consonant. But if the Feminines were to be derived from the Masculines, we would need a separate operation for each consonant: add [ʃ] to form *blanche*, [g] for *longue*, etc., etc. This has become the standard example of subtraction or of 'minus formation', dealt with many times since Bloomfield's classic exposition in the 1930s (BLOOMFIELD, p. 217).

However, some analysts would have it differently. The basic form of *bon*, for example, may be established as the 'liaison' form [bɔn] (basic form in the sense of Ch. VI; liaison as at the end of Ch. VI), *bonne* then being the same plus a suffix [ə] which corresponds to the 'silent' *e* in the spelling. Thus Masculine [bɔn] → Feminine *[bɔn]+[ə] by a straightforward process of affixation. In the Masculine the final consonant will normally fall by processes of sandhi; in the Feminine the final [ə], though falling itself, will nevertheless protect the consonant from falling also. The merits of this issue need not concern us here. The crucial lesson is that the same facts may be handled in an entirely contrary way by different analysts. Hence the same process (in a real sense) stands in danger of falling under two quite contrary typological headings.

RELATED READING

For zero morphs, replacive morphs and related arguments compare *Inflectional Morphology*, §6.1. For zero the leading article is Bloch's on the Verb: B. Bloch, 'English Verb inflection' (in *RiL*). The earliest criticism is by Nida, the fullest and most important by Haas: E. A. Nida, 'The identification of morphemes' (in *RiL*: see pp. 256, 263); W. Haas, 'Zero in linguistic description', in *Studies in Linguistic Analysis* (Supplement to *TPhS*: Oxford, 1957), pp. 33–53. For replacement as a 'morphemic segment' see HARRIS, pp. 167f.; also Nida, 'Identification . . .' (pp. 262–4 in *RiL*), NIDA, p. 54. Nida's discussion in *RiL*, which ends by talking of a 'replacive morpheme', refers to that of BLOOMFIELD, p. 216; but Bloomfield's category is still that of 'phonetic modification'. For immediate criticism (of another exposition by Harris) see C. E. Bazell, 'The correspondence fallacy in structural linguistics', §2 (in *RiL* II, pp. 273f.). For a partial summary of the entire controversy see Hockett's set of alternatives for *took* (HOCKETT, *Models*, pp. 393f. in *RiL*); brief textbook discussion in ROBINS, pp. 204f. See also my own summary in *New Horizons*, pp. 99f.

For morphological processes and sandhi see my account of 'Item and Process' in *Inflectional Morphology*, §7.4.2 and in *New Horizons*, pp. 104ff.; also generativist references in Ch. XII. For **hit-t → hit* see PALMER, p. 48.

For the typology of processes compare SAPIR, Ch. 4; E. M. Uhlenbeck, 'Limitations of morphological processes', *Lingua*, **11** (1962), pp. 426–32; A. Koutsoudas, 'The handling of morphophonemic processes in transformational grammars', in *Papers in Memory of George C. Pappageotes*, ed. R. Austerlitz (Supplement to *Word*: New York, 1964), pp. 28–42; BLOCH & TRAGER, pp. 56ff. My main categories are basically those of Uhlenbeck, except that I treat composition or compounding separately. It will be clear that I am not wedded to my earlier article: 'The inflectional component of a Word and Paradigm grammar', *JL*, **1** (1965), pp. 139–71 (see §2.2, pp. 147ff.).

For the various vowel changes in English Verbs see again PALMER, pp. 46ff., or, in his own terms, Bloch, 'English Verb inflection'. For an analysis of French Adjectives contrary to that of Bloomfield see S. A. Schane, *French Phonology and Morphology* (Cambridge, Mass., 1968), pp. 5f.

For the problems of typology in general see Bazell's inaugural lecture: C. E. Bazell, *Linguistic Typology* (London, 1958); reprinted in P. D. Strevens, ed., *Five Inaugural Lectures* (London, 1966).

VIII
Properties and their exponents

Word and Paradigm v. morphemics: sequential and non-sequential representations of the word; sequence justified by patterning of allomorphs; different patterning in some languages; ambiguity of formatives (Spanish Subjunctives); multiple identification of properties (Greek *elelýkete*); attractions of Word and Paradigm. *Exponence:* defined by rules for morphological processes; by rules for affixes; central v. peripheral categories; cumulation; v. fused and overlapping exponence; extended exponence. Exponents of marked/unmarked oppositions.

At the grammatical level, a word is traditionally referred to by the lexeme to which it belongs and the place which it occupies in the paradigm. Thus Latin *legebat* 'he was reading' would be represented as belonging to the lexeme LEGO 'choose, read' and as occupying the place in the paradigm defined by the terms Imperfect, Indicative, 3rd, Singular, and Active: briefly, the '3rd Singular Imperfect Indicative Active of LEGO' (see Chs. II and IV). In such a representation the ordering of terms such as '3rd', 'Imperfect' or 'Singular' is purely a matter of convention. They are properties of the word considered as a whole, and like the properties of any other object may in principle be listed in whatever order we please. The birch which I see from my window has lightish-green leaves and a silver bole. Alternatively, it has a silver bole and lightish-green leaves; it means the same. *Legebat* is a form of the Imperfect Indicative, or alternatively of the Indicative Imperfect; they both mean simply that the word in question has both these properties. We do not usually say that it is a Singular 3rd Person. But if we did it would be no different from saying that it is a 3rd Person Singular.

In Ch. IV we referred to categories such as Tense, Person or Number as 'morphosyntactic' categories. If we follow this style of representation we may similarly refer to their individual terms (Imperfect, 3rd, Singular, etc.) as **morphosyntactic properties**. They are properties of the word which, once again, have a rôle in both morphology and syntax. The traditional representation of *legebat* will therefore mean: 'that form or member of the lexeme LEGO which has, in addition, the unordered set of morphosyntactic properties 3rd, Singular, Imperfect, Indicative and Active'. Similarly, English *begotten* would be 'that member or form of BEGET which has, in addition, the morphosyntactic property Past Participle'. A feature of this representation is that the lexeme (e.g. BEGET) is a different sort of primitive or elementary term from the morphosyntactic property (e.g. Past Participle). This is reflected by the different rôles which they are said to play in the derivation of word-forms: the lexeme as the source of the root, and the morphosyntactic properties (plus in some cases the inflectional class – see Ch. IV) as the features which select the operations which are applicable to it.

But is this anything more than the legacy of a tradition? The modern alternative, as we have seen, is to represent the word as a sequence of morphemes: within such a sequence order is potentially contrastive (PAST PARTICIPLE + BEGET would not be the same as BEGET + PAST PARTICIPLE) and in addition all elements are of the same primitive class. This is in one sense simpler, in that the construction of words can be stated in the same format as that of phrases and clauses (see the beginning of Ch. V). And at least some languages have a morphology which can be described very neatly within this framework. Is there any reason, therefore, for continuing to handle certain other well known systems in the traditional way?

The answer is bound to be controversial, but in the author's view the case for the traditional model (the Word and Paradigm model as we called it in Ch. IV) is quite convincing. There can be no language, of course, which literally cannot be described in terms of morphemes – just as there can be none, indeed, which literally cannot be described in terms of lexemes and morphosyntactic properties. As so often in linguistics, it is not possible to give knock-down arguments on behalf of either model. The morpheme is simply an abstract grammatical unit: for very few linguists is it still defined as a class of allomorphs (see Ch. V). Its necessary properties, therefore, are simply those of combining in grammatical constructions. So far as its modes of realisation are concerned, one must at least allow for suppletive alternations (compare the suppletive morphological process for *go* → *went* in Ch. VII). One must also allow for zero realisation (as suggested in Ch. VII for the PAST PARTICIPLE morpheme in *come*). But by these means alone we could relate any word-form, by hook or by crook, to whatever sequence of morphemes we desired. Indeed, many linguists would wish to allow for even more drastic possibilities.

However, although the morpheme is no longer DEFINED in terms of its allomorphs (and is therefore invulnerable, as we said, to strictly knock-down arguments), nevertheless it is hard to see how morphemics could be JUSTIFIED otherwise. If we say that *sailed* is the 'Past Tense' of SAIL – or simply that its grammatical elements are Past Tense on the one hand and SAIL on the other – this in itself is enough to distinguish it from every other word in English syntax. We add nothing, so far as the needs of grammatical or syntactic representation are concerned, by saying that there is a sequence with SAIL coming first and 'Past Tense' after. The same holds for the relationship between any English lexical element and any of the grammatical elements that go with it. Although the sequence of morphemes can in theory be contrastive (according, that is, to the morphemic model) it is never so in fact. But in that case what is the point, we may reasonably ask, in establishing morpheme sequences at all? If word order is contrastive within sentences, but morpheme order is invariant within words, one might fairly conclude that the principles of word and sentence construction are not after all the same. Why persist with a model in which the relationship of sequence is distinctive within the word as well as outside it?

The answer can only be based on the segments or morphs by which the elements are identified. *Sailed*, for example, does consist quite plainly of a segment *sail* followed by another segment *-ed*. As we have seen in Ch. v, this is part of a pattern by which Bloomfield's insight into 'sames of form and meaning' is substantially confirmed. In that case it is only sensible (the argument would run) to establish a grammatical ordering of elements which corresponds to the sequences of segments so discovered. This we already do in our representation of phrases and clauses: in *I have sailed* the reason for saying that the word HAVE (or the Present Tense of HAVE) precedes the word SAIL + PAST PARTICIPLE or the Past Participle of SAIL) is that the forms identifying them (*have* and *sailed*) are in that order already. In *sailed* we have before us the segments *sail* and *-ed*. Therefore we say that SAIL precedes PAST PARTICIPLE.

In the author's view this is not, in itself, a sufficient justification for representing words as sequences of morphemes. One can establish a pattern of inflectional formatives (the 'morphemes' in Bloomfield's or a common European sense) without having to add that the relationship of lexical and grammatical elements (the morphemes in our present sense) is the same as that of the larger units in syntax. However, for a language such as English the argument is at least available: the patterning of identifying formatives does exist (with certain irregularities of the types already examined). We can therefore see how the morphemic case might be made out. The problems arise with other groups of languages, and in particular with the older Indo-European systems for which the Word and Paradigm model was developed. In many cases, which we will illustrate in a moment, the tidy patterning of formatives simply is not there. On the one hand, an individual 'morph' may be highly and even systematically ambiguous: indeed in English, as we have already seen in Ch. V, the ending [s], [z] or [iz] will represent one 'morpheme' in *Jack's*, another in the Verb *sails*, and still another in the Noun *sails*. In itself such a 'morph' has little identifying power: its precise rôle can only be clear within the word as a whole (or indeed the wider syntactic context). On the other hand, a single grammatical or semantic unit may be realised by two or more quite separate features of the word-form. In English this happens irregularly: as we remarked in Ch. VII, the Past Tense or Participle element of *told* or *sold* is identified by both the vowel change and the suffix. But in many languages examples are common in regular paradigms. Moreover, the features identifying one element will overlap, include or coincide with those identifying another. In such systems we cannot say that the 'morphemes' actually 'are' located in specific formatives. Can there be any reason at all, in that case, for preferring the morphemic to the traditional Word and Paradigm approach?

This book is not concerned to preach one view or the other. The reader may study the literature and make up his own mind. But it is important to be familiar with the type of phenomena that have been used to support the Word and Paradigm case. For an illustration of formative ambiguity, we may take the contrasts between the Present Indicative and Present Subjunctive in Spanish (examples from Italian, Portuguese, or other similar Romance dialects would serve equally well). The following are the forms for COMPRAR 'buy':

	Indicative	*Subjunctive*
'I'	compro	compre
'thou' (Familiar)	compras	compres
'he', etc.	compra	compre
'we'	compramos	compremos
'you' (Familiar)	compráis	compréis
'they', etc.	compran	compren

(*compro* ←, we will assume, **compra-o*) – from which it will be seen that the Subjunctive is most consistently identified by an *e* as opposed to an *a* in the second syllable. But then we look at the forms for COMER 'eat':

	Indicative	*Subjunctive*
'I'	como	coma
'thou' (Familiar)	comes	comas
'he', etc.	come	coma
'we'	comemos	comamos
'you' (Familiar)	coméis	comáis
'they', etc.	comen	coman

(*como* ← **come-o*), in which the pattern is the reverse: it is now the Indicative which has *e* and the Subjunctive *a* instead. Similarly, in the forms for VIVIR 'live', the Subjunctives again have an *a* throughout (*viva*, *vivamos*, etc.) and the Indicatives can be established with at least a basic *i*: *vivo* (← **vivi-o*), *vives* and *vive* (← **vivi-s* and **vivi*), *vivimos*, *vivís* (← **viví-is*), *viven* (← **vivi-n*). With allowance for a few irregularities (e.g. Indicative *sale* 'he goes out', Subjunctive *salga*), there is a pattern by which all Verbs with an Infinitive in *-ar* follow the paradigm of COMPRAR, all those with an Infinitive in *-er* follow COMER, and those in *-ir* follow VIVIR.

It will be clear that this is not a mere irregularity. The whole system of contrast works by a rule of vowel-reversal, the Subjunctive having the open *a* whenever there is a front vowel *e* or *i* in the Indicative or Infinitive, but the front *e* whenever they have *a* instead. Both classes, we must add, have many members. But in that case one can hardly say that Subjunctive is identified by either formative as such. The 1st Plural *pidamos* happens to be Subjunctive; but if the reader does not know Spanish, or has momentarily forgotten the lexeme PEDIR 'ask', he has no means of telling this from the presence of *a* before the final *-mos*. *Pasamos* happens to be Indicative, but if its lexeme PASAR 'pass' was a member of the other conjugations the *a* would have to mark the Subjunctive. The Mood can only be identified (the 'I' forms apart) from the particular stem *pida-*, *pasa-*, *viva-*, *come-*, *compre-*, etc., taken as a whole. What is the point, therefore, in saying that 'SUBJUNCTIVE' is an element in sequence which is located in its allomorphs *e* or *a* specifically? Obviously we CAN say so if we must. But the traditional view seems more revealing. Mood is a category of words as wholes, which is identified by the oppositions of whole stems or word-forms in the individual paradigm.

For an elaborate example of the *told/sold* type of point we may return to Ancient Greek. The form *elelýkete* 'you had unfastened' (ἐλελύκετε)[1] enters into the following oppositions within morphosyntactic categories. Firstly, it is 2nd Plural as opposed to 2nd Singular or Dual, 1st or 3rd Plural, 1st Singular, and so on. These properties are identified ('marked', let us say) by the ending *-te*: the same form appears in every 2nd Plural (*lý:ete* (λύετε) 'you are unfastening', *elý:ete* (ἐλύετε) 'you were unfastening', etc.) throughout the Active paradigm. But note that this only holds for the Actives (see below). A further point is that there is no distinction, within this 2nd Plural formative, between recurrent markers of Number on the one hand and Person on the other. It is conceivable that an analyst might make such a distinction in certain Duals (though it would also be bound up with the Tense and Mood oppositions), but never so in the Singulars and Plurals: compare *elelýkete* with 1st and 3rd Plural *elelýkemen* (ἐλελύκεμεν) and *elelýkesan* (ἐλελύκεσαν), or with 2nd Singular *elelýkɛ:s* (ἐλελύκης).

Secondly, it belongs to the Perfective Aspect as opposed to the Imperfective and Aorist. But whereas Number and Person were marked together by a single affix, in this case a single property is identified in concert by three separate features. One of these is the reduplicative prefix *le-* (as in Ch. VII); compare the corresponding Imperfective *elý:ete* (ἐλύετε) and the Aorist *elý:sate* (ἐλύσατε). This is a regular feature of Verbs whose roots begins with a consonant (again, see examples in Ch. VII), and holds throughout the Perfective paradigm. Another marker is the length of the root vowel itself: short *ly-* as against long *ly:-*. The third is the suffix *-k-* which follows: this recurs throughout the Perfective Active paradigm, and is regular for this type of vocalic root. But note that there are other paradigms in which it does not appear: in the corresponding forms for the lexeme meaning 'leave' the reduplicative prefix is backed up not by a suffix but by a pattern of vowel change (also in Ch. VII): Perfective *eleloípete* 'you had left' (ἐλελοίπετε), Imperfective *eleípete* (ἐλείπετε), Aorist *elípete* (ἐλίπετε). Note also that the *-k-* is another marker which holds only for the Actives.

Next, it is Past Tense as opposed to Present or Future. Leaving

[1] Given as the normal form by GOODWIN, p. 101. But there is an alternative *elelýke:te* (ἐλελύκειτε) with a different vowel before the ending ('not classic' according to GOODWIN, § 684.2). In all the forms to be cited the accent is predictable by general rules applying regularly to Verb forms (GOODWIN, pp. 29f.); we can therefore ignore it for the purposes of our present analysis.

Future aside, the distinction between Past Perfective *elelýkete* and Present Perfective *lelýkate* (λελύκατε) is evidently made by two features: the prefix *e-* (traditionally called the 'augment') and the quality of the vowel (Past *e*, Present *a*) before the final *-te*. The former has a fairly consistent identifying rôle; however, it also marks the Aorist – e.g. in the corresponding 2nd Plural Active *elý:sate* (ἐλύσατε). The second is not consistent (and note indeed the alternative *elelýke:te*). In other parts of the paradigm the distinction may be made by the augment alone (e.g. Imperfective Present *lý:ete* (λύετε) versus Past *elý:ete* (ἐλύετε)) or by the augment plus a different termination (e.g. the Imperfective 1st Singulars *lý:ɔ:* (λύω) 'I am unfastening' versus *ély:on* (ἔλυον) 'I was unfastening'). Moreover, both *e* and *a* recur independently of Past and Present specifically: compare the Aorist cited above, and the Future Imperfective *lý:sete* (λύσετε) 'you will be unfastening'. But still it is systematic at this particular point: compare 1st Plural Past *elelýkemen* (ελελύκεμεν) with Present *lelýkamen* (λελύκαμεν), or 2nd Singular *elelýkε:s* (with long *ε:* as a further complication) with *lélykas* (ἐλελύκης, λέλυκας).

Next, the word belongs to the Indicative Mood as opposed to the Subjunctive, Optative or Imperative. In these other Moods there is no distinction between Past and Present, the forms being correspondingly without an augment. However, the distinctions between the Present Perfective Indicative, Perfective Subjunctive and Perfective Optative are most consistently marked by the same pre-termination vowel: if we take the 2nd Plurals alone the forms are *lelýkate* as above, *lelýkε:te* (the vowel in the Subjunctives being regularly *ε:* in some Person/Number forms and *ɔ:* in others), and *lelýkoite* (*oi* being found in every Optative).

Finally, it is Active in Voice as opposed to Middle or Passive. As may be clear already, this is another distinction which is marked by more than one formative. The following are the Plurals for the Past Perfective:

	Active	*Middle/Passive*
1st Pl.	elelýkemen (ἐλελύκεμεν)	elelýmet^{h}a (ἐλελύμεθα)
2nd Pl.	elelýkete (ἐλελύκετε)	elélyst^{h}e (ἐλέλυσθε)
3rd Pl.	elelýkesan (ἐλελύκεσαν)	elélynto (ἐλέλυντο)

– from which it may be seen that the whole ending of the word-form differs from the first column to the second. The Middle/Passive has no *-k-* (as we have already remarked) and no following vowel. Furthermore, there is a different set of terminations: just as 2nd Plural *-te* is general for the Actives, so Middle/Passive *-st^he* is systematically contrasted with it. A similar pattern is found in the Duals and also in the Singulars: for the latter and for the 3rd Plurals, however, the Middle/Passive terminations also vary systematically for Past versus Present Tense (Perfective 3rd Singular *elélyto* (ἐλέλυτο) versus *lélytai* (λέλυται), likewise Imperfective *elý:eto* (ἐλύετο) versus *lý:etai* (λύεται), and so on).

To sum up, the form *elelýkete* may be analysed into its formatives as follows:

e – le – ly – k – e – te

(the accent falling predictably on the antepenultimate syllable), where each particular marker is isolated by its recurrences elsewhere in the paradigm. Its own place in the paradigm is as indisputably defined by the morphosyntactic properties Perfective, Past, Indicative, 2nd, Plural and Active. But properties and formatives are in nothing like a one-to-one correspondence. Perfective is in part identified by the reduplication *le-*, but it is also identified by the suffix *-k-*. At the same time *-k-* is one formative which helps to identify the word as Active, another being the *-te* which, however, will also identify it as 2nd and Plural. The following table shows each marker in sequence, with each of the properties which it helps to identify shown above it:

		(Root)	*Perfective*	*Indicative*	*Active*
Past	*Perfective*	*Perfective*	*Active*	*Past Active*	*2nd Plural*
e	le	ly	k	e	te

As can be seen, the markers for a given property need not even be next to each other; Perfective and Past are both identified at once by prefixes before the root and by suffixes following.

None of this involves any crucial irregularity. The paradigm of the Verb 'to loose' or 'to unfasten' is the first which the author and generations of schoolboys have committed to memory. Where then would we stand if we wanted to speak of sequences of morphemes? Does the PAST morpheme come before PERFECTIVE or after it, and how does either stand in relation to the Verb morpheme LY-? Perhaps we shall say that PAST is the first morpheme in the word, since the augment (*e-*) is its most consistent marker. But why, in a form such as *ély:on* 'I was unfastening' or *elélyto* (see above) is it the conditioning factor for a choice of termination (compare again *lý:ɔ:* 'I am unfastening' and *lélytai*) which is up to five morphemes away? Finally, which is the right sequence for Person and Number – 2ND + PLURAL or PLURAL + 2ND? There seems no way of deciding. Some theorists would try to avoid the issue, saying that *-te* is the allomorph of a single morpheme '2ND PLURAL', which happens to have '2nd' and 'Plural' as two independent 'morphemic components'. But is there any other reason for regarding the Person and Number as a different sort of element from 'PAST', 'PERFECTIVE', and so on?

The reader may be left to ponder these questions. By insisting on the morphemic model one would create an apparently gratuitous problem of explanation. Why should an element in sequence be identified by features scattered before and after the root? Why should a 'morpheme' which comes at the beginning of a word select an alternant of the one which comes at the end? Why, in the Spanish example which we gave earlier, should two 'morphemes' be contrasted as *x* and *y* in one paradigm but *y* and *x* in another? The Word and Paradigm answer is that the so-called 'morphemes' are not sequentially organised but are properties of each word as a whole. Hence the contrasts too are drawn within the word-form as a whole. It is not surprising that they can, in fact, be localised in certain instances (for example, the identification of Greek Person and Number is always made by the termination); nor is it surprising that in other cases they are not.

* * *

Within the Word and Paradigm model the features which identify a morphosyntactic property may be referred to as its **exponents**. Thus in our Greek example *-te* is an exponent of 2nd, Plural and Active. Another way of wording this is to say that a relationship of exponence holds between them (i.e. between the formative *-te* and each of these properties). In writing grammars there are various techniques by which this relationship might be stated, but the most obvious, in the light of the tradition and of our own earlier discussion, would be the method of roots and stems which we introduced in Chs. IV and VII. Taking Greek *elelýkete* for illustration, we might begin with a sequence of three operations (shortening of the root vowel to *ly-*, reduplication to form *le-ly-*, suffixation of *-k-* to form *le-ly-k-*) each of which is associated at least with the Perfective. If a word has this property then, one rule would say, the root will normally undergo reduplication: we may interpret this as defining an exponence-relationship between the formative resulting from the process in question (i.e. the reduplicative prefix *le-*) and the morphosyntactic property (Perfective) which selects it. According to another rule, the suffixation of *-k-* will be selected as appropriate to any word (of the regular inflectional class) which is both Perfective and Active: both these properties thus have the formative *-k-* among their exponents.

From *lelyk-* we might then go on to predict the more specific stem *elelyk-*. For any Past Tense word, the rule would say, the corresponding word-form is derived via the prefixation of *e-* to the root or stem already determined. Accordingly, *e-* is an exponent of Past. Another rule, inevitably far less neat and general, would extend this stem in turn to the form *elelyke-*. For this particular word it will have to refer at least to the three morphosyntactic properties Past, Indicative and Active: if any of these was different (Present instead of Past, Subjunctive or Optative instead of Indicative, Passive instead of Active) the basic word-form would certainly be different at this point. Although the suffix *-e-* has a very weak identifying rôle (bearing in mind, again, the alternative with long vowel *elelýke:te*), it is technically among the exponents of each of these categories. Finally, the termination *-te* is added (sc. to whatever stem the earlier rules have predicted) if and only if the word has all three properties 2nd, Plural and Active. Again, therefore, *-te* is an exponent of each. The table which summed up our exposition of this form (see above) is in effect a table of the exponence relation as it should be defined by any grammar which derived the paradigm correctly.

This is a method, of course, in which the concept of a morphological process (the SUFFIXATION of *-k-*, the PREFIXATION of *e-*, and so on) is applied throughout the inflectional description. In fact, the languages for which the Word and Paradigm model is appropriate (those with the types of patterning illustrated earlier in this chapter) tend, in addition, to be among the languages requiring at least a partial process treatment (i.e. those which raise the type of problem argued at the beginning of Ch. VII). But the issues are logically independent, and it may be that there are systems with clear-cut affixes throughout which, nevertheless, do not lend themselves to assignment as the 'allomorphs' of morphemes. Leaving aside irregularities, a language such as Spanish is very close to this type. If so, a statement without processes might seem a more attractive possibility. Instead of deriving the word-form by successive operations, we could say instead that its structure has a number of successive affixal positions, each of which is either blank or filled by affixes selected in a similar way. For example, the Spanish Present Subjunctive might have the general structure Root + Stem suffix + Termination: for particular words the 'Stem suffix' slot would be filled by *e* or *a*, and the Termination slot left blank (in the 'I' and 'he' forms *compre* or *coma*) or filled with *-s*, *-mos*, etc. The rule for the Stem suffix would state that *e* or *a* are selected (according to the inflectional class or conjugation) if the word has both the properties Present and Subjunctive. By the same principle of interpretation, both have the vowel among their exponents. The rules for Terminations would state that *-n*, for example, is selected for any word which has the 'they' properties (hence *compr-e-n*; also Indicative *compran* and other forms throughout the paradigm), that the position is blank for any word, among others, that has the 'I' properties and is also Subjunctive (hence in *compr-e* etc. 'I' has no exponents), and so on.

Whichever method one adopts, the exponence relation will be as complex as the contrasts within the paradigm require. At any stage in the derivation of a word-form (alternatively, in any of the affixal positions) a rule may in principle refer to any or all of the morphosyntactic properties which define its place in the paradigm. Nor is it helpful, at least in the author's experience, to restrict the properties which are in general referred to at one stage or another. For any affixal position, accordingly, the particular affix might in principle be selected according to one set of morphosyntactic categories in one form and quite a different set in another. Restrictions which would simply rule this out do not sit naturally within the total Word and Paradigm model. In practice, however, the rules of exponence usually do make some sort of pattern. In Ancient Greek and Spanish, the Person and Number are consistently identified at the periphery of the word-form – the periphery being the termination in a language where suffixation predominates. In Ancient Greek the Tense is also relatively peripheral, Mood being more central and Aspect (marked by formatives in and around the root) most central of all. In Spanish both Tense and Mood are relatively central, Tense being arguably more so.

Now in fact there seem to be no substantive universals ('substantive' in the sense of Ch. IV) in any of this patterning. Person and Number are identified peripherally in many familiar languages; but Huave (a Mexican Indian language on the South side of the Tehuantepec

Isthmus) is one example in which, conversely, the Person is central in comparison with the Tense.[1] In Ancient or Modern Greek, Voice is relatively more central. In Latin, however, it is at the absolute periphery: compare Active *amo* 'I love' with its Passive *amo-r*, Active *amabat* with Passive *amabat-ur*, and so on. But even if the patterns are not universal, they are real enough in particular languages, particular groups or particular areas. It is therefore useful to have at least a partial typology within which the formal character of different exponence-relationships ('formal' likewise in the sense of Ch. IV) can be distinguished.

One type which is often referred to is the case in which two or more categories are never identified by separate formatives. This is notoriously true of Case and Number in the older or more conservative Indo-European languages. In Russian, for example, the Masculine Inanimate STOL 'table' (стол) has a paradigm as follows:

	Singular	*Plural*
Nominative	stol	staly̍
Genitive	stalá	stalóv
Dative	stalú	stalám
Accusative	stol	staly̍
Instrumental	stalóm	stalám'i
Prepositional	stal'é	staláx

(unstressed $o \rightarrow a$; the prime in two forms is a mark of palatalisation). In the columns, it will be clear that no feature consistently identifies Plural versus Singular. In the rows there is arguably a consistent Vowel + *m* (plus or minus *-'i*) in the Instrumental. But no exponent recurs for any of the other Cases (Nominative, Dative, etc.). The same observations hold for other classes of Nouns, the terms in both categories being identified simultaneously throughout the paradigm.

This can best be referred to as the phenomenon of **cumulative exponence** or **cumulation**. We will say that Case and Number in Russian are identified **cumulatively**, or that their combinations have **cumulative exponents** in each particular termination. It is important, however, to distinguish this type of case from at least two others which are superficially similar. The first is the type of **fused exponence** which results as a special case from processes of sandhi. In Spanish *vivís* 'you live' the final *-ís* at once identifies the word both as 'you (Familiar)' and as Present Indicative or at least not Subjunctive; again,

[1] For references see the Reading at the end of this chapter.

it cannot be divided into two strictly recurrent formatives. But we are dealing here with a phonological and not a morphological regularity. From the rest of the paradigm one would expect *viviis* (compare *compráis* 'you buy' and other forms cited earlier). But *íi* would be contrary to the rules for phoneme combination. Accordingly, *vivís* may be handled as a sandhi-form (in the sense of Ch. VI) for basic **viví-is*; at the basic level the exponents are separate. Even if fused exponents are found throughout a paradigm (compare the Greek forms for 'golden' which were one of our main examples in Ch. VI), they should still be distinguished from cumulation in the proper sense. By contrast, there is no phonological reason why Russian STOL should have a Genitive formative *-á* in the Singular but *-óv* in the Plural, Dative Singular *-ú* but Plural *-ám*, and so on.

The second case which must be distinguished is the special instance of overlapping at the basic level. In Ancient Greek, the Verb termination is a regular exponent of Person and Number. It is also a consistent exponent of Voice, and in certain parts of the paradigm an exponent of Tense: in the Perfectives compare again the Past Middle/Passive *elélyto* (ἐλέλυτο) with the corresponding Present Middle/Passive *lélytai* (λέλυται) and with the Past Perfective Active *elélyke:* (ἐλέλυκει). But whereas Person and Number are never identified separately (at least in the Singular and Plural sections of the paradigm), both Voice and Tense can have a further marker (the augment *e-* in *elélyto* and *elélyke:*, the *-k-* in *elélyke:*) elsewhere in the word-form. The exponents of Person and Number coincide completely. Those of Person/Number, Tense and Voice merely overlap. We will accordingly say that there is cumulative exponence for the first two categories only.

The same distinction can be illustrated with the *-o* of Spanish *compro* 'I buy' or *como* 'I eat'. This is the only 'I' form in which a termination *-o* appears: compare, for example, the Subjunctives *compre* or *coma*, the Imperfect Indicative *compraba* or *comía*, and the Future *compraré* or *comeré*. It is therefore as much an exponent of Present and Indicative as it is of the Person properties 'I'. But this does not form part of a regular pattern. In general, the terminations tend to be constant for different Moods and Tenses: compare, for instance, the *-mos* of *compramos* 'we buy', Subjunctive *compremos*, Imperfect Indicative *comprábamos* 'we were buying', and so on. At the same time, Tense and Mood are regularly marked by independent features: Imperfect Indicative, for example, by the *-ba* of *compraba* and *comprábamos* or the *-ía* of *comía* or the 'we' form *comíamos*. We will not, therefore, speak of *-o* as the cumulative exponent of the 'I' properties and of Present Indicative. In these particular forms (*compro*, *como*, etc.) it is true that Mood and Tense are without additional exponents. But this is merely a special case of **overlapping exponence** – as we may reasonably call it – in relation to the paradigm as a whole.

It is not clear how far it may be helpful to distinguish other general types of exponence. The reverse of the cumulative case would be one in which a category, if positively identified at all, would have exponents in each of two or more distinct positions. But it would be very hard to exemplify a pattern as precise and general as this. In Ancient Greek the Perfective seems at first suggestive: in the Actives *lélyka* 'I have unfastened' (λέλυκα), *léloipa* 'I have left' (λέλοιπα), etc., the Aspect is regularly marked both by reduplication and by a suffix or internal variation in the root. But this only holds for the Actives, as we have shown. Nor does it hold for Aspect in general: although the Imperfectives might be said to fit by sleight of definition (the Imperfective part of the paradigm being characterised by the absence of either feature), the identification of Aorist cannot. In comparison, cumulation is defined for the paradigm as a whole – or at least for a regular or non-trivial section of it.

It seems more realistic for this type of exponence-relationship – that of **extended exponence**, let us call it – to be defined for particular words and word-forms only. In Greek *lélyka* and in many other such forms we will say that there are **extended exponents**, *le-* and *-k-*, of the morphosyntactic property Perfective. As such, extended exponence is often no more than a trivial concomitant of overlapping (see above). But it is not necessarily so. One interesting case, for example, is where a property is identified in position *a* in one class of words, in position *b* in another, and then in both positions *a* and *b* in a third. This is true, as we have seen, of the Past Tense and Past Participle formations of English Verbs: in *sailed* the identifying feature is an affix, in *sank* or *stole* it is the particular vowel-quality, in *told* or *sold* there are both. Another obvious but more regular illustration is provided by the Plurals of Nouns in German. Taking just the Nominatives, we find the types of contrast shown as follows:

	Singular	*Plural*
'arm'	Arm	Arme
'picture'	Bild	Bilder

	Singular	*Plural*
'father'	Vater	Väter
'earth'	Boden	Böden
'painter'	Maler	Maler
'apostle'	Apostel	Apostel
'worm	Wurm	Würmer
'neck'	Hals	Hälse

In the first two forms, the Plural is marked by an affix (another possible affix at this point would be *-en*). In the next two it is marked by a vowel-change (phonetically, [ɑː] in *Vater* → [ɛː] in *Väter*, [oː] in *Boden* → [øː] in *Böden*); this is traditionally referred to by the term 'Umlaut'. In the next two neither feature is present (though Singular and Plural are distinguished sporadically in other Cases). Finally, in the last two we have the non-overlapping case of extended exponence, in which Plural is identified both by an affix (the terminations *-e* or *-er* as before), and by the Umlaut ([ʊ] in Wurm → [y], [ɑ] in *Hals* → [ɛː]) in addition.

* * *

As an appendix to this discussion, it is worth asking how far there is a natural relationship between the exponents of a category and the semantic oppositions between the grammatical properties themselves. If we return to the paradigm of STOL in Russian, it will be seen that the Plural endings are consistently longer than the Singular. Where the Singulars have the bare root (Nominative and for this class the Accusative) the Plurals have a vowel as termination: Nominative/Accusative Plural *stal-ý*. Where the Singular itself has a vowel (Genitive *stal-á*, Dative *stal-ú*, Prepositional *stal-'é*) the Plural has a Vowel + Consonant: Genitive *stal-óv*, Dative *stal-ám*, Prepositional *stal-áx*. Where the Singular has a Vowel + Consonant (Instrumental *stal-óm*) the Plural has Vowel + Consonant + Vowel: Instrumental Plural *stal-ám'i*. Although the vowels and consonants vary separately in the individual Cases, the general pattern is clearly there.

At the same time, some scholars would maintain that Plural is semantically the **marked** and Singular the **unmarked** term in the opposition. 'Singular', that is, should more properly be analysed as 'Non-Plural' – the term in the Number category which lacks the 'mark' of Plurality specifically. If this can genuinely be confirmed – confirmed FOR THIS LANGUAGE, since it does not appear to hold universally – then the increased length of the endings would find an explanation. It has also been suggested that Nominative is the unmarked Case – the 'casus rectus' or 'straight', 'uninflected' Case (as the older grammarians would have said) as opposed to the 'casus obliqui' (the 'oblique' or 'inflected' Cases) such as Genitive, Dative, etc. If this can be justified in terms of syntax and semantics (again the 'if' is important), perhaps there is a reason why the Russian Nominative forms (bare root or root + Vowel) should often be the shortest of all.

Another specific example is suggested by the work of my colleague Irene P. Warburton in the field of Modern Greek.[1] The following table:

	Present	*Past*
1st Sg.	-o	-a
2nd Sg.	-is	-es
3rd Sg.	-i	-e

shows the regular Verb endings in the Singular (excluding the Passive 'Present' and 'Imperfect'). For illustration compare the Present Active Imperfective *γráfo* 'I write' (γράφω) with the corresponding Past Active Imperfective *éγrafa* 'I was writing' (ἔγραφα),[2] *γráfis* 'you write' (γράφεις) with *éγrafes* (ἔγραφες), and *γráfi* '[he, etc.] writes' (γράφει) with *éγrafe* (ἔγραφε). Now it will be remembered from our discussion of external sandhi (see the end of Ch. VI) that the vowels of Modern Greek may be ordered according to a scale of phonological strength or dominance. According to this scale, the vowels of the Past Tense terminations are stronger than those of the Present (*a* stronger than *o*, *e* stronger than *i*), and those in the 1st Person (*o* and *a*) are again stronger than those in the 2nd and 3rd (*i* and *e*). In addition, it will be seen that the 3rd Persons have the vowel alone (*-e* or *-i*), whereas the 2nd Persons have the same vowel with an *s* in addition. In general, therefore, we may say that the terminations are 'stronger' or 'weightier' as one moves from bottom to top or left to right in the table – those with the weaker and phonetically less sonorous front vowels (rows 2 and 3) being 'lighter' than those with the stronger and more sonorous *o* and *a* (row 1), those without *s* (row 3) being lighter than those with it (row 2), the one with *o* (row 1, column 1) being lighter than the one

[1] Compare her article, 'Modern Greek Verb Conjugation', *Lingua*, **32** (1973), pp. 193–226.

[2] The Tense and Aspect categories are essentially those of A. Koutsoudas; see Householder *et al.*, *Reference Grammar of Literary Dhimotiki*, p. 104.

with the phonologically stronger *a* (row 1, column 2), and those with *i* (remainder of column 1) being at least arguably lighter than those with *e* (remainder of column 2).

That, then, is the patterning within the formatives themselves. However, according to many authors a similar progression would also hold for the patterns of semantic marking. In the category of Tense the 'Present' is often characterised as essentially 'Non-Past': the unmarked term in a binary Tense category, and the maximally unmarked (e.g. both 'Non-Past' and 'Non-Future') in more elaborate systems. In the Person category, the 3rd Singular has often been presented as unmarked in relation to the 1st and 2nd: in effect, neither the 'I' nor 'You' participant in the speech situation. Finally, it has been suggested that the 1st Person is marked in opposition to the 2nd – the former being 'I' and the latter essentially 'not I'. In accordance with these theories, one proceeds from maximally unmarked (3rd Singular Present or 'Not I', 'Not You', 'Non-Past') to maximally marked (1st Singular Past) just as one proceeds from less weighty to more weighty exponents.

Patterns of this kind are of particular interest when they are repeated from one language to another. In the Nouns of other Indo-European languages there is the same tendency for the Plural and 'oblique' endings to be longer or more weighty than the Singulars and Nominatives. Russian is merely one of the neatest instances. There is also the non-cumulative pattern which we have illustrated from Turkish (Ch. v), in which it is precisely the Singular and the Absolute – the latter functionally similar to a Nominative – which lack morphological identity altogether. It is this general tendency which has tempted many scholars to accept the marking explanation. Again it is more usual, at least, for the 3rd Singular to lack exponents in opposition to the 1st and 2nd than for the 2nd, let us say, to lack them in opposition to the 3rd.

But it is a scholar's duty to be cautious and honest. Patterns of this kind are sometimes confirmed, but often they are not. Even in the Russian Case-forms it is not clear why the Instrumental ending in Nouns is longer than the Genitive, Dative and Prepositional. Is this property semantically more 'oblique' than the 'oblique'? According to the author's information, there is no independent justification for saying so. In this field it is very easy to 'explain' the things which fit, and relegate as exceptions or aberrations those which do not. Inflections are basically arbitrary, just as roots and lexical formations are also arbitrary. In the end one has to resign oneself to it.

RELATED READING

For the basic characteristics of the Word and Paradigm model (morphosyntactic properties, categories, and so on) see *Inflectional Morphology*, §9.1 (already referred to for lexemes etc. in Ch. II); also my earlier version in 'Some concepts in word-and-paradigm morphology', *FL*, **1** (1965), pp. 268–89. For an alternative formulation see the references for syntactic features in Ch. XII. The model is also discussed in a more general way in *Inflectional Morphology*, §7.1.

For Word and Paradigm v. morphemics see R. H. Robins, 'In defence of WP', *TPhS*, 1959, pp. 116–44, and *Inflectional Morphology*, Part 2 (especially from §6.4 onwards); other illustrations are discussed more briefly in *New Horizons*, pp. 107f. It may also be helpful to look at two more extended reanalyses: P. H. Matthews, 'The main features of Modern Greek verb inflection', *FL*, **3** (1967), pp. 262–84, and 'Huave verb morphology: some comments from a non-tagmemic viewpoint', *IJAL*, **38** (1972), pp. 96–118. These may then be compared with equivalent morpheme-based descriptions by A. Koutsoudas, *Verb Morphology of Modern Greek* (Supplement to *IJAL:* Bloomington, 1962), and by Emily F. Stairs and Barbara Erickson Hollenbach, 'Huave verb morphology', *IJAL*, **35** (1969), pp. 38–53. (The last paper is also the source for the factual statement made in the text.)

The present use of 'exponent' and 'exponence' is defined, within the Word and Paradigm setting, in *Inflectional Morphology*, §9.3.3. In Firthian linguistics it is usually used more widely, to refer to the relationship between any linguistic unit (e.g. a phonological unit) and, ultimately, the data from which it is abstracted; see ROBINS, pp. 46f. I have naturally no wish to preempt it for morphology especially. For types of exponence (cumulative, and so on) see *Inflectional Morphology*, pp. 65ff., 82, 93ff., 132ff. Of these, only cumulation is usually discussed as such; for the diverse terms in which it IS discussed see *Ibid.*, §6.2 (footnotes in particular), also §7.4.1.

For marked/unmarked oppositions the leading references are two of Jakobson's pre-war papers: R. Jakobson, 'Zur Struktur des russischen Verbums' (reprinted in *RiL* II, pp. 22–30), and 'Beitrag zur allgemeinen Kasuslehre' (*Ibid.*, pp. 51–89). For beginners, the most accessible account is that of LYONS, pp. 79f. (and examples, p. 306 and passim). As Lyons points out, the notion has been explored at all linguistic levels; for phonology (where it is particularly important) compare TRUBETZKOY on privative oppositions and correlations, HOUSEHOLDER, Chs. 9–10 (well worth study on any account), and, for example, any of the generativist references in Ch. XI. Of the morphological categories discussed that of Person is perhaps the most interesting; see in particular E. Benveniste, 'Structure des relations de personne dans le verbe', in *Problèmes de linguistique générale* (Paris, 1966), pp. 225–36, and compare the brief account by LYONS, pp. 276–8. My own article on Huave may also be of interest, p. 112 in particular. For the other categories LYONS may be taken as the starting point.

IX
Inflectional morphology and syntax

Morphology and syntax in traditional theories; syntagmatic and paradigmatic relations; alternative analyses: morphemics and syntactic paradigms; governance reanalysed in terms of allomorphs; words the crucial unit in traditional argument.
The word in Latin and in other languages: as a unit of phonology; as smallest sentence unit: bound and free forms, minimal free forms; cohesiveness; fixed ordering of elements; non-recursiveness; logical independence of different characteristics; divergencies in some languages (problems of the word in French): between grammatical word and phonological word; full words and clitics; the word in 'isolating' languages (Vietnamese); in 'agglutinating' languages (Turkish).
Inflected and periphrastic formations: semantic equivalence; words still valid at grammatical level.

'Peut-on poser une définition universellement valable des domaines respectifs de la morphologie et de la syntaxe?' ('Can one define the fields of morphology and syntax in a way which will be universally valid?') The question is the last of three proposed for discussion at the VIth International Congress of Linguists: in the conference proceedings the answers are gathered together with a summary and comments by the Czech linguist Bohumil Trnka, and supplemented by further interventions from the same participants.[1] According to one of the few North American scholars who took part the answer was simply 'No'. For us it will also be No – except that there is just a little more that ought to be said. The point was also argued ably, though in varying terms, by some of the European respondents. Now, after more than twenty years, we are in an even better position to justify it and explore its implications.

Traditionally, morphology is concerned with the INTERNAL STRUCTURE of words and their relationship to other words WITHIN THE PARADIGM. Syntax, on the other hand, is concerned with their EXTERNAL FUNCTIONS and their relationship to other words WITHIN THE SENTENCE. Any

[1] M. Lejeune (ed.), *Actes du VIe congrès international des linguistes* (Paris, 1949), pp. 19–30, 261–302, 473–96.

simple example from an inflecting language will help to put these terms into correspondence with our earlier discussion (Ch. I). In Latin, the word *aevum* (Nominative or Accusative Singular of the Noun meaning 'age, time, eternity') has an internal structure of root (say, *aevu-*) followed by the Case and Number termination (*-m*); we may express this by saying that *-m* is the allomorph of a 'Nominative Singular' or 'Accusative Singular' morpheme (Ch. V), or that it is the exponent of these combinations of properties (Ch. VIII), or by whatever other form of statement seems appropriate. As such, it stands in opposition to other words which hold the *aevu-* or *aev-* element constant: Genitive Singular *aevi*, Dative and Ablative *aevo*, etc. It is also opposed to others which hold the *-m* or more generally the Nominative or Accusative Singular constant: *bellum* 'war' or *corpus* 'body' (the latter being from a different inflectional class or declension). These oppositions are contracted by the words IN ISOLATION, considered as individual units within the grammatical and lexical system of the language. Amongst the network of relations which are so established, a particular type defines the paradigm as it is usually understood.

At the same time, in the specific phrase *in aevum* or *in omne aevum* 'for eternity' (see our quotation from Horace in Ch. II), the Noun *aevum* is the element syntactically 'governed' by the Preposition *in*. It also enters into a relationship with *omne* 'all', the Adjective functioning as its Modifier or Determiner. Here we are concerned not with relationships of words in isolation, but of words STANDING WITHIN A SPECIFIC CONSTRUCTION. If we take another line from the *Epistles*:

Forte meum si quis te percontabitur aevum

'If perhaps someone asks you my age' (I, XX, 26), the same word in terms of its internal structure and place in the paradigm ('the Accusative Singular of AEVUM') is now in a different construction, functioning as one of two Objects of the Verb *percontabitur* 'will ask'. Relations and functions such as these (Modifier, 'Object of', 'Governed by', and so on) were described by Saussure as relationships 'in praesentia' – obtaining, that is, between elements which are 'present' in a given speech-chain.[1] According to a more normal usage, they are **syntagmatic relations**, relations between different constituents (or 'syntagms') in a construction. It is these that form the domain of syntax. By contrast, the oppositions of *aevum* to *aevi*, *aevum* to *corpus*, and so forth, are

[1] SAUSSURE, p. 171.

relationships 'in absentia' – obtaining between elements of which only one is selected (the others being accordingly 'absent') for any given function. Alternatively, they are **paradigmatic relationships** in the most general sense of this term. It is the particular relationships in absentia within 'paradigms' that form the domain of morphology.

This, as we said, is quite traditional and on the face of it seems all very well. But everything hinges on the unique and central status of the word. As we have seen in Ch. V, this unit could itself be subjected to a form of syntax-like analysis. Thus *aevum* would have *aevu-* 'functioning as root' just as *meum te percontabitur aevum* '[he] will ask you my age' has the whole word *aevum* (alternatively, the whole phrase *meum... aevum*) functioning as Object. A corollary of morphemics was that the forms of statement which have traditionally been used in syntax (*x* functioning as *y*, preceding *x* standing in such and such a way to following *y*, and so on) could also be extended to internal word structure. Whereupon, as we have seen, the distinction between the 'grammar of words' and the 'grammar of units larger than the word' would begin to lose its point (Ch. I).

Conversely, one could also speak of clauses, sentences, etc., entering into structures similar at least to paradigms. In English *will help* is an Active Verbal phrase and *will be helped* its Passive equivalent. Likewise *The police will help you* is an Active clause with Passive equivalent *You will be helped by the police*, and on other dimensions it is a Declarative as opposed to the Interrogative *Will the police help you?* and a Positive as opposed to the Negative *The police won't help you*. One article of the middle 1960s had the precise title 'A syntactic paradigm':[1] is this any different, it is implied, from saying that within 'Word paradigms' *help* is Present in opposition to Past *helped*, *men* Plural in opposition to Singular *man*, and so on? In the later work of Halliday and his pupils, a quasi-paradigmatic classification has been extended to the entire discussion of grammatical constructions. Alongside the Yes/No Interrogative *Will the police help you?*, the Declarative is also opposed to a *Who*-type Interrogative with the Subject questioned (*Who will help you?*), to another with the Object questioned (*Who will the police help?*), to a Relative clause with or without *who* as Object ([*the people*] *the police help*), etc. There is thus a tendency, within this school in particular, to extend to units 'larger than the word' a form of statement which has traditionally been typical of morphology only. But if 'mor-

[1] K. L. Pike, 'A syntactic paradigm', *Lg*, **39** (1963), pp. 216–30.

phology' is made more like 'syntax' in one way, and 'syntax' more like 'morphology' in another, is there (it will be asked) a real distinction between them?

Now perhaps these last parallels are not exact. The clauses which we have given may form a 'paradigm' of oppositions: Declarative opposed to Interrogative, Yes/No Interrogative subsidiarily opposed to *Who*-type, and so on. But they are not the PARADIGM OF something, in the sense that *man* and *men* form the traditional paradigm of MAN, or *aevum* etc. that of AEVUM. Following this approach to syntax, the clause or sentence *Who will the police help?* might be assigned the classification 'Interrogative, *Who*-type, Transitive, Object questioned', and so forth, but there is no specific lexical unit (not even the whole collocation of POLICE and HELP) to which it in any sense belongs. Whereas the word can still be regarded as a 'lexeme-carrying' unit, the clause has instead a pattern of functions with various different lexemes entering into it. However, the case is not so clear when we come to phrases such as *will help* versus *will be helped*. Why do we not describe these as, let us say, the 'Simple Active and Passive *will*-forms of HELP' (Simple as opposed, e.g., to Progressive *will be helping*; *will*-forms as opposed, e.g., to the *may*-forms *may help*, *may be helped*)? In the author's view this is still not the same as a morphological paradigm. Although the phrases are certainly Non-Progressive, although they certainly have *will* as one member, and so on, nevertheless it is the forms *help* and *helped* (the 'Infinitive' and 'Past Participle' of HELP) that are in a special sense the vehicle of the lexeme itself. But why so? Although there is more to be said on this kind of example (see the end of this chapter), the pin-pointing of *help* and *helped* as WORDS would seem an essential step in the argument.

Still more radical restatements are possible. In the Latin phrase *in aevum* 'for eternity' we said that the word *in* governs the Accusative Noun *aevum*. In other phrases, such as *in nostro aevo* 'in our time', the same Preposition is said to govern a Noun in the Ablative (*aevo*) instead. But in theory at least there is an alternative. First, we could say that there are two different Prepositions '*in*': 'IN^1', traditionally said to 'govern the Accusative', and 'IN^2', which 'governs the Ablative'. But then we could also say that the endings *-m* and *-o* are representatives of an identical morpheme (simply SINGULAR), the former being merely the 'allomorph' (Ch. v) which is selected by the morphemic environment IN^1 AEV-, and the latter another 'allomorph' selected, e.g., by

IN² AEV-. In our other example *meum te percontabitur aevum* 'will ask you my age', the *-m* allomorph would be selected by another grammatical environment which includes the Verb PERCONTOR 'ask, make inquiry' (traditionally a Verb 'governing a double Accusative'). Likewise the *-m* of *meum* (*meum...aevum*) could be treated not as an Accusative Singular determined by a rule of agreement (compare Ch. III for agreement in Italian), but merely as an alternant of 'SINGULAR' determined by an otherwise equivalent rule of alternation.

A further refinement of this approach can be found in the literature. In *meum aevum*, again, one might say that Accusative and Singular are selected only once: instead of *aevum* being *aevu-* + Accusative Singular ending, and *meum* separately *meu-* (Neuter stem) + another Accusative Singular ending, the whole phrase is morphemically *meu-* + *aevu-* + ACCUSATIVE SINGULAR, with the last morpheme represented by a 'discontinuous allomorph' *-m...-m*. Likewise the *-m* of *in aevum* could be regarded as part of a discontinuous allomorph *in...-m*, which is a cumulative exponent (compare Ch. VIII) of 'IN¹', as above, and SINGULAR. Putting these two alternatives together, the more elaborate phrase *in omne aevum* (with the added Adjective *omne* 'all') would have a three-part 'morph' *in...-e...-m*. If such analyses were accepted the whole basis for the division of morphology and syntax would be swept away.

Of course, any student of Latin would reject such analyses out of hand. The reader is not invited to describe this or any other language in that way. But like other peculiar analyses they help to focus our attention on the reasons for their peculiarity. Why are they rejected, except precisely because they violate word-boundaries? The *-m* of *in aevum* is certainly determined by general rule; why should it be a rule of word connection (the Accusative Noun as a whole being selected by the particular construction with *in*) instead of one selecting *-m* individually (e.g. as a conditioned allomorph of SINGULAR)? The answer, it seems, is precisely that we want to preserve the integrity of *aevum* as a unit. Hence we reject an analysis which says that *aevu-* and *-m* are related less directly than *in* and *-m*. The reader may have felt a similar objection, in Ch. I, to the transformational analysis of *were trying*: surely *try-* and *-ing* simply ARE related more closely, as it were. But this makes clear the structure of the argument. The word is not itself justified by the traditional model of paradigmatic and syntagmatic relations which we spoke of earlier. On the contrary, it is because we recognise its special status that we set up paradigms and 'syntagms' in that way. It is this special status which we now have to examine.

* * *

It will be well to continue with the word in Latin, partly because our concepts spring from the classical tradition, and also because the classical languages are among the neatest exemplars of a particular linguistic type. As may already be clear from the closing section of Ch. II, one pointer to its special status is that it is a unit both on the grammatical and on the phonological level. In phonology it is the unit within which the accent is determined: *percontábitur áevum* is so accented because, among other things, the word boundaries are where they are. Of the languages which we have cited, the same is also true of Egyptian Arabic: *kitáab* 'book' is accented finally because the final syllable is long but *kátab* 'he wrote' and *káatib* 'clerk' initially because it is short, *kátaba* 'clerks' is accented initially because all three syllables are short, *maktába* 'library' medially because the third is short but the first long, and so forth.[1] In many other languages the accent is not determined by phonology alone. But even then it is often restricted to a certain part of any polysyllabic word. In Modern Greek, for example, a word of four or more syllables may be accented on the last syllable (ἀδιαφορῶ *aðjaforó* 'I don't care'), on the second to last or penultimate (ἀδιαφορία *aðjaforía* 'indifference') or on the third from last or antepenultimate (ἀδιάφορος *aðjáforos* 'indifferent'), but not on any other syllable preceding.[2] Accent apart, there are other phonological features or restrictions which are peculiar to word boundaries. In Italian, for example, the final syllable regularly ends in a vowel although initial and medial syllables may readily end in a consonant. The native exceptions to this rule are certain monosyllables (*per* 'through', etc.), which for that reason might not be regarded as full words at the phonological level.

This last example reminds us that there are sometimes discrepancies between phonological words and grammatical words. As we pointed out in Ch. II, the form *virum* in *arma virumque* 'arms and the man' is a word at one level (a member of the paradigm of VIR 'man') but only part of a word at the other (the first two syllables of the accentual unit *virúmque*). But it is the agreement rather than the discrepancies which

[1] Mitchell, *Colloquial Arabic*, pp. 26f.

[2] Mirambel, *La langue grecque moderne*, pp. 25f.

ought to strike us more forcibly. There is no reason why units of phonology and grammar SHOULD correspond. In Latin, it is not so for the smaller units – *percontabitur*, for example, being phonologically a series of syllables *per-con-ta-bi-tur* but morphologically a complex stem *per-cont-* (*cont-* crossing a syllable boundary) with formatives *a-*, *bi-* or *b-i-*, *t-* and *-ur* (the last two splitting a syllable between them). Nor NEED they correspond for word-sized units either: we will discuss the example of French later in this chapter. That they largely DO correspond, for Latin and for many other languages, is a sure sign of the importance of the word within the overall system.

The grammatical characteristics of the word are themselves significantly diverse. One of those discussed most widely is its status as the **smallest sentence unit** – no smaller unit being able to form a sentence in its own right. In Latin (as in English) a word could often be uttered on its own. A character in Plautus interrogates another: 'Tell me in good faith (*dic bona fide*), you didn't get at (*surrupuisti*) that gold?' The other replies *bona* '[in] good [faith]'. A little later: 'And if you know who took it, you'll tell me?' Answer: *faciam* 'I'll do so'. To the next question the answer is simply *ita* 'just so' (*Aulularia*, IV. x). But one does not find stems on their own (unless, of course, they happen to form words as well); in answer to the first question our character in Plautus could not have said simply *bon-* (the stem of the word meaning 'good'). Nor does one find isolated inflectional formatives. The second question ends with the word *indicabis* 'you'll tell', of which the *-bis* is the Future 2nd Person Singular inflection; but in answer one could not simply pick this up and say *-bo* (1st Singular 'will do', as it were). In Bloomfield's classic formulation, forms such as *bon-*, *-bo* or *-bis* are **bound forms** (or sequences of one or more **bound morphemes**): forms which can only appear as part of a larger form or larger sequence of morphemes. However, *bona*, *bona fide*, *dic bona fide*, *mihi indicabis* 'you will tell me', and so on, are all **free forms**: capable, that is, of appearing on their own. Of these last, all but *bona* can be divided into two or more smaller free forms: *bona fide* into *bona* and *fide*, *mihi indicabis* into *mihi* and *indicabis*. They are what Bloomfield called 'phrases'. But *bona*, *fide*, *indicabis*, etc., cannot themselves be so divided; it is to such **minimal free forms** that Bloomfield applied the term 'word'.

As a basis for DEFINING the word this has often been criticised. Latin *et* 'and' would normally be called a 'word', and so would English *my* or *the*. But do these, in fact, appear on their own? *My* seems especially unlikely; apart from exclamation (*My!*), when would one use it instead of *mine*? In the case of *et*, no isolated syntactic usage is attested in the dictionaries. Perhaps we might have heard it (as it were, in the context 'Did you mean *et* or *aut*?'), but then parts of words can also appear alone in that kind of circumstance: e.g. question *Did you say révise or dévise?*, answer *Re* (attested by my colleague Dr Crystal). The difficulty with *the* is one which Bloomfield himself recognised; he argued, however, that since an article is in other respects syntactically similar to *this* or *that*, and these can certainly occur freely in conversation, therefore it could be accorded word-status too. But then could not the Comparative *-er* be a word, since functionally (though not positionally) it is equivalent to *more*? For such reasons, the 'minimal free form' is regarded with misgiving by many linguists. Nevertheless, as a characteristic of words as a class (and as one criterion by which they are recognised), it is beyond dispute.

By the same token, speakers are able to split up utterances into words (e.g. to help the analyst or the learner). This cannot always be explained by writing conventions: fifty years ago, Sapir reported similar experiences with an unwritten language (SAPIR, p. 34) and the author, at least, cannot recall a later report to the contrary. Indeed, who developed the orthography to start with, and why do children learn to space words readily? A further point is that fragments of a word do not appear alone in sentence constructions. A Roman could not, for example, coordinate two different endings of Verbs – say, *indicabit vel -avit* ('will indicate or has [indicated]'), with both Future and Perfect inflections linked to the same stem. Again, one does find exceptions. My colleague Dr Lepschy supplies an example from Italian, in which a speaker asked *È proprio -accio?* 'Is it really bad?', with a pejorative derivational suffix (*-acci-*) used on its own with a Masculine ending. This too would be an obstacle to any strict DEFINITION. One would have to say that our Italian speaker made a 'mistake' (but, as reported, neither speaker nor hearer reacted as if it WAS a mistake), or was engaged in 'rule-breaking creativity' (see Ch. XII), or whatever. But, again, the general PROPERTY of the word cannot be doubted.

This leads naturally to a second main characteristic (that of **cohesiveness**) which could in principle be independent. Just as a part of a word does not as a rule appear on its own (unless, of course, it is itself another word), so the parts cannot as a rule be separated by other forms (unless, of course, the whole is then a new word). In Latin, the words in a phrase may often appear with quite extraneous items intervening. For example, in our second line from Horace (*forte meum si quis te percontabitur aevum*) the members of the Object phrase *meum...aevum* 'my age' are separated by the Conjunction introducing the whole clause (*si* 'if') and also by the Subject, Verb and the other Object (*quis* 'someone', *percontabitur* 'will ask', *te* 'you'). By contrast the word is absolutely cohesive. One could say nothing like *percont- aevum -abitur*, *me- si quis -um aevum*, and so on. In English, there are marginal exceptions with expletives. The following, for example, is from an Australian song of the First World War:[1]

> Get a —— move on, have some —— sense,
> Learn the —— art of self de- —— -fence.

where the interrupted word *defence* might itself be regarded as the second member of a compound. A less marginal exception is provided by the phenomenon usually referred to by the Greek term **tmesis** (literally, a 'cutting'). In German, for example, the members of a compound Verb (e.g. AUSGEHEN 'go out') are regularly separate in some constructions. Nevertheless, cohesiveness in general holds – and even in tmesis the members tend to be words themselves by independent criteria.

Another important characteristic concerns the **fixed ordering** of constituent elements. In Latin, the order of words in the sentence is strikingly free: in the same example, *te meum aevum percontabitur* would do as well (metre apart) as the variant actually cited. In English, word order often carries a difference of meaning, *John loves Mary* being not the same as *Mary loves John*. But in both languages the order of stems and inflections is at once fixed and non-contrastive. In *per-cont-a-bi-t-ur* the formative elements appear only in that sequence; there is no alternative order, such as *per-cont-ur-a-bi-t*, which can serve either as a rhythmic variant or as another member of the paradigm. In the Perfect *cu-curr-is-ti* 'you have run' the stem *cu-curr-* is formed by prefixal reduplication (see Ch. VII), whereas in *sur-rup-u-is-ti* 'you have got at' its counterpart *sur-rup-u-* is formed by suffixing *-u-*; but that a 'Perfect morpheme' should come before the root in one case (*cu-*), while coming after it in another (*-u-*), is a fixed feature of these

[1] The lines are to be sung to the refrain of 'Onward Christian Soldiers', with the blanks supplied according to taste; see 'Headway in Australia's quest for new anthem', *The Times*, 3 July 1973.

forms and has no syntactic or semantic import. It is this characteristic which makes it natural to regard the grammatical properties of the word as unordered, to say that *sailed* is merely the 'Past Tense of SAIL' (see Ch. VIII), and *cucurristi* the traditional '2nd Singular Perfect Indicative Active of CURRO' rather than 'PERFECT morpheme followed by root morpheme CURR-' and so on.

With this characteristic, however, the qualifications become more serious. Firstly, it is particularly true of the classic inflecting type of language (Ch. I). In Turkish, which of our European languages is most removed from this type, a pair of 'words' may indeed be distinguished by their different ordering of morphemes. *Türktürler* 'They are Turkish' is a 'word' (i.e. at least a phonological word) by the test of vowel harmony; it consists of a Noun *Türk* 'Turk, Turkish', followed by a morpheme with the basic form *-dIr* 'be', plus the basic *-lEr* (Plural) already established in Chs. V and VI. However, in *Türklerdir* 'They are the Turks' we have another 'word' in which the same morphemes appear in the order *Türk-lEr-dIr*.[1] Of course, these COULD be handled as grammatical words within the inflecting pattern. It would be possible, that is, to arrange and label them in paradigms somehow. But the facts remain: the 'word' in Turkish, unlike the word in Latin, does have a potentially contrastive ordering of formatives. Moreover, this difference coincides (for these two languages, at least) with the positive arguments for and against the Word and Paradigm model. Turkish, as we have seen, may be handled very neatly by a morpheme-based approach (Chs. V and VI). Latin, however, will raise the same problems of allomorphs that we illustrated from Spanish and Ancient Greek in Ch. VIII. In Turkish it is the morpheme and in Latin the word that is the basic unit for morphological statements.

A second qualification is for lexical formations as opposed to inflections. In composition the same elements can obviously appear in different orders: English *outlet* is different from *let-out*, *cart-horse* from *horse-cart*, *shotgun* from *gunshot*, *pack ice* from *ice-pack*, and so on. In some of these examples it is hard to point to any other difference in construction, except precisely that *a* is Modifier of *b* in one but *b* of *a* in the other. A similar point may be made for 'derivational' formations.

[1] Examples from LEWIS, p. 98. The alternation between *-tür* and *-dir* is determined partly by the pattern of vowel harmony (*Türk-* having a Rounded vowel and *-ler* an Unrounded), and partly by the assimilation already illustrated in *kitap-tan* versus *köy-den* (Ch. VI).

In English, again, one may derive an Adjective from a Noun by suffixing *-al* (*nation* → *national*), then derive a Verb from that by adding *-ise* (*national* → *nationalise*), and then a Noun from that by adding *-ation* (*nationalise* → *nationalis(e)ation*). But one may also have a Noun in *-ation* to which *-al* and *-ise* are added subsequently. *Sensation*, for example, is from *sense*+*-ation* and itself serves as a base for the Adjective *sensational*; this in turn is the base for the Verb *sensationalise*. The result is that the formatives appear in the order *-al*+*-ise*+*-ation* in one word but *-ation*+*-al*+*-ise* in the other.

Another related characteristic must be subject to similar qualifications. In Latin, as in English and other languages, one may often build a sentence by repetition of the same or essentially the same construction. For example, one may take a phrase which includes a Relative clause (*milites quos saucios vidisti* 'the soldiers who you saw wounded'), make this the Object of a Verb (*adiuvabat milites quos saucios vidisti* 'was giving aid to the soldiers who...'), then put this in a larger Relative clause construction (*feminam* 'the woman' *quae* 'who' *adiuvabat milites*, etc.), and then, since *feminam* is Accusative, have the whole form from *feminam* to *vidisti* as the Object of another Verb. This is one aspect of what is generally called the **recursiveness** of language (Relative clauses being one example of a **recursive construction**). But this is not possible within the word. One cannot, as it were, derive a Future stem for the Verb ADIUVO 'help' (*adiuvabi-*), then derive an Imperfect stem from that (*adiuvabi-ba-*), then a Future again from that (*adiuvabiba-bi-*), and then, with the Person/number ending (*adiuvabibab(i)-unt*), have a form which would mean something like 'will be in a position where [they] were about to give help to'. If one wants to say that one has to use several words instead. The Latin word is throughout built up by **non-recursive** formations. There is no case where a stem of type *a* has another stem of the same type *a* included within it.

Again, this does not hold for a language such as Turkish. There one may certainly find recursive constructions within the word: for example, the stem of the Intransitive Verb form *öldü* '[he, etc.] died' may be extended with a Causative suffix to yield *öl-dür-dü* 'killed' (i.e. 'caused to die'), and this in turn might be extended with a further Causative suffix (different merely because *-dür* is excluded by the phonological context) to yield *öl-dür-t-tü* 'got [someone] to kill'.[1] Nor, again, does

[1] Examples from LEWIS, p. 147; for the contextual restrictions on *-t* and basic *-dIr* (here *-dür*) see LEWIS, pp. 144f. N.B., this *-dIr* is merely homonymous with the *-dIr* of *Türklerdir* (see above).

this characteristic strictly hold for compositional and derivational formations. From English *sense*, as we have seen, we can have *sensation* and then *sensational* and *sensationalise*. But to that could we not add another *-ation* to form *sensationalisation*? With two *-ation*'s together it may seem something of a jingle, but can one say that it is morphologically excluded? My colleague Mr Brasington points out that I have myself written *institutionalisation* (with two *-ion*'s) in a later chapter. If we play around with the same suffixes we find derivations of the type *organ-* (also in *organic*) → *organ-ise* → *organis(e)-ation* → *organisation-al* (note, with a third possible ordering). Would it not be possible to add *-ise* again to form *organisationalise*? No doubt most readers will not like it, but can one swear that one has never heard it? With prefixes there are even examples where a formation is repeated immediately: e.g. [*in his*] *pre-pre-school* [*days*] (attested by Dr Crystal). With compounds one can find at least sporadic cases of recursiveness: e.g. [*This is a knife-and-fork soup, not a*] *soup-spoon soup*. Of course, it is hard to find established examples; but would they really be anomalous? Here we have further reasons for not handling lexical stems in paradigms (see Ch. III) or, more precisely, for not applying to them the Word and Paradigm model which we have since developed (Chs. IV and VIII). And, of course, we have yet another reason for not applying paradigms to 'words' in Turkish.

Each of the properties which we have considered is logically independent of the others. One could imagine a language where *ab* and *c* could be minimal sentence-units (the first of our grammatical characteristics), but *ab*, when construed with *c*, could nevertheless yield the non-cohesive ordering *a- c -b* – i.e. a systematic instance of the pattern *self de- bloody -fence*. Again, two such units CAN contrast by the ordering of elements only: in our actual Turkish example neither *Türklerdir* nor *Türktürler* can be split into a smaller sequence of free forms. Nor does cohesiveness in turn rule out recursive derivations (*institutionalisation* still functions as a continuous whole within the sentence). But in fact these features DO coincide in Latin and in many other languages, and particularly so if we restrict ourselves to words that are lexically simple. Even more widespread is a matching between the first two (minimal sentence-hood and cohesiveness). WHY should different grammatical criteria fall together in this way – while also falling together, more or less, with the phonological criteria referred to earlier? It is because there is no a priori reason that we are led to assign to this unit such preeminent descriptive status.

Finally, it is within the word that we are typically faced with problems in relating formatives to morphosyntactic properties (Ch. VIII). We have therefore every reason to adopt the traditional Word and Paradigm treatment of inflections, and with it the morphology/syntax division in its most hallowed form. But difficulties arise with languages of other types, in which the phalanx of criteria begins to break apart. How many words are there, for example, in the simple French phrase *des enfants* 'of the children'? The spelling will suggest that there are two: *des*, phonetically [dɛz] with liaison (see the end of Ch. VI), and *enfants* [ɑ̃fɑ̃]. But as far as phonology is concerned this is certainly not so. Firstly, the piece as a whole carries only one accent, [dɛzɑ̃ˈfɑ̃]; just as there is an accent-carrying unit in Latin (the 'phonological word'), so in French there is a similar unit (whatever we call it) which carries the stress on its final syllable. From this viewpoint, therefore, the phrase is a single unit at the phonological level. In addition, the boundary between *des* and *enfants* appears to have no consequences for the syllabification: in terms of these smaller phonological units the division is simply between [dɛ], [zɑ̃] and [fɑ̃]. There is no intermediate phonological unit to which *des* and *enfants* as such could belong.

Let us accept, then, that there is a discrepancy between phonology and grammar. Are *des* and *enfants* two grammatical words instead? Certainly they are grammatical units of some kind, in the sense that one would normally say that there was a grammatical boundary between them. Furthermore, the phrase is not cohesive: for example, we may insert an Adjective to form *des grands enfants* 'of the tall children' (again with liaison [degrɑ̃zɑ̃fɑ̃]). But we must then consider the class of elements to which *des* 'of the' belongs. In *les enfants* 'the children' we have the bare Definite Article (liaison form [lɛz]); so far so good. But the Definite Singular is simply *l'enfant* [lɑ̃fɑ̃]; do we want to say that we have a 'word' consisting of the single consonant [l]? Now of course this *l'* is a sandhi form, for a morpheme which in other phrases (e.g. *le père* 'the father') appears with the variant [lə]. Moreover, we have already acknowledged a certain discrepancy between phonological form and grammar. But do we want to take the discrepancy that far? A further problem arises with another series of *C* or *Cə* elements. In the sentence *je ne le vois pas* 'I can't see him', there are three of them: *je* 'I', *ne* (combining with *pas* to form the negative), and *le* 'him'. These are much more cohesive with the following *vois* '[I] see', in that although they may be separate from the lexical Verb itself (*je l'ai vu*, with Auxiliary Verb *ai*, 'I've seen him, I saw him'), nevertheless no other lexical unit can intervene in sequences of the form *je ne le* + Verb, *je le* + Auxiliary, etc., in general.[1] Nor are any of them (or *des* and *les* for that matter) Bloomfieldian 'free forms'. One cannot say just *je* 'I' (and the form one would utter, *moi* 'me', is systematically different in shape). Surely we do not want all these as 'words' in the same sense that *enfants* is a 'word'?

In effect, we can only segment French into words if we are prepared to throw either our grammatical or our phonological caution to the winds. Phonologically, we could simply cleave to the position of accent (or potential accent), saying that *des enfants* is one word, *des grands enfants* two (with possible accent on [grɑ̃] as well as [fɑ̃]), *je l'ai vu* one, the whole of *je ne le vois pas* one, and so on. The only compromise we would make with the grammar is to divide words at the morpheme boundary rather than the syllable boundary in cases where the two conflict (so [degrɑ̃z ɑ̃fɑ̃] rather than [degrɑ̃ zɑ̃fɑ̃]). For *je*, *ne* and Object *le* this would be grammatically tolerable; it will be clear already that they are as much prefix-like as word-like in character, and many writers have spoken of them in such terms. But for *des*, *les* or the Article *le* it is not satisfactory. In *des enfants* the *des* would then be a 'prefix' to the Noun (the Head element of the Noun-phrase), in *des grands enfants* to the Adjective (the subsidiary or Modifier element), and in *des enfants stupides* 'of the stupid children' to the Noun again. Why should it be a 'prefix' to the Adjective if the latter comes before the Noun, but to the Noun if it comes after? If it is a 'prefix' of one given word then why does it not move with it? The answer, of course, is that it cannot be a 'prefix': syntactically it belongs neither with the Adjective nor with the Noun, but is a third constituent within the Noun phrase as a whole.

Conversely, we could cleave to grammatical criteria and insist that *des enfants* is two words, *des grands enfants* three, *l'enfant* again two, *je l'ai vu* at least two (with a division between *ai* and *vu*), and *je ne le vois pas* again at least two (*pas* at least being separable in tags – *tu viendras, pas?* 'you're coming, aren't you?' – in *pas un* 'not one', and so forth). We are then left with a continuing dispute concerning the grammatical status of *je*, *ne* and the like. But at this point one is bound to wonder whether the question we have asked is wholly sensible. Is it

[1] Indeed there are only a few (as my colleague Mr Brasington reminds me) that can come between the lexical Verb and the Auxiliary – pattern: *je ne l'ai probablement pas vu* 'I probably haven't seen him'.

reasonable, in fact, to require that the sentence in French should be divided exhaustively into 'words'? The crux here is the requirement of exhaustiveness. If *vois* or *enfant* is a 'word', is that any reason why their partners in construction (*je*, *ne*, *le* or *l'*) should also be words in the fullest sense? Why should we expect to be able to segment a phrase or sentence (*je le vois* or *l'enfant*) exhaustively into units of any given type?

It is with this clue that many scholars would resolve the problem (in so far as it is possible to resolve it). In *je le vois* or *je l'ai vu* the morphemes *je* and *l(e)* are neither full words nor, in the strict sense, merely prefixes or parts of a word. Instead they belong to an intermediate class of 'clitic words' or **clitics** – unaccented words which must lean for support (the term 'clitic' is ultimately from the Greek word for 'leaning') on a neighbouring full word in their construction. In *je le vois* there is only one word in the fullest sense, the Verb *vois* 'see'. The Pronouns *je* 'I' and *le* 'him' are still its grammatical partners, but they are not viable as full words on their own. In *l'enfant* or *des grands enfants* we may establish a further class of clitics (*l(e)*, *des*, *les*, etc.) which are even more 'word-like' in syntactic function, but which again can only appear supported by a full word such as *enfant* or *grands*. At this point many problems remain (particularly in phonology and phonetics), but at least we are in a position to distinguish morphology and syntax satisfactorily. On the one hand, certain types of full words may be grouped into rudimentary paradigms: for example, the Finite *vois* (in *je le vois*) and the Participle *vu* (in *je l'ai vu*) are two members of the paradigm of VOIR 'see'. So also may certain of the clitics: thus the Masculine Singular *l(e)*, Feminine Singular *la* (in *la chambre* 'the room') and Plural *les* form the paradigm of the definite Article LE. The statement of these belongs to morphology in the normal way. On the other hand, the constructions of *je* and Object *le*, or the Article *les*, etc. as a whole, are as much a part of syntax as the external relationships of *vois* or *enfant*.

Clitics are at least a marginal phenomenon in many languages. In the French examples which we have given, *je*, *le*, etc., are more precisely proclitic words or **proclitics** – words that lean forwards ('pro') onto a full word which follows. But a language may also have enclitic words or **enclitics** (in fact 'enclitic' is the original of this group of terms) which instead lean backwards onto a full word preceding. For example, in the Latin tag *arma virumque* 'arms and the man' (see earlier and Ch. II) the element *que* 'and' can now be seen as an enclitic attached to the last member of the coordination. A case that has been widely discussed is that of the English *'s* (Possessive). In *John's chances* the first member of the construction is apparently a word *John's* with *'s* as suffix: it is still called the 'Genitive Case' suffix. But *a man of twenty's chances* means 'the chances of a man of twenty', the *'s* going syntactically not with *twenty* alone (the stem to which it is apparently suffixed), but with the whole phrase *a man of twenty*. An alternative, therefore, is to say that *'s* is properly an independent but enclitic element, which forms a 'word' (phonologically) with whatever full word happens to precede. In English, clitics are not a usual feature (at least, it is not usual to speak of English in these terms), and in Latin *que*, as we originally observed, is one of only three such elements. But in French they are very common, and in forms such as *je ne le vois pas* they pile up in sequence. There are similar sequences in Italian, and moreover the same form may be proclitic in one construction (e.g. *lo* 'it' in *lo fa* 'he's doing it') but enclitic in another (e.g. *lo* in the Infinitive *farlo* 'to do it').

In comparing language-types such as French and Latin it is reasonable to argue that there are no more than differences of degree. In Latin there are few clitics, the word is especially clear-cut, and the inflections are rather complex. Conversely, in French there is a wide variety of clitics, the word is problematic, and the inflections few. Certain other languages (such as Italian) may fairly be placed in the middle in all respects. But in the traditional isolating languages (such as Vietnamese) or agglutinating languages (such as Turkish) we are faced instead with a difference of kind. In Vietnamese it is now thought that some concept of a 'word' is necessary: although the vast majority of words will still contain a single morpheme and a single syllable (which is the traditional picture of this sort of language), in certain cases there does appear to be a unit intermediate between the morpheme and the phrase. However, it does not form paradigms in the sense that words in Latin form paradigms. Of the forms in question the most striking, perhaps, are those with a partly reduplicative formation: for example, *nết-na* 'be well behaved' alongside *nết* 'morals, [good] manners', *rầy-rà* 'be troublesome, complicated' alongside *rầy* 'annoy, pester', *đẫy-đà* 'be very fat' alongside *đẫy* 'be stocky, fat'.[1] But this

[1] Examples are from L. C. Thompson, 'The problem of the word in Vietnamese', *Word*, **19** (1963), pp. 39–52; they are cited in the normal spelling (the accents being tone-markers). The traditional view of the Vietnamese word had earlier been rejected by P. J. Honey, 'Word classes in Vietnamese', *Bulletin of the School of Oriental and African Studies*, **18** (1956), pp. 534–44; see also Thompson's later *A Vietnamese Grammar* (Seattle, 1965).

recalls the European category of lexical 'derivation' (Ch. III), if anything. There are also compounds, some with a member that cannot appear in separate constructions: for example, *quốc* in *quốc-gia* 'nation, country' (*gia* on its own meaning 'household, establishment') or *Mỹ-quốc* 'America' (*Mỹ* also meaning 'America'). But there is nothing that might be called an 'inflection'. To talk of inflectional morphology would be fatuous, since no 'paradigm' could be established with more than a single member.

In Turkish, the reality of the phonological word is beyond dispute. In particular, it is the unit within which rules of vowel-harmony operate – within which syllables vary between Front or Back, Close Rounded or Close Unrounded, in harmony with the invariant final syllable of a Noun or other element (Chs. V and VI). But grammatically, again, the make-up of a word differs crucially from its make-up in Latin. One point that is often stressed concerns the incidence of Case, Plural and other morphemes within the Noun-phrase: whereas in Latin *omne aevum*, for example, has a marking of Accusative and Singular in each of its constituent words (Adjective *omne* 'all', Noun *aevum* 'age, time'), in Turkish the Case morpheme would be attached to the Head Noun only. The same is true of the Plural morpheme *-lEr* (as indeed of the Plural in English, *big boot-s* not *big-s boot-s*). Even in coordination a phrase such as *Ankara ve İzmire* [*gideceğim*] '[I am going] to Ankara and Smyrna' appears with a single Case morpheme (Dative *-e*) to be construed with both Nouns.

For our purposes, however, it is the general nature of Turkish word structure that is more important. As we have seen already, a word in Turkish cannot always be characterised by a listing of its constituents: in *Türklerdir* we must add that the morpheme 'to be' (*-dIr*) is construed with the Head morpheme *Türk* accompanied by Plural *-lEr* (hence 'they are the Turks'), whereas in *Türktürler* the Head *Türk* is construed with the morpheme 'to be' plus the Plural (hence 'they are Turkish'). The words are distinguished by what can only be called a different pattern of syntactic relationships. The same point emerges from the example of recursiveness which we referred to earlier. Within the word, the rôle of morphemes must be described directly by syntactic forms of statement. Indeed, would we speak of 'words' at all were it not for the patterns of vowel-harmony, of consonant assimilation (e.g. of *-dIr* to *-tür* in *Türktürler*), and other essentially phonological matters?

These typological remarks are not complete. Indeed it would be hard to make them complete; in many languages the descriptive status of the 'word' (if any) has still not been sufficiently clarified. But at least we have an answer to the question posed at the very beginning of this chapter (can morphology and syntax be defined universally?). It must, as we said, be 'No'. In Latin, the traditional division seems justified. In French or English it is tolerable, although the rôle of inflections is more restricted. But in Vietnamese it would be nonsense, and in Turkish the most we can say is that there must be rules for the incidence of different allomorphs (Ch. V). Of course, it is disappointing not to be able to find specific universals (see Ch. I). But the differences which we have outlined appear to be broadly true.

* * *

There is one final qualification, which arises especially in quite familiar European languages. In English, *help* is a Present and *helped* the Past form of HELP; but why (to return to our discussion earlier in this chapter) can one not take *will help* as the 'Future' or '*will*-form' of the same lexeme, *will be helped* as its Passive, *is helping* and *was helping* as the Progressives corresponding to *helps* and *helped*, and so on? Likewise in French we have said that *vois* '[I] see' and *vu* 'seen' are two members of the paradigm of VOIR; but although a specialist in French would agree with this, he would also say that in *je l'ai vu* 'I saw, have seen him' there is another Tense (the 'passé composé' or Compound Past) which has its exponents in *ai vu*, and in a form such as [*quand*] *je l'ai eu fait* '[when] I've done it' there is yet another Tense (one of the 'temps surcomposés' or Double-compound Tenses) with exponents in *ai eu fait*. In Latin, a schoolboy learns *amo* 'I love' as Present Active, *amor* 'I am loved' as Present Passive, *amavi* 'I loved' as Perfect Active, but then *amatus sum* (a form consisting of a Masculine Nominative Singular Participle, *amatus*, and the form for 'I am', *sum*) as the Perfect Passive. There is a paradigm, it is implied, with both single words and groups of words among its members. Again, must we insist on a morphology/syntax division at the expense of these oppositions?

From the semantic viewpoint the answer is most certainly not. In the Latin case, the traditional treatment of the Verbal paradigm may perhaps be regarded with suspicion. One can object that only some of the forms with SUM are included: for example, the 'Future Infinitive Active' *amaturus esse* 'to be about to love' but not the corresponding Perfective *amaturus fuisse* 'to have been about to love'. In brief, it is restricted to the forms which fill a gap (e.g. for 'Future Infinitive') in the intersections of the traditional categories or 'accidentia' (see Ch. IV). But this does not invalidate the principle, namely that a two-word form (such as *amatus sum* and its variants) may have the same relationship to a single word (*amavi*) that other single words (such as *amo* and *amor*) have among themselves. In French, the oppositions of Tense are a much-debated semantic problem; but no contributor would dream of treating the Compound Tenses (as in *ai vu* or *ai eu fait*) as a different semantic system from the 'Simple' or one-word Tenses (*vois* or Imperfect *voyais*). If one did the oppositions of meaning would make no sense at all, either synchronically or diachronically. The same is true of the forms with and without Auxiliaries in English (*helps*, *is helping*, *helped*, *has helped*, and so on).

Grammatically, however, the distinction between inflected and 'compound' forms may stand. Perhaps 'compound' is not an entirely satisfactory term, since in lexical morphology it has already been used of forms which are one word by every external test (Chs. II and III). Moreover, one may often speak of one-word compounds in inflectional morphology: for example, the Agau Desiderative *destagi* 'I wish you studied' incorporates a particle *-gi* (here merely a means of forming the Desiderative) which also appears in syntactic constructions with the meaning 'all'.[1] Perhaps, therefore, the Greek term **periphrastic** might be less misleading. Latin *amatus sum* would thus be a **periphrastic form** of the Passive (a form involving 'periphrasis' rather than a single word), and French [*j'*] *ai vu* a periphrastic Tense-form as opposed to the simple Tense-forms *vois* etc. But, terminology apart, the crucial point is that they are still divisible into separate words. In Latin, *amatus sum* is no more cohesive than any other group of words; in fact, its constituents may be separated widely for rhythmic or other reasons. At the same time *amatus* participates in rules of agreement just like any normal Participle or Adjective. In English, the constituents of a phrase such as *has helped* are regularly separated in the Interrogative (*Has he helped?*). Just as the student of meaning would be

[1] See R. Hetzron, *The Verbal System of Southern Agaw* (Berkeley/Los Angeles, 1969), p. 21. Agau is a Cushitic language of Northern Ethiopia; in citing one lesser-known example I do not mean to imply that there is anything unusual in the pattern.

unwise to treat inflected and periphrastic separately, so for our present purposes it would be unhelpful not to do so.

RELATED READING

Pike's 'A syntactic paradigm' is reprinted in the collection *Syntactic Theory 1: Structuralist*, ed. F. W. Householder (Harmondsworth, 1972); see also his 'Dimensions of grammatical constructions', *Lg*, **38** (1962), pp. 221–44. For Halliday's more recent work see, for example, 'Options and functions in the English clause', *Brno Studies in English* **8** (1969), pp. 81–8 (also reprinted in Householder's collection); the fullest discussion is in R. A. Hudson's *English Complex Sentences* (Amsterdam, 1971), but this is quite stiff going.

For 'discontinuous morphemes' see HARRIS, pp. 182ff. (on Swahili), p. 205 (for Adjective and Noun agreement in Latin). These analyses should be distinguished from those proposing discontinuous morphs within the word (e.g. in HOCKETT, *Course*, pp. 271f.).

The properties of the word are discussed in most general introductions: see in particular LYONS, pp. 200–6, ROBINS, pp. 193–9, ULLMANN, Ch. 2 (naturally from a semanticist's viewpoint); also, at a more popular level, F. R. Palmer, *Grammar* (Harmondsworth, 1971), pp. 41–51. There is a useful introductory article by Martinet: A. Martinet, 'Le mot', *Collection Diogène* **2** (Paris, 1966), pp. 39–53 (more satisfactory than MARTINET, §§4.15–17). For Bloomfield's definition of the word see BLOOMFIELD, pp. 178f.; for further discussion, and the related criterion of potential separation, see HOCKETT, *Course*, Ch. 19 (also BOLINGER, pp. 52f. on points of hesitation). For cohesiveness, fixed ordering and non-recursiveness see *Inflectional Morphology*, pp. 97f.; the section as a whole (§6.4.3) will supply a number of supplementary references. For recursiveness in general see LYONS, pp. 221f., or Palmer, *Grammar*, p. 151; the notion has been stressed by the transformationalists (references for transformational syntax in Ch. X).

For a recent discussion of French see R. Harris, 'Words and word criteria in French', in *History and Structure of French: Essays in Honour of Professor T. B. W. Reid*, ed. F. J. Barnett *et al.*, (Oxford, 1972), pp. 117–33; Harris's references cover both the general and the specialist literature. Of the earlier accounts, that of Bally is thought-provoking: see C. Bally, *Linguistique générale et linguistique française*, 2nd ed. (Berne, 1944), pp. 287–302, especially his conclusion (§§493–4). For 'enclitic' and 'proclitic' see BLOOMFIELD, p. 187; the terms originate in Greek grammar (e.g., for Ancient Greek, GOODWIN, pp. 31ff.). For 'clitic' ('clitique') as a general term for unstressed words see, for example, P. Garde, *L'accent* (Paris, 1968), pp. 70–4 (with examples from French and Italian); however, even 'enclitic' and 'proclitic' are rarely explained in the general literature.

For the semantics of the French verbal system see T. B. W. Reid, 'Verbal aspect in Modern French', in *The French Language: Studies Presented to Lewis Charles Harmer*, ed. T. G. S. Combe & P. Rickard (London, 1970), pp. 146–71. For English see PALMER.

X
Syntax and lexicon

Preamble: lexical relations as syntactic functions; contrast with traditional view.
The transformationalist hypothesis: relationships between constructions; deep structure, surface structure, transformations; embedding; reductionist principle in transformational analysis; extension to the lexicon (English abstract and agentive nominalisations); special qualifications: restrictions in surface structure, abstract deep structure elements; semantic complications; how does it help?
Compounds: in transformationalist model; v. syntactic constructions; criteria from morphology; from semantics; from phonology; from syntax; all criteria relevant.

In Ch. III we cited a remark from Lyons's *Introduction*, according to which a great deal of derivational morphology 'can be, and ought to be', integrated with the rules of syntax (LYONS, p. 196). This perhaps leaves open what degree of integration is envisaged; certainly various views are possible. But let us consider the suggestion as it arises within the theory of morphemes. According to the model of Ch. V, the Noun *seas* was morphemically SEA + PLURAL, the two morphemes standing within what we called the 'Root + Qualifier' construction. *Generations* would have the same construction, only the Noun (*generation-*) being different. But what now of this Nominal 'Root' itself? According to the morphemic model it too would be represented by successive morphemes: GENERATE and, let us say, -ION. Can we not say that these too stand in a grammatical construction? The function of -ION would be that of a 'Nominaliser' – i.e. an element combining with a Verb to form a Noun. The Verb GENERATE itself might (for the sake of a term) be said to function as a 'Base'. The analysis of *generations* as a whole could thus be displayed as follows:

Root		*Qualifier*
Base	*Nominaliser*	
GENERATE	-ION	PLURAL

where the relationship of Base and Nominaliser, within the inflectional root, would be of the same order as the relation of Root as a whole and Qualifier. In such an analysis, the 'integration' of syntax and derivational morphology is complete. As with inflections in Ch. v, so with lexical formatives here; they are merely one subfield of the general study of syntactic functions.

Since it is now Ch. x, it will be clear that the author must have little sympathy with such a treatment. Otherwise, it would certainly have been expounded earlier! Nor will many readers wish to challenge the more usual view assumed as our starting-point in Ch. III. However, the possibility is worth exploring further, if only because an unconventional analysis (as at one point in Ch. IX) will help to draw our attention to the arguments justifying the convention. According to the tradition, *generation* represents a single syntactic unit. It is related lexically to the Verb GENERATE and its meaning may, in *the generation of electricity* and similar phrases, have what we called a Verbal force. But that does not mean that it has a construction with the Verb as one of its members. Why, then, should this traditional treatment be preferred? In Ch. III we discussed the criteria for dividing lexical and inflectional formations – taking for granted, that is, that the division should be made. But WHY should it be made? To suggest an answer, we must at least be prepared to give the opposite view an airing.

* * *

So far we have spoken merely of a 'possibility': given the general theory of the morpheme (-ION being a morpheme just as PLURAL or SEA are also morphemes), it is tempting to propose an equally general theory of constructions (GENERATE + -ION forming one construction just as SEA + PLURAL forms another). But it is within transformational syntax that the 'integration' of the lexicon has proved particularly attractive. According to some transformationalists, a lexical process is indeed no more than a special type of process in the syntax: just as the Gerund *generating* may be derived syntactically by adding *-ing* to the Verb stem *generate*, so also may the Noun stem *generation* be derived by adding *-ion*. It must be said at once that Chomsky himself would disagree. He would support a more conservative analysis – the 'lexicalist hypothesis' as opposed to the 'transformationalist hypothesis' of many of his pupils. But it is easy to see the origins of their view within the general transformational theory of syntax. To understand it, we must therefore begin with relations that are indisputably syntactic (or at least non-lexical) in character.

A stock illustration is the English Passive construction. *The caretaker closes the door* is an Active sentence, containing the Active Verb or Verb phrase *closes* with *the caretaker* as Subject and *the door* as Object. Equally, *the door is closed by the caretaker* is a Passive sentence, in which the Passive Verb phrase *is closed* has *the door* as grammatical Subject and *the caretaker* (preceded by the Preposition *by*) as Agent. So much is conventional. But between these two constructions there is a double parallel. On the one hand, the Subject of the Active is in the same semantic relationship to the Verb as the Agent of the Passive; this is brought out, in particular, by a correspondence between the possible Subjects for *closes* (*the caretaker*, *the guard*, *my husband*, etc.) and the possible Agents for *is closed* (*by the caretaker*, *by the guard*, etc.). On the other hand, the Active Object is also in the same semantic relationship as the Passive Subject; this is brought out, in turn, by a correspondence between the possible Objects of the Active Verb (*the door*, *the book*, *his garage*, etc.) and its possible Subjects in the Passive. How, it may be asked, are these relations to be made explicit in linguistic theory?

The transformationalist answer has already passed into the general literature. In the following schema:

[the caretaker]^{1} [close-^{2} -es^{3}] [the door]^{4}
[the door]^{4} [BE -es^{3}] [close-^{2} -ed] by [the caretaker]^{1}

we establish a point-to-point correspondence between the two constructions: thus *the caretaker* in the Active (first line) corresponds to *the caretaker* in the Passive (second line) as shown by the superscript '1', *close-* in the Active (combining with a suffix *-es* to form *closes*) corresponds to *close-* in the Passive (combining with *-ed* to form *closed*), *-es* in *closes* corresponds to *-es* in *is* (the same suffix with the Verb BE), and *the door* as the last element of the Active (superscript '4') corresponds to *the door* as the first element of the Passive. In this schema *the caretaker* and *the door* are both Noun phrases, *close-* a Verb (or Verb stem), and *-es* is a Tense (more strictly Tense and Number) element. We may accordingly establish a more general schema:

[Noun phrase]^{1} [Verb^{2} Tense^{3}] [Noun phrase]^{4}
[Noun phrase]^{4} [BE Tense^{3}] [Verb^{2} -ed] by [Noun phrase]^{1}

showing, among other things, that whatever phrase appears first in the Active (i.e. as Subject) will also appear last in the Passive (i.e. as Agent), and conversely whatever phrase appears last in the Active (i.e. as Object) will appear first in the Passive (i.e. as Subject). With appropriate extensions, the schema could be generalised to cover every possible correspondence between Active and Passive constructions.

We then require a theory of syntax which can express or incorporate correspondence schemata of this kind. According to Chomsky, the solution is to say that these are different **surface structures** (see already Ch. I) which are related by different rules of correspondence, or different sequences of such rules, to an identical **deep structure**. The precise nature of this structure need not concern us. But the rules of correspondence will be such that a phrase in a certain position within it (let us call it the 'Deep Subject') will be put in correspondence with a phrase in Subject position ('Surface Subject') in the Active and in Agent position ('Surface Agent') in the Passive. Likewise a phrase in another position in deep structure ('Deep Object') will be put in correspondence with one in Object position in the Active ('Surface Object') and in 'Surface Subject' position in the Passive. The same semantic relationships (Deep Subject to Verb, Deep Object to Verb) will thus underlie the description of both constructions.

The rules of correspondence (rules relating deep and surface structure) are called **transformations**, and it is from these that transformational syntax takes it name. But before we can proceed, another more basic insight must be added. Conventionally, once again, the phrase *a very angry man* contains a Noun *man* (the 'Head' of the construction) modified by an Attributive Adjective phrase (*very angry*). In another construction the same Head might be modified by a Relative clause with *angry* as Complement: thus *a man who is very angry*. In yet a third, *angry* may appear in a main clause with *the man* as Subject: *the man is very angry*. But although these are different on the surface again, the transformationalist will argue, we can see a constant semantic relationship running through them. This too may be brought out by a similarity in collocations: just as the Subjects and Objects of *closes* matched the Objects and Agents of *is closed*, so here the Adjectives which can appear directly as the Modifier of *man* (*an angry man*, *a tall man*, etc.) are to a significant degree the same as those which can appear as Complement to *the man* in a main clause (*The man is angry*, *The man is tall*) or as Complement of *who* in a Relative clause which modifies *man* (*A man who is angry*, *a man who is tall*). By contrast, one would not normally speak of *a man who is very cloudy*, nor, by the same token, of *a very cloudy man*. How, one asks, is this 'by the same token' to be rendered?

The transformationalist answer is again general currency. As a first step, the main clause *The man is very angry* will be related to a deep structure (again its precise form need not concern us) in which the phrase corresponding to *the man* will function as 'Deep Subject' and the phrase corresponding to *very angry* as 'Deep Complement'. The same structure may also be made to underlie the Relative clause: *very angry* will correspond again to the 'Deep Complement', but *who*, as the 'Surface Subject', will be substituted by transformation for a Deep Subject with *man* specifically. In this way, the grammar would establish a correspondence-schema as follows:

[the man]^1 is^2 [very angry]^3
[who]^1 is^2 [very angry]^3

which may obviously be generalised thus:

[Noun phrase]^1 is^2 [Adjective phrase]^3
[Relative Pronoun]^1 is^2 [Adjective phrase]^3

(Indeed this too may readily be generalised further.)

Of these surface constructions, the main clause can appear as a sentence on its own. But the Relative clause does not; instead it appears as a subordinate member (the 'Modifier') in a Noun phrase which is itself normally part of a larger clause. For example, *I can see a man who is very angry* has a surface structure in which *a man who is very angry* functions in its entirety as Surface Object. To represent this at the deep level, the structure which as a main clause would underlie *The man is very angry* is accordingly **embedded** within a structure which would otherwise underlie *I can see a man*. Taking '*X*' in inverted commas to mean 'the deep structure corresponding to *X*' (*X* being any phrase, clause or whatever), this combined structure could be roughly schematised as follows:

['I can see a man' ['The man is very angry']]

– the most important transformation, as we have seen, being the one which substitutes the Relative Pronoun *who* for the Deep Subject of '*is very angry*'.

But now, as a final step, the same structure can also underlie *I can see a very angry man*. The deep embedded clause would simply be reduced, by further transformations, to the bare Attributive Adjective.

Similarly, the deep structure of *A man who is tall will visit me tomorrow*:

['A man ['The man is tall'] will visit me tomorrow']

(embedded '*The man is tall*' as part of the Deep Subject) will also correspond to the surface structure of *A tall man will visit me tomorrow*. For the phrases in isolation, the grammar will accordingly establish correspondence-schemata such as the following:

a^{1} [very angry]^{2} man^{3}
a^{1} man^{3} [who is [very angry]^{2}]

– or in general:

$$\text{Article}^1\ [\text{Adjective phrase}]^2\ \text{Noun}^3$$
$$\text{Article}^1 \qquad \text{Noun}^3 \left[\begin{bmatrix}\text{Relative}\\ \text{Pronoun}\end{bmatrix} \text{ is [Adjective Phrase]}^2\right]$$

– by virtue of which any Noun and Adjective pair which can appear in the Attributive construction (Article + Adjective phrase + Noun) can also appear (barring some special rule to the contrary) as Head and Surface Complement in the Relative. Conversely, any pair which appears in the latter construction can also appear (again barring a special rule) in the former. Since the Relative clause is in turn in correspondence with the main clause (see above), the same collocations can thus be related in all three surface constructions.

It will be seen that a transformational analysis proceeds by what we may call a strong REDUCTIONIST PRINCIPLE. If there are two constructions x and y, and a and b in x are in the same semantic relationship as a and b in y, then, it is argued, both x and y should reduce to the same structure at a more fundamental level. Hence, in the first illustration, both Active and Passive reduce to the same structure of Deep Subject, Verb and Deep Object. Furthermore, if x is a complex construction (a construction including a clause or something judged equivalent to a clause), then at the deep level it should reduce to a complex of simple structures, each of which could correspond to a sentence on its own. So, in the second illustration, both the phrases with Relative clauses (whose complexity is self-evident) and those with Attributive Adjectives (whose complexity flows from their relationship to the former), are related to a complex of simple structures which includes that of a sentence with an Adjectival Complement. This principle has been central to transformational syntax throughout its development.

But now let us apply this to our lexical relations. In *the generation of electricity* the Noun *generation* might, as we have remarked, be said to have a 'Verbal force'. So also might *action* in *the action of the government*, *arrangement* in *her arrangement of the flowers*, *surrender* in *the surrender of the garrison*, and so on. But surely (a transformationalist will argue) there are two SORTS of Verbal 'force' that are involved. In *the generation of electricity*, the Verbal Noun stands in the same semantic relation to *electricity* as the Verb itself in *They generate electricity*, *Electricity is generated cheaply*, and so on. In brief, its 'force' is that of a Verb in relation to its Deep Object. But *the action of the government* is different; the relation of *action* to *government* is rather that of *act* in the Intransitive sentence *The government acted.* The 'force' is now that of a Verb in relation to its Subject. In the remaining examples the two types of 'force' are still more sharply distinguished. *Her arrangement of the flowers* has a Noun *arrangement* in the Object or 'Objective' relationship to *the flowers* (compare *arranged the flowers*) but at the same time in the Subject or 'Subjective' relationship to *her* (compare *She arranged...*). *The surrender of the garrison* is, one might argue, ambiguous: the relationship of *surrender* to *the garrison* could be Subjective on one interpretation (compare *The garrison surrendered*) but Objective on another (compare *The commanders surrendered the garrison*).

Granted the reductionist principle, the way ahead will now be clear. For *the action of the government* the analysis requires, in effect, a correspondence schema as follows:

[the government]^1 [act-^{2} *Tense*]
the [act-^{2} ion] of [the government]^1

where *act-* is accompanied by a Tense marking (e.g. as Past Tense *acted*) in the first construction, and a suffix *-ion* (which we have previously called a 'derivational' formative) in the second. A sentence *The action of the government was very helpful* might accordingly be assigned a deep structure:

[['The government acted'] 'was very helpful']

in which the structure which would otherwise correspond to *The government acted* is embedded as Subject (note, AS Subject and not here merely part of the Subject) to '*was very helpful*'. By one of the necessary transformations the suffix *-ion* would be added to the Verb stem *act-* to form the Noun stem *action*: we will describe this as a 'nominalising' transformation (compare the 'Nominaliser' function at the beginning of this chapter), and the corresponding surface structure as a 'nominalised' construction.

By contrast, *the generation of electricity* would enter into a correspondence schema as follows:

Subject [generate-[1] *Tense*] electricity[2]
the [generate-[1] -ion] of electricity[2]

(here neither the specific Tense nor the specific Subject are relevant), where the relationship of *generation* and *electricity* corresponds, as required, to that of Verb and Object. The deep structure of *They began the generation of electricity* could accordingly be set up roughly as follows:

['They began' ['They generated electricity']]

or, perhaps more appropriately:

['They began' [*Subject* 'generate'- *Tense* 'electricity']]

with Subject and Tense still unspecific at the underlying level. In a similar spirit, *I like her arrangement of the flowers* might on first sight be assigned a deep structure:

['I like' ['She has arranged the flowers']],

His surrender of the garrison was unjustified another which would look something like:

[['He surrendered the garrison'] 'was unjustified'],

and *They encouraged the surrender of the garrison* (if we may take this Subjectively) one which would be roughly:

['They encouraged' ['The garrison surrendered']]

(although this could, of course, be taken Objectively also).

So far as the formatives are concerned, *action* and *generation* would be formed (as we said) by adding *-ion*, *arrangement* by adding *-ment*, and the nominalised *surrender* with no addition at all. According to Ch. III, this would all form part of the lexical or 'derivational' section of the grammar – the last example being a case of zero derivation (derivation by an identity operation – see Ch. VII) or, according to some scholars, of 'conversion' (the Verb *surrender* being 'converted', as such, into a Noun). But according to the transformationalist hypothesis, this can all be integrated into syntax in the strongest possible sense. Just as

BE and the 'Past Participle' *-ed* were added by transformations in the Passive construction (*is closed* corresponding to *closes* in the illustration given earlier), so the nominalisation of *act*, *generate*, and so on is again simply part of the syntactic correspondence between deep structures and surface structures. We have, of course, to state the shape of the nominalising formative. But this may be handled in the same way as, indeed, the shape of the Past Participle formative: allomorph *-ion* in one set of environments, *-ment* in another, 'zero' in a third, and so on (compare Ch. V). As we suggested in passing at one point in Ch. III, the formation itself would be as much a part of the construction as the morphemes traditionally called 'inflectional'.

For a second 'lexical' illustration let us take the sentence *He is a bad actor*. In surface structure, *bad* is just an Adjective which goes with *actor*: that (it would be argued) is the most that can be discovered at the 'superficial' level. But their meaning relationship differs from, for example, that of *tall* and *actor* in *He is a tall actor*. There we are saying of someone, firstly, that he is tall and, secondly, that he is an actor: his 'tallness' and his 'being an actor' are not connected. But in *He is a bad actor* we are not saying simply that someone is an actor and, independently, that he is bad. He is 'bad' precisely qua 'actor'; he may be good in other respects, but he is 'bad at acting' or 'acts badly'. Similarly, *He is a superb painter* means that he 'paints superbly', *He is an appalling bore* that he 'bores people appallingly', and *He is a lousy cyclist* perhaps one of two things: either 'He is a cyclist' and cyclists are 'lousy people' (*lousy* functioning as an 'epithet' rather than a modifier), or, commonly with a different intonation, that he 'cycles lousily' or is 'lousy at cycling'. The semantic relationship between an Adjective and an Agentive can thus correspond exactly (it would be said) to the relationship between a Verb and its Adverb (*He acts badly*, *He paints superbly*), between a Gerund and Complement Adjective (*His acting is bad*, *His cycling is lousy*), and so on.

Again, the way ahead is clear. According to our earlier analysis, the sentence *He is a tall man* would have a deep structure:

['He is a man' ['The man is tall']]

(compare *an angry man*, meaning 'a man who is angry'). But since an actor is 'a man who acts', the apparently simple *He is an actor* could likewise be reduced to a deep structure with embedded '*The man acts*':

['He is a man' ['The man acts']]

– and then, of course, *He is a bad actor* might at the deep level be:

['He is a man' ['The man acts badly']]

For Adjective + Noun and Verb + Adverb a correspondence schema could accordingly be established as follows:

[act-^{1} -s]	[bad-^{2} -ly]
a bad^{2}	[act-^{1} -or]

where *-or* (or AGENTIVE) is a morpheme introduced directly by a nominalising transformation (and *-ly*, we may add, could likewise represent a morpheme introduced as part of an 'adverbialisation'). In *a superb painter* the AGENTIVE morpheme is spelled as *-er* instead; in *cyclist* it takes the form *-ist*, and in *an appalling bore* there is again a zero derivation or conversion of the Verb *bore* into the Noun *bore*.

So far the transformationalist proposal looks attractive, maybe. But if we take it further we will find a host of special problems, requiring a host of special elaborations. Still with the Agentive what, for example, is the deep structure of *a great actor* or *an important painter*? Again, the former means someone who is 'great' as an actor: in the sentence *Irving was a great actor, not just a good actor* surely *great* and *actor* are entirely parallel to *good* and *actor*. But there is no corresponding Adverb *greatly*: even with the contrast, one does not say *Irving acted greatly, not just well.* Likewise *Cézanne was an important painter* means that he was 'important' considered as a painter; this is not just parallel to *a tall painter* or *an angry painter*. But can one say *Cézanne painted importantly*? Perhaps one could, meaning something like *He painted pretentiously*; but that is not the meaning we want for *important* as an Adjective. Turning to the Nouns, what is the deep structure of *a bad poet* or *a superb artist*? Semantically, these are no different from *a bad writer* or *a superb painter* (except that *poet* and *artist* have been substituted). But there are no Verbs to which they can be assigned as nominalisations – only the further Nouns *poem* and *art*. How then could *a good poet* and *a good writer* be derived by the same transformation? *A good athlete* seems even more intractable. Morphologically, the Noun is simple; how then can *a tall athlete* and *a good athlete* (let alone *a great athlete*) be syntactically distinguished?

Ah, but (our transformationalist would say) one has to realise that deep structures are established at an abstract level. We agree, he would argue, that *a great actor* parallels *a good actor*, and that the latter parallels (in relevant respects) the Predicate *acts well.* But this is precisely to say that *great* has a semantically 'Adverbial' function; it modifies the Verbal sense of *actor* and not the Noun *actor* itself. How then could it possibly NOT derive from an Adverb in deep structure? The fact that it does not have a corresponding 'surface' Adverb is neither here nor there. Similarly, *a good athlete* parallels (we agree) *a good runner* and the latter is related to the Predicate *runs well.* But this is precisely to say that *athlete* has an underlying Verbal sense, and it is this that *good* modifies. How can it possibly NOT derive from a Verb in deep structure? The Verb underlying *athlete* might be conveniently represented as 'to ATHLETE'; the deep structure of [*He is*] *a good athlete* would thus be:

['a man' ['The man ATHLETES well']]

– the only detail being that a simple '*The man* ATHLETE*s well*' would be prevented (by special provisos in the transformations) from having a surface structure on its own. Similarly, the Adverb underlying *great* (or this sense of *great*) could be represented as GREAT, and the deep structure of [*Irving was*] *a great actor* would be something like:

['a man' ['The man acted GREAT']]

Putting this together, the deep structure of *a great athlete* would naturally be:

['a man' ['The man ATHLETES GREAT']]

The apparent problems, it would be argued, are merely gaps in the realisation of elements in surface structure.

What, though, of *poet*, *artist* or, for example, *pianist*? Well, actually (our transformationalist might say) the structures which have been given are still unwarrantably dominated by surface syntax and surface lexical elements. Why, in particular, is *a painter* or *an actor* specifically 'a man' who paints or acts? At the deep level all we need is some form of 'abstract' Noun (a Noun not itself viable in surface structure) to which the embedded structure is subordinated. Let us represent this as -ER – thus:

['an -ER' ['The -ER acts']]

and so on. But is there any reason (he would continue) why we should not establish whole 'abstract Predicates'? In *a great athlete* we are naive if we think of ATHLETE as specifically a Verb: it is simply some sort of element or complex of elements which has the ability to combine with -ER to form a sentence-like structure. Equally, why should '*acts*' or '*paints*' (the deep structures underlying *acts* and *paints*) consist of Tense and the mere surface Verb stem? All we need is some abstract Predicate-like structure (call it ACT- or PAINT-) which can be put in correspondence with the surface Verb in some sentences and the surface Agentive in others. But then a similar abstract Predicate ('to PIANO', let us say) could also underlie both *John is a pianist*:

['John is an -ER' ['The -ER PIANOS']]

and *John plays the piano*:

['John PIANOS']

Similarly for any other case (*artist*, *poet*, etc.) that a critic cares to mention.

But our transformationalist must also parry a host of semantic criticisms. In the first illustration we implied that *arrangement* was semantically parallel to *surrender*. But really this is not so: *I deplore his surrender of the garrison* refers to the FACT that he surrendered it, but *I like her arrangement of the flowers* to the WAY she has arranged them. How are these to be distinguished – by adding an 'abstract Noun' FACT to one deep structure and an 'abstract' WAY to another? And why can Subjective *surrender* appear only in the Singular (we cannot say *the surrenders of the soldiers*), whereas Subjective *action* can be Plural also (*the actions of the government*)? We can hardly appeal to the mere surface 'lexemes'; there must be a further subdivision of deep structures (or further provisos in the transformations) to deal with it. Returning to the Agentive examples, a *poet* may indeed be someone who 'writes poetry' (or 'POEMS') and a *pianist* someone who 'plays the piano', but in the usual sense an *artist* is someone engaged in graphic 'art' specifically. As so often with lexical formations (see Ch. III), the use of the derived element is not simply predictable from its base. How is this to be taken care of? Is the deep Predicate underlying *artist* ('to ART') quite different from whatever underlies *art*? But surely we do not want to say that *art* and *artist* are unrelated. So perhaps *artist* does not correspond to 'ART' on its own, but rather to 'ART' with a specific modifier – 'to ART GRAPHIC', as it were. There must then be special provisos to ensure that a deep structure with any other modifier –

['an -ER' ['The -ER ARTS LITERARY']]

for example – cannot have as its surface structure *an artist* as such.

Amendments of this last sort can be added indefinitely. We have discussed two Nouns formed from *act*, the Agentive *actor* and the Abstract *action*. But their Verbal senses are different: the government is not *an actor* if it decides to 'act' or 'take action', nor, because he 'acted Hamlet', do we talk of *Irving's action of* (or *as*) *Hamlet*. Will our transformationalist say, then, that there must be two 'deep Predicates' (ACT[1] and ACT[2]), of which one is a structure corresponding to *action* but not *actor*, and the other vice versa? If so, does their base *act-* have any real unity? To this last the transformationalist answer might indeed be No: the so-called relationship of derivation (*act* → *actor*, *act* → *action*) is a mere surface reflex of the deep relationships to be established. Similar distinctions would be made for any other discrepancy in these or any other examples.

However, there is another sort of semantic problem. Where, for example, is the line between an 'ordinary' Adjective and a 'deep Adverbial' Adjective? We have suggested that *a tall painter* has one structure and *a great painter* the other; but what, say, is *a busy painter*? Is it someone who is 'painting busily' or someone who is 'a painter' and happens to be 'busy'? Again, *a diligent painter* appears to be someone who 'paints diligently'; but is its structure really different from that of *a diligent man*? Semantically it seems nonsense to say so. Is the latter then Agentive also – ['*an* -ER' ['*The* -ER MAN*s* *diligently*']]? That would be even more preposterous. Unfortunately, if *a diligent painter* is syntactically just like *a tall painter* (the meaning differences springing simply from the meanings of the Adjectives), then we can go back and say the same of *a great painter* or *a good painter*! Returning to the Abstracts, does a Noun such as *generation* always have a 'Verbal' deep structure? In Ch. I we drew a parallel between *three generations ago* and *fifty years ago*. Do we now deny this, saying that *generations* is related to a deep Predicate and *years* not? Or do we accept it, saying that *years* must therefore come from a Predicate too? Either choice is absurd. Perhaps then we could take a third line, saying that this *generation* has nothing at all to do with the *generation* of *the generation of electricity*. Unfortunately, there are other examples which cannot be pushed off so confidently. *The relation of X to Y* would plainly correspond to *X is related to Y*; but what, let us say, of *our nearest relations*? Does this really have a different syntactic construction from *my eldest brother*? Surely the answer is No. Yet by the light of our earlier analyses, *nearest* has a clear Adverbial sense ('The people related to us most nearly'). How could analysis at the deep level extract us from this impasse?

In the author's judgment, the transformationalist proposal has now been given more than enough rope to hang itself. Technically it might be made to work – in that in principle we could establish more and more abstract structures until the semantic distinctions and parallels were exhausted. But as a theory it creates problems of explanation instead of resolving them. Why should we have these problems in the distribution and relationships of 'surface' elements? Why should *actor* and *action* fail to match either *act* or one another? Why should *athlete* appear to allow an 'Adverbial' modifier, but at the same time lack a Verb? If *arrange* and *surrender* are both Transitive Verbs (entering, collocations apart, into similar relationships), then why should the properties of *arrangement* and the Noun *surrender* diverge? Why, again, should *relations* look like an ordinary Noun from one angle, but like a partner of *relate* and *related* from another? The traditional answer is that these are individual 'words' or lexemes, and as such they have a life of their own. Why should we expect it to be otherwise? But the whole point of the transformationalist hypothesis is to deny to the lexeme more than a superficial reality. Unless its proponents have a better answer then they are surely wrong.

Indeed, is there even a prima facie argument in their favour? In the Active and Passive, we spoke of Noun phrases standing in the 'same semantic relationship' to their Verb. The main support was the evidence from collocations. Although there are exceptions, as a basic rule 'if S_1 is a grammatical sentence of the form [schema for Active construction], then the corresponding string of the form [Passive schema] is also a grammatical sentence' (Chomsky, *Structures*, p. 43). It is this generalisation that the common deep structure was intended to capture. We also established a general correspondence-schema for the Adjectives: if there is a Subject-Complement clause with Noun *n* and Adjective *a* then (broadly speaking) there will also be an Attributive phrase with *n* as Head and *a* as Modifier. Again, it was to account for this correspondence that Chomsky's transformations were postulated. But we did not give similar support for our analysis of *generation* or *action*, and for *actor* we merely appealed to paraphrases of the sort 'a man who acts'. In retrospect, could the evidence have been provided? It seems not. To say that for any construction of Verb + Object there is also a construction of Abstract Noun + of + Object is not even broadly true.

What, then, did we think we were trying to explain when we applied the reductionist principle to them?

* * *

So far in this book we have said comparatively little about compounds. We pointed to their existence in Ch. II, and in Ch. III we drew a distinction between composition and derivation within the lexical field. We also referred to the difficulty of determining this boundary in certain cases: was the [mən] of *postman* a member of a compound or merely a lexical formative (end of Ch. III)? But otherwise their problems are in large part those of the lexicon in general. In the development of the 'transformationalist' view, it was in fact the compounds that were first subjected to full analysis: *madman*, for example, was related syntactically to *a man who is mad*, *girlfriend* to *a friend who is a girl*, *arrowhead* to *the head of an arrow*, *garden party* to *party in a garden*, *eggplant* (perhaps less appropriately) to *a plant like an egg*, and so on.[1] The case for such analyses was similar to the one already illustrated for derivational formations: although *girlfriend* and *arrowhead* are on the 'surface' merely Noun + Noun, their types may be distinguished semantically in the same way that sentences with a Nominal Complement (*The friend is a girl*) may be distinguished from whole-part Possessives (*The arrow has a head*). The arguments against are also of the same sort. One talks of a *girlfriend* and a *boyfriend*, but not usually of a *manfriend* and still less of a *childfriend* or an *adultfriend*. Why so? This cannot be explained by syntax, but only by the particular properties of GIRLFRIEND and BOYFRIEND as semantic units. Many problems hit one even more forcibly. Readers not already satiated may work out the deep embedded sentences underlying *a carhop* or *a striptease*, *a cuptie* or *an offside*, *slap-up* (in *a slap-up dinner*), *a stitchwort* or *a nuthatch*, etc., etc.

There is, however, one special and serious problem, which concerns the boundary between a compound and a syntactic construction. The definition itself is clear: a compound (such as *madman*) is 'one word', and a construction (such as [*a*] *mad man*) two or more separate 'words'. But in practice what are the criteria for distinguishing them? GIRLFRIEND, for example, could be written in any of three ways: as two words (*girl friend*), as one word hyphenated (*girl-friend*), or unhyphen-

[1] Examples given as types by R. B. Lees, *The Grammar of English Nominalisations* (Supplement to *IJAL*: Baltimore, 1960), Ch. 4.

ated. It is certainly a lexeme in the widest possible sense (see Ch. II), but should it be classed as a 'word lexeme' or merely an idiomatic use of FRIEND with Modifier GIRL? Our original example in Ch. II is written either as *ice-cream* or as *ice cream*. Does it make sense to say that it is sometimes a lexeme and sometimes not? In inflecting languages the distinction is often straightforward: see our discussion of Latin LIQUEFACIO and TRIBUNUS MILITARIS in the same passage of Ch. II. But in a language such as English it is a notorious crux.

Relevant criteria can be drawn from every level: from morphology and semantics, from phonology and syntax. Where a morphological criterion is available it may, of course, be decisive one way or the other. *Socio-economic* is certainly a compound, because its first member is a stem or stem-variant plus suffix (compare *soci-al*, *soci-o-logy*, etc.) which cannot appear as a free form (Ch. IX) as such. The same is true of the type *Anglo-American*, *Franco-Chinese*, *Italo-Celtic*, etc. On the other hand, *heir apparent* is not a compound, because in the Plural (*heirs apparent*) HEIR is still inflected as a separate unit. Unfortunately, only positive results prove anything. *Social Democratic* MAY be a compound, in that *Social* is not inflected separately; but then how could it be? Equally, it may NOT be a compound, in that *Social* can appear independently; but then so can *mad* in *madman*, *girl* in *girlfriend*, and so on. The types which do allow positive results (*socio-economic* or *heir apparent*) are only the extreme cases. In addition, the Plural test reveals considerable free and other variation. In *solicitor general*, the first member is not usually inflected (e.g. *the solicitor generals in the last three governments*). But perhaps a pedant will insist that it should be, and there are certainly styles in which *solicitors general* would be more normal. Turning to a more ordinary situation, could three people in a restaurant order *three prunes and custards* or *three tournedo Rossini's*? For the author, at least, both are more acceptable than *three apple-pie and creams* or *three sole bonne-femme's*. There are several factors at work, and it is not easy to be sure of the facts.

Semantic criteria have often been emphasised. The phrases *a black bird* and *a blue jay* have meanings predictable from the individual words and their construction: the former refers to any 'bird' which is 'black' (e.g. a rook), and the latter to a 'jay' which is 'blue' (whatever that means, a European reader may say!). But the compounds *blackbird* and *bluejay* have meanings which are not predictable; both are names for particular species (the latter more familiar to North Americans).

Other compounds are still less transparent. A *blackbird* is at least a sort of 'bird', but a *ladybird* is a genus of beetle and a *silverfish* is not (even in the popular mind) a sort of 'fish'. Nor are a *blackcap* and a *redcap* types of 'cap'; the former is a species of warbler which 'has' a 'black cap', and the latter a military policeman (who wears one). Traditionally, the types represented by *blackbird* and *blackcap* are put into different semantic categories; according to a Sanskrit classification which is sometimes referred to, the latter is a type of 'bahuvrihi' compound, whose Head member cannot be substituted for the whole. In the same spirit, the transformationalists would set up different deep structures: ['*a bird*' ['*The bird is black*']] versus ['*a* Noun' ['*The* Noun *has a cap*' ['*The cap is black*']]]. But some compounds are not even transparent to that extent. Still on bird names, is a *yellowhammer* a type of 'hammer' which is 'yellow', or a type of finch which 'has' a 'yellow hammer'? Both make equally bad sense.

Unfortunately, semantic criteria are not sufficient on their own. *A madman* may be opposed to *a mad man* just as *a blackbird* may be opposed to *a black bird*; but is the meaning of MADMAN in fact unpredictable from MAN and MAD? Certainly we do not want to conclude that *madman* is merely two words in a different construction. *Apple-tree* and *pear-tree*, *oak-tree* and *yew-tree*, *strawberry-tree* and *tulip-tree* are all names for trees; intuitively, at least, they should fall on the same side of the line. But the first two pairs are in regular meaning correlations (*apple* is to *apple-tree* as *pear* to *pear-tree*, *oak* to *oak-tree* as *yew to yew-tree*), while the last pair are not: 'strawberry-trees' and 'tulip-trees' cannot be identified from the meanings of *strawberry* and *tulip*. If they ARE to be classed together then other criteria must come into play. In other cases the notion of a 'compound' would be extended much too far. In Ch. II we have noted the special meaning of '*to pull one's socks up*'; but for morphological reasons at least (compare now *heir apparent* and *heirs apparent*) we will still class this as an idiomatic construction. *Sickbed* and *madhouse* are compounds because (in part) their collocations would otherwise be odd: one does not speak of a 'bed' being 'sick' or (at least in any relevant sense) of a 'house' being 'mad'. But *a topless bar* bears little relation to *The bar is topless*, and *a refrigerated butcher* equally little to *The butcher is refrigerated*; must these be classed as compounds too? One objection is that they are not cohesive (see Ch. IX), in that one could presumably talk of *a topless sandwich bar* or *a refrigerated pork butcher*. But of course these could be compounds too, with *sandwich* and *pork* as subsidiary members. Somewhere between *sickbed* and that kind of conclusion a line must be drawn by other criteria.

In many of our examples the phonology is obviously relevant. *Bláckbird* and *yéllowhammer* are stressed on the first member, as shown: [ə'blæk'bəːd] and [ə'jelou'hæmə] can only be *a black bird* and *a yellow hammer*. But *mádman* and *oák-tree* have the same stress pattern vis-à-vis *a mad man* and, let us say, *a single tree*. Therefore they do belong to the same compound class (with the addition that *madman* also has the reduced vowel [ə] of *postman* etc.). The same criterion is decisive for *síckbed* versus *topless bar*; indeed the distinction is just as clear between the latter and (we may certainly say) the compounds *sándwich bar* or *mílk bar*. As the last examples show, this is not always captured by the spelling (even where spelling practices are consistent). *Gárden party* and *shérry party* are phonological compounds as compared with [*a*] *rotten party* or [*a*] *merry party*, even though they are not consistently hyphenated (*garden-party*, *sherry-party*). *Mental hospital* is always written as two words, although its stress pattern is still that of *madhouse* and not, say, of [*a*] *large house* or *Christ's Hospital*. So is *black man* (a Negro etc.), although it is only the quality of the vowel ([mæn]) that sets it apart from *madman*. For the stress compare *The Green Man*, for example.

Unfortunately, while the semantic criterion allows too many 'compounds', the phonological criterion (it might be argued) will allow too few. A case in point is when the Head loses its ordinary meaning. Just as a *ladybird* was not a 'bird' so, for example, a *red admiral* and a *purple emperor* are species of butterflies and have nothing to do with 'admirals' or 'emperors'; are these constructions merely because their stresses are like *a tall admiral* rather than, say, *a reár-admiral*? Even more arguable are those which are semantically of the type of *blackcap* or *redcap*: for example, *Red Beret* (paratrooper) or *black belt* (judo expert entitled to wear such a belt). These too have phrasal stress, but in meaning they are not phrasal constructions with BERET and BELT as Head. Are they compounds, or merely fixed instances of metonymy (figures of speech in which an attribute or adjunct stands for the whole)?

Furthermore, this is another criterion whose results are subject to variation. One reason is that the distinction may often be obliterated by sentence stress and intonation. Thus a 'phonological compound' CAN have its second member prominent: e.g. *I'd say that's an oak búsh rather than an oak trée.* Conversely, a phrase may lack stress on its Head: e.g. *It's a funny sort of bláck bird* (not, say, a brown one) may be identical to *a funny sort of bláckbird* (not, say, a starling). Some forms then vary freely: the author is not sure, for example, whether he says *mílk sháke* or *mílk-shake*, *óffice párty* or *óffice-party*, *téddy beár* or *téddy-bear*. Many vary from dialect to dialect or speaker to speaker: *ice-cream* is a well known example, and *striptease* or *orange squash* are others. The author remembers the confusion when he asked for a *hót dóg* in the United States.

Syntactically, one might think of testing whether the subordinate member can enter into its own construction. One could talk of *reed and corn buntings* or *a flock of white and red admirals*; therefore, it might be argued, *red admiral*, *corn bunting*, etc., cannot be compounds. Again, the members would be separated in *a hospital – mental, isn't it?* or *parties, cocktail and otherwise*; therefore *mental hospital* and *cocktail party* would not be compounds either. But in fact this is more a reflection of transparency and possible semantic contrast. One does not talk of *sick- and death- beds* or of *birds, black and otherwise* (meaning 'blackbirds') – the latter because it would only be understood non-idiomatically. But one type of compound allows coordination readily (e.g. *macro- and micro-economic studies*), and many others are not objectionable: e.g. *missel- and song-thrushes.* On another aspect, it is certainly possible for a member to be picked up individually by a Pronoun: e.g. [*historians*] *do not sit open-mouthed waiting for something to fall into it* (example from *The Times Literary Supplement*), or *He's a lady-killer because he likes them so much.*

A more important criterion is based on the arrangement of forms within the compound. Often it recalls that of a true syntactic construction: although we reject the transformationalist conclusion, *blackbird* does have the Modifier + Head arrangement of *black bird*, and *jack-in-the-box* does parallel [*a*] *pen in the box.* It is here that the boundary is most troublesome: again, if *a pig in a poke* is an idiom, and *jack-in-the-box* a compound, which is *toad in the hole*? But in other cases the arrangement is one which is never fully productive. One talks of an *arrowhead*, a *pinhead* or a *masthead*, but far less readily (either as one or as two 'words') of a *dart head*, a *tack head* or a *pole head.* Unlike the arrangement of Adjective + Noun, that of Noun + Noun is always semi-productive (Ch. III). It follows that *arrowhead* etc. are lexical formations. If they were two-word idioms then what construction would they be idiomatic instances of?

The boundary between ordinary and partial productivity is delicate and crucial. In Ch. III we referred briefly to the type represented by *woman-hater* or *lady-killer*, citing *schoolgirl-hater* as a marginal instance. But with some roots this pattern has more productivity than a dictionary, at least, can be expected to handle. Taking *drink-* we can have [e.g. *a heavy*] *whisky-drinker*, *wine-drinker*, *gin-drinker*, and why not, for example, *Beaujolais-drinker*, *Crême-de-Menthe-drinker*, and so on? *Smoke-* yields *cigar-smoker*, *cigarette-smoker*, *pipe-smoker* – and why not, say, *cheroot-smoker* or *Gauloise-smoker*? Shall we say, then, that this is the free construction (limited perhaps to Verbs of the class of DRINK, SMOKE or EAT) of which *lady-killer* etc. are the fossilised parallels? Unfortunately, there are still some collocations which give one pause. One can say of someone that they are *a great cheese-eater* or *meat-eater*, but *butter-eater* seems less secure and *egg-eater* even more so. Why so, given that some people do indeed eat striking quantities of eggs? There seems no simple answer, except that *cheese-eater* has acquired clearer status as a unit. But possibly not all readers will agree with the author's judgments. Here we are very close to the boundary between syntactic and lexical 'creativity' (see Ch. XII).

The criteria which we have discussed tend to give different results. *Red admiral* is a compound by the test of meaning, but by the phonological test it would be taken merely as a fossilised or non-transparent metaphor. *Heir apparent* is morphologically two words, but syntactically the arrangement of Noun + Adjective is unproductive. However, it would be a mistake to conclude that one of them must be THE criterion par excellence. In the history of a language, collocations and figures of speech may often be INSTITUTIONALISED (as clichés or idioms) without also being LEXICALISED as single units: this is true, for example, of *a sick joke*, where *sick* can still have its own Modifier (*a very sick joke*). Alternatively, lexicalisation may follow (either at once, as for *dishwasher*, or later, as for *son of a bitch*) and this may lead to the fossilisation of at least one member (e.g. *whinchat*), to a purely derivational formation (e.g. *childhood*) or to virtual morphological unity (e.g. *chaffinch* [tʃæfintʃ]). In a language such as English, how can we expect a single criterion to mark the boundary between lexicalisation and mere institutionalisation? This is not to say that the distinction is spurious; it is often the mark of a genuine unit that one has trouble with it! But as with the word in general (Ch. IX) criteria at all levels may be relevant.

RELATED READING

For transformational syntax in general the best starting-point is still CHOMSKY, *Structures*. For deep and surface structure see CHOMSKY, *Aspects*; also CHOMSKY, *Mind*, pp. 28ff.; also his *Topics in the Theory of Generative Grammar* (The Hague, 1966), pp. 16f. and Ch. 3. With these later works the rôle of transformations effectively changes (though not the way they operate within the theory); for a brief survey of successive developments see, for example, Lyons in *New Horizons*, pp. 115–39. One of the best introductions to transformational syntax (apart from Chomsky's own writings) is Lyons's *Chomsky* (London, 1970).

Chomsky's early work is in part an outgrowth of Harris's distributional programme; for the link see, in particular, Z. S. Harris, 'Cooccurrence and transformation in linguistic structure', *Lg*, **33** (1957), pp. 283–340. In Chomsky's account, transformations were initially justified by criteria of distribution and simplicity (including 'collocability' or 'cooccurrence restrictions'); see CHOMSKY, *Structures*, Chs. 5 and 7 ('purely formal and non-semantic', *Ibid.*, p. 93), and compare, e.g., E. Bach, *An Introduction to Transformational Grammars* (New York, 1964), pp. 65f. Chomsky THEN pointed to their merit in explaining ambiguities and semantic similarities (CHOMSKY, *Structures*, Ch. 8). In fact, formal criteria will not suffice: see now, e.g., Chomsky's 'Remarks on nominalization', in *Readings in English Transformational Grammar*, ed. R. A. Jacobs & P. S. Rosenbaum (Waltham, Mass., 1970), p. 186. But the problems remain obscure, and in much recent work not only is syntactic ambiguity treated as a datum, but a heavy reliance is put on so-called 'paraphrase' relations between sentences; for 'paraphrase' see already J. J. Katz & P. M. Postal, *An Integrated Theory of Linguistic Descriptions* (Cambridge, Mass., 1964), e.g. p. 76. I have tried to minimise this tendency in my own exposition.

For reductionism compare S. C. Dik, *Coordination* (Amsterdam, 1968), pp. 72–4. I believe that this interpretation is correct; but it must be emphasised that Chomsky himself does not talk in precisely these terms.

For the transformationalist view of derivational morphology see G. Lakoff, *On the Nature of Syntactic Irregularity* (Mimeographed report: Cambridge, Mass., 1965), especially §5.4; the work was later printed under the title *Irregularity in Syntax* (New York, 1970). For earlier explorations see Lees, *Grammar of English Nominalizations*, Ch. 3, passim (e.g. pp. 70f.). See also the brief example in LYONS, p. 249. In the late 1960s this was caught up in the wider movement known as 'generative semantics'; according to a characteristic view, not only would *X's action* be related transformationally to *X acted*, but, e.g., *X killed Y* to *X caused Y to die*, *X walked* to *X went on foot*, and so on. For relevant articles see J. D. McCawley, 'The role of semantics in a grammar', in *Universals in Linguistic Theory*, ed. E. Bach & R. T. Harms (New York, 1968), pp. 124–69, and, for this point in particular, J. M. Anderson, 'On the status of "lexical formatives"', *FL*, **4** (1968), pp. 308–18. See also Lyons's more cautious discussion in his *Introduction* (Lyons, §8.2, especially p. 360); but note that his notion of 'lexicalisation' (see also *New Horizons*, p. 138) differs from the sense in which I use the term in the last paragraph of this chapter.

For the contrary 'lexicalist' view see Chomsky, 'Remarks on Nominalization'. For a non-transformational treatment compare Jespersen's theory of 'nexus-substantives': O. Jespersen, *The Philosophy of Grammar* (London, 1924), especially pp. 169–72; also *Analytic Syntax* (London, 1937), pp. 67–9, 159f. For a full discussion of English 'conversion' or zero derivation see Marchand, Ch. 5.

For the transformationalist treatment of compounds see Lees, *Op. cit.*, also R. P. Botha, *The Function of the Lexicon in Transformational Generative Grammar* (The Hague, 1968). Lees returns to the subject in his contribution to Jacobs & Rosenbaum, *Op. cit.*: 'On very deep grammatical structure', pp. 139ff. For criticism I hope I may still refer to my own review, 'Transformational Grammar', *Archivum Linguisticum*, **13** (1969), pp. 196–209; see also references for semi-productivity in Ch. xii.

For compounds v. phrases the best discussion is still that of Bloomfield, pp. 227ff. For morphological features of compounds see *Ibid.*, pp. 229f. For semantic criteria see O. Jespersen, *A Modern English Grammar*, Vol. 6 (Copenhagen, 1942), Ch. 8. For phonological criteria in English see Bloch & Trager, p. 66; for stress in particular see Bloomfield, p. 228; Hill §10.2 for 'fixed phrases' (e.g. pp. 180f.); Hockett, *Course*, pp. 316f. (for 'phrasal compounds'); Lees, *Op. cit.*, pp. 119f. (where the distinction is called 'traditional'); Chomsky & Halle, pp. 16f. and passim (the 'compound rule'). All this depends rather heavily on the received American theory of English stress; for criticisms see Bolinger's *Forms of English*, Part i (Reading for Ch. i). For syntactic and non-syntactic relationships in compounds see Bloomfield, pp. 233–7; for problems of productivity see again Ch. xii.

For thorough surveys of the semantic and other types of English compounds see Jespersen, *Op. cit.*; Marchand, Ch. 2; briefly in Quirk *et al.*, pp. 1020ff.

XI
Morphology and phonology

Preamble: connections between phonology and sandhi; problems of unified statement; approaches of different schools: of Post-Bloomfieldians; of generativists; morphophonemics; diversity of interactions.
Survey (examples of interaction in Italian): purely morphological alternation; v. purely phonological; phonological conditioning (nasals before consonants); Post-Bloomfieldian and generativist arguments; neutralisation, archiphonemes; phonotactic motivation (consonants plus *s* or *t*); v. inferrability; sandhi without motivation; with varying reflexes; lexically restricted sandhi (palatalisation of velars); morphophonemes; phonetic plausibility as limiting criterion.
Conclusion: no simple boundary between levels.

In Ch. IV we cited a passage from Priscian's *Institutiones Grammaticae* (*Principles of Grammar*) in which the *p* of *scripsi* 'I wrote' was connected with the general absence of *bs* clusters (the cluster one would expect from *scribo* 'I write') before a following vowel. But what is the nature of this connection, and how is it to be expressed in a description? Now Priscian's inflectional rule may certainly be reformulated. Instead of relating *scripsi* and *scribo* as wholes, or even the stem *scrips-* to the stem *scrib-*, we will say that the basic root *scrib-* is followed by a further element *-s-* (the allomorph of the Perfective morpheme, or a formative suffixed to form the Perfective stem), and we will postulate a rule of sandhi, or of phonologically conditioned alternation, by which the *b* is assimilated. The sandhi will also be generalised to other consonants; the same assimilation (voiced → voiceless) is found in Perfects such as [fiːksiː] (spelled *fixi*) 'I fixed' as compared with Present [fiːgoː] (*figo*) 'I fix'. But the essential insight remains and is still not captured. On the one hand we do have an assimilation; that, if we like, is a fact of morphology (of the alternations or adaptations of morphological elements). On the other hand we do find, as a fact of phonology, that there are no clusters which were phonetically [bs] or [gs]; although Priscian's statement was qualified ('at the beginning of a syllable' or before a vowel), the written clusters which require this qualification (e.g. in *plebs* 'the people') were without doubt [ps] also. These 'facts' are obviously related. Indeed they are surely facets of the same 'fact'.

Similar connections can be illustrated from later chapters. In Ancient Greek (Ch. VI) there were no clusters of the type *k*^{h}*s* and *gs* as distinct from *ks*; that can be stated as a matter of phonology, regardless of morphological boundaries. But in addition a basic *k*^{h} or *g*, as in *t*^{h}*rik*^{h}- ('hair') or *aig*- ('goat'), fell together before *s* to yield a cluster identical to one with basic *k*: thus *t*^{h}*rík-s*, *aík-s*, *p*^{h}*ýlak-s* (the last with root *p*^{h}*ýlak-*). Just as the assimilation in *scripsi* is a reflection of rules in Latin phonology, so these are EXPLAINED (we may reasonably say) by similar rules in Greek. How is this explanatory relationship to be brought out?

These examples involve consonants. But the point can also be made repeatedly for vowels. In Turkish (Ch. V), the restrictions of vowel-harmony are not confined to variations of suffixes. Just as a monosyllabic root in *u* cannot be followed immediately by a Case or other suffix in *i*, so a disyllabic root would break the pattern if, likewise, it had an *u* in one syllable and an *i* in the next. If we look at each case in isolation, we will say that the first reflects a recurrent alternation, and the second a rule for the phonological structure of items in the lexicon. But taken together they are facets of the SAME rule, which is concerned with the sequences of syllables in word-forms. At this point a more fundamental question may present itself. If this is one rule, then to what linguistic level should it be assigned? Is it the job of the morphologist or the phonologist to explain what is going on? The phonologist seems more directly concerned. But in that case might not the phenomenon be removed from the domain of morphology altogether?

Unfortunately, different schools of linguists have given very diverse answers to such questions. According to the Post-Bloomfieldians, phonology and morphology should be kept very rigidly apart. The former is concerned purely with the identity and distribution of phonemes; for that purpose any grammatical unit (such as the grammatical word or the morpheme) is irrelevant. The phonologist will merely establish that /bs/ does not appear in Latin, that certain sequences of syllables do not normally appear in Turkish, and so on. Morphology, in its turn, is concerned purely with the identity and realisation of morphemes. So, at that level, we will establish that Latin had a Verbal morpheme with the allomorphs /skriːb/ and /skriːp/ (/b/ and /p/ being different phonemes), that there is a morpheme in Turkish with allomorphs *-i*, *-ü*, *-ı* and *-u*, and so on. Not only are these levels different, but it would be a serious confusion to suggest that they should be treated together. To a Post-Bloomfieldian, our questions are therefore misconceived. Returning to the Greek examples, the correct course is indeed to say, firstly, that there is a cluster *ks* but no $k^h s$ or *gs* and, secondly, that morphemes with basic $-k^h$ and *-g* have allomorphs in *-k* before *s*. Any conflation of these statements would involve a 'mixing of levels', and is to be avoided.

The view of the generative school is very different. Firstly, the phoneme is rejected; according to their scheme of levels, it is wrong to distinguish rules relating morphemes to phonemic allomorphs (e.g. the Latin morpheme meaning 'write' to the phonemically written /skri:b/ and /skri:p/) from other rules relating phonemes to their phonetic realisations. The argument for this is important, and we will illustrate it later. Secondly, there can be no rules for the distribution of phonological elements, except those which apply either within the basic forms of morphemes (these continue to serve as the elements of generative syntax) or to the sandhi of one morpheme with another. Taking the Greek example, a statement of one sort would exclude both $k^h s$ and *gs* within morpheme boundaries: more precisely, any cluster of Velar + s (e.g. in *éksɔː* ἔξω 'outside') would automatically be $k+s$ in particular. This is technically known as a 'morpheme-structure rule'. A rule of another sort would add that k^h- or *g*- are modified in positions of assimilation. This is known as a 'phonological rule' proper, the term 'phonology' being applied to the whole process of relating 'surface structures' to 'phonetic signals' (Chs. I and XII).

The present author does not agree with either American approach (as may be clear from the way in which the examples have been presented). But the problem is difficult, and these and other views are still debated. A further solution, for example, is to postulate yet a third field (that of **morphophonemics** or **morphophonology**) which lies between phonology on the one hand, and morphology on the other. On an extreme view, this might form a third descriptive level – one level (morphology) being concerned solely with grammatically conditioned or irregular alternants, the next (morphophonemics) with any that are phonologically conditioned, and the next (phonology) purely with the characterisation of phonemes. Apart from this scheme, the term 'morphophonemics' is often applied to rules of sandhi in particular: so, for example, there would be a **morphophonemic rule** for

Ancient Greek by which **aíg-s* is modified to *aíks*. Of course, there is then the problem of relating this third field to both the others.

In the circumstances, it would be rash to inculcate a single theoretical solution. But in addition the facts themselves are not as simple as our three illustrations may so far have suggested. Morphology and phonology interact in varying degrees, and at certain stages one can see the arguments which lead to one theoretical position or another. It will therefore be instructive to take a single language, and work through the range of possibilities (from pure morphology at one end to pure phonology at the other) which a description must take account of. This will at least provide the groundwork on which the reader may develop his own judgment.

* * *

Let us take Italian as the language of illustration. At one extreme, there are naturally many alternations which Italian phonology does not explain at all. For a regular Verb such as FERIRE 'wound', the Past Participle is formed with the vowel of the Infinitive (*fer-i-*[*re*]) and a suffix *-t-*: thus *fer-i-t-* (Masculine Singular *ferito*). Other regular examples are *sal-i-to* 'gone up', *and-a-to* 'gone' (Infinitive *and-a-re* 'to go'), and so on. One might expect, therefore, that APPARIRE 'appear' or MORIRE 'die' would have similar Participles of the form *apparito*, *morito*. But they do not. In the case of MORIRE the suffix *-t-* is added to the bare root: thus *mor-t-* (*morto*). For APPARIRE even the formative is different: thus *appar-s-* (Masculine Singular *apparso*). This is the type of case referred in Ch. V to the category of non-recurrent, grammatically conditioned alternation. Although the majority of Participles do go with *ferito* or *andato*, there is simply a substantial minority (further examples later) which go with either *morto* or *apparso* instead. There is no general rule which explains why this should be so. Nor is there any reason why *apparso* should have an *-s-* while *morto* still has a *-t-*. Although there is some partial system for the roots in occlusives (see the very end of this survey), here at least we are forced to refer to the individual lexeme. Both roots end in *r* (*mor-*, *appar-*) and both Verbs belong to the same broad inflectional class (shown by the vowels of the Infinitive: *mor-i-re*, *appar-i-re*); what more general factor COULD be responsible?

At the other extreme, it would be easy to set up 'alternations' which are purely phonetic in character. In the forms *cade* '[he] falls' and *cadde* 'fell', the difference in consonant length (shown by the single and double *d*'s in the spelling) is matched by a complementary difference in vowel length. The *a* in *cade* is noticeably long ([kaːde]), but the one in *cadde* is short ([kadde]); that is undoubtedly how we would transcribe them if we were not already familiar with the language. Morphologically, both forms contain a root of the shape *CVC*, followed in one case by a bare vowel (*cad-e*) and in the other by a reduplication of the final consonant (*cad-d-e*, with the same vowel following). For the root itself we might therefore be led to establish an alternation between a variant in [aː] ([kaːd]) and another in [a] ([kad]), the conditions being, apparently, the presence of a vowel (e.g. *e*) or a consonant (e.g. *d*) as the element following. But in fact we will do no such thing. According to the accepted phonological analysis, consonant length is distinctive (the *d* of *cade* being phonemically opposed to the *dd* of *cadde*), but vowel length is merely an accident of the type of syllable in which the vowel appears. In non-final stressed open syllables ('open' = ending in the vowel itself), the phonetic variants or allophones are at their longest: this is the case in *cade* (with the syllabic structure ['kaː]+[de]). In closed syllables (syllables ending in a consonant) the allophones are shorter: thus *cadde* is ['kad]+[de]. This can be discovered and stated without any reference to the grammar. In analysing the morphology we may therefore take it as read and assume that *a* is identical throughout.

For all linguists but the generativists, it is these extremes that justify the two main levels of description that we are considering. On the one hand, the 'alternation' in *cad-* is explained entirely as a repercussion of the phonology. That indeed no one would dispute. Once the phonologist has stated the distribution of allophones, the student of morphology need not pay the slightest attention to it. On the other hand, the variation in the Past Participle falls entirely in the morphological domain. The phonologist, qua phonologist, will not be aware that there is any problem; it cannot arise until the forms are also subjected to grammatical analysis. Nor will anything he can say provide the slightest explanation for it.

These then may be taken as the endpoints of our discussion. But between these extremes there are many alternations (those of the phonologically conditioned type in Ch. v) which are less easily assigned to one level or the other. Let us begin with the sandhi of nasals before consonants. At the beginning of a syllable, Italian has three distinct nasal phonemes: written *m* [m] as in *matto* 'mad', *n* [n] as in *nostro* 'our', and *gn* [ɲ] as in *gnocchi* 'dumplings'. But at the syllable ending any nasal is simply homorganic (identical as to its place of articulation) with whatever consonant follows. Before a bilabial we find only the bilabial [m] (written as *m* in *impossibile* 'impossible' or *ambedue* 'both'). Before a labiodental there is only the labiodental [ɱ] (written as *n* in *infelice* 'unhappy' or *inverno* 'winter'). Before a dental there is only the dental [n] (compare *insolito* 'unusual' or *andare* 'to go'), before an alveolo-palatal only the matching [ɳ] (e.g. *ingiusto* 'unjust' or *lancia* 'launch'), and before a velar only the velar [ŋ] (written as *n* in *incolto* 'uncultivated' or *lungo* 'long'). This is a feature of syllable structure (or of medial clusters across syllable boundaries), which may be stated quite independently of the grammatical elements in question.

At the same time it also has morphological repercussions. The first of each pair of examples (*impossibile*, *infelice*, *insolito*, *ingiusto*, *incolto*) is an Adjective formed with a Negative prefix written as *im-* or *in-*: compare *possibile* 'possible', *felice* 'happy', *solito* 'usual', *giusto* 'just' and *colto* 'cultivated'. Even in the spelling this has two 'allomorphs', and in phonetics it has all five separate variants [im], [iɱ], [in], [iɳ] and [iŋ]. Since the dental variant [in] is also found before vowels (compare *inelegante* 'inelegant', *elegante* 'elegant') that must be the basic form; the others will be due to assimilation in one form or another. A second, slightly different repercussion can be found in the Past Participles of ASSUMERE 'take up, assume' and SPEGNERE 'put out, extinguish'. Before a vowel their roots have different nasal consonants: bilabial [m] in *assum-* (e.g. Infinitive *assum-e-re*), palatal [ɲ] in *spegn-* (*spegn-e-re*). But in the Participles both have a dental [n] (*assun-t-o*, *spen-t-o*), the morphological formation being that already illustrated by *morto* 'died'. Here too we must speak of assimilation: just as basic *in-* is assimilated as *im-* in *impossibile* so, conversely, basic *assum-* is assimilated as *assun-* in *assunto*. Likewise in *spento* basic *spegn-* is assimilated as *spen-*.

At what level, then, are the assimilations to be stated? It is with this kind of example that our different schools will begin to fall apart. According to the Post-Bloomfieldians, some would be purely phonological and others purely 'morphophonemic'. As we have seen, Italian has no phonemic contrast between [m] and [ɱ], or between [n], [ɳ] and [ŋ]; therefore the variations of *impossibile* and *infelice* ([iɱ]), or of *insolito*, *ingiusto* and *incolto* ([iŋ]), have no more than an allophonic ('sub-phonemic') status. They are similar to that of *cad-* in *cade* and *cadde*, [m] and [ɱ] being different allophones of the Labial phoneme /m/ (the latter appearing before a labiodental, the former elsewhere), and [n], [n̪] and [ŋ] different allophones (it would usually be said) of the Dental /n/.[1] The student of morphology may accordingly assume the phonemic spellings /im/*possibile*, /im/*felice*, /in/*solito*, /in/*giusto*, /in/*colto* – and, once again, does not have to bother any further.

But there ARE phonemic contrasts between [m], [n] and [ɲ]; this we have already established at the beginning of a syllable. The nasal in *impossibile* or *assumere* is thus a different phoneme from that of *insolito*, *inelegante* or *assunto*, and that of *spegnere* different from that of *spento*. This in turn puts a different complexion on the alternations which they enter into. Speaking as phonologists, we can of course remark that the phonemes have limited distributions: at the end of a syllable, /m/ (allophones [m] and [ɱ]) appears only before a bilabial or labiodental, /ɲ/ at best before another /ɲ/ (phonetically, at least, forms such as *spegnere* have a geminate, ['spɛɲɲere]), and /n/ ([n], [n̪], [ŋ]) only before other consonants where /m/ and /ɲ/ are excluded. These statements would form part of what is often called the **phonotactics** (a section of the phonology dealing with the possible 'arrangements' or 'tactic behaviour' of phonological units). But only a morphological analysis can reveal the alternating roots and prefixes, and it is only at that level, therefore, that the problem of relating *im-* and *in-*, *spegn-* and *spen-*, etc., will arise. These are accordingly four different morphs (Ch. V), and must be related by techniques appropriate to the morphemic section of the description. So, following Ch. VI, the basic form *in-* would be modified by sandhi rule to *im-*, basic *assum-* to *assun-*, and basic *spegn-* to *spen-* wherever the relevant phonological conditions are fulfilled. It is to this type of rule, as we said, that the term 'morphophonemic' is particularly applied.

Other scholars have objected to such a division on various grounds. The obvious comment is still that the morphophonemics and phonotactics are unconnected. There are rules of one sort in one section (e.g. $n \rightarrow m$ before a Labial), and of another sort in the other (e.g. $n +$ Labial cannot appear as a cluster), but no relationship is established between them. As we remarked earlier, this is conscious and deliberate. But is it satisfactory? A proponent will answer, perhaps, that it is simply necessary. It is a premiss of phonemic analysis (according to his prin-

[1] Cf. Ž. Muljačić, *Fonologia generale e fonologia della lingua italiana* (Bologna, 1969), p. 449.

ciples, that is) that if two sounds are contrastive then on any occurrence they must be different phonemes – the principle of 'once a phoneme, always a phoneme', as Householder once called it.[1] Alternations between phonemes MUST belong to morphology, whereas, naturally, their distribution cannot but belong to phonology. But surely distribution and alternation are opposite sides of the coin. Phonemic principles aside, is there any sense in separating them?

Furthermore, why should an assimilation that is phonetically the same throughout (nasals assimilate to the position of whatever consonant follows) be split in half between a 'sub-phonemic' and a 'supra-phonemic' section of the description? Given the basic form ***in-possibile***, we require a rule (whether 'morphological' or 'phonological') which will indicate that its phonetic form has [m]. Given basic ***in-colto***, we likewise need a rule which will show that the nasal is phonetically [ŋ]. Why can it not be the SAME rule? The Post-Bloomfieldian answer is, once again, that ***m*** is a different phoneme from ***n*** whereas [ŋ] is merely an allophone. But we can turn this round the other way. We want to formulate a generalisation (with the wording given above). If the only objection to it is that some nasals are 'phonemes' whereas others are not 'phonemes', then surely that is a good reason for abandoning the concept of the phoneme. This argument is central to the generativist case as it has developed since the end of the 1950s. The object of our statements, it has been said, is to relate a representation of grammatical elements (the 'surface structure') to the phonetic 'signals' corresponding. Naturally, this should be done by rules which are as general and illuminating as possible. If phonemes intervene, we are often forced (as here) to obscure a generalisation by dividing the rule between the 'morphophonemics' and the 'allophonics'. Therefore any representation in terms of phonemes must be rejected.

The generativist view here stands at the opposite extreme from the Post-Bloomfieldian. But there is a compromise way of handling this kind of example. According to the theorists of the Prague school, we are dealing with a case of phonological **neutralisation**: although the nasal phonemes are distinct before vowels, the oppositions between them are suppressed or **neutralised** whenever another consonant follows. The nature of this neutralisation may be expressed in terms of distinctive phonological features. As a phoneme, ***m*** is Labial (let us say) and Nasal, ***n*** Dental and Nasal, and '***gn***' Palatal and Nasal; it is by

[1] Picked up again in HOUSEHOLDER, p. 206.

these features that the units are distinguished both from each other and from the occlusives (e.g. Labial Voiceless Occlusive *p*), fricatives (e.g. Voiceless Dental Sibilant *s*), and so on, which make up the remainder of the consonant system. When the oppositions are neutralised the phonemes lose the features which are individual to each (in this case, Labial, Dental and Palatal), and we are simply left with those which they have in common (in this case, Nasal). According to this theory, pre-consonantal [m], [ɱ], [n], [ɲ] and [ŋ] are all phonologically identical: their more specific features bilabial, labiodental, etc., belong purely to the level of phonetic realisation. The unit which they are said to represent (the **archiphoneme**, as it is usually called) is neither the same as any of the individual phonemes *m*, *n* or '*gn*', nor yet wholly different from them. It is the unique set of distinctive features ('Nasal') common to all three.

That much we can again say simply qua phonologists. But then is there anything that the morphological statement need add? In forms such as *inelegante* the prefix is basically *in*-; here both *m* and '*gn*' would be possible, and to identify *n* it must be [n] specifically. In *insolito*, *ingiusto*, *impossibile* or *incolto* the basic form is also *in*-, just as in *spento* the basic root is again *spegn*- and in *assunto* it is again *assum*-. But here *n*, *m* and '*gn*' cannot be distinct. In the position of neutralisation all must reduce to the same archiphoneme: *i* + Nasal + *solito*, *i* + Nasal + *giusto*, *i* + Nasal + *possibile*, and in precisely the same way *spe* + Nasal + *to*, *assu* + Nasal + *to*. The remaining details belong, as we said, to the level of phonetic realisation. In *insolito*, *assunto* or *spento* the Nasal archiphoneme is realised as [n]; it merely happens that in one case (*insolito*) the basic phoneme is dental also. In *impossibile*, *ingiusto* and *incolto* it is realised as [m], [ɲ] and [ŋ]. Since ALL these assimilations are 'sub-phonemic' (concerned with the 'allophones', if we like, of an archiphoneme), we can easily generalise the rule by which they are handled.

Whatever interpretation we adopt, examples of neutralisation form a large part of the sandhi in many languages. In Italian the pattern of SPEGNERE, for example, may at once be extended to the corresponding forms of SCEGLIERE 'choose'. Phonologically, just as the Palatal *gn* contrasts before vowels with the Dental *n*, so also a Palatal Lateral (written *gl* or *gli*) contrasts with a Dental Lateral *l*. It is these Palatals which appear in the basic roots: *spegn-e-re* (with long [ɲɲ], as we said), and *scegli-e-re* (likewise with long [ʎʎ]). But before *t* both oppositions are equally neutralised: the archiphonemes are characterised by the features Nasal (as before) and simply Lateral (the only feature common to Palatal Lateral and Dental Lateral). It is this last archiphoneme which is accordingly realised in the Participle *scelto* 'chosen'. Although the *l* here is phonetically dental (and there is thus an apparent morphological alternation between *scel-* and the *scegli-* of *scegliere*), this is entirely a consequence of the neutralisation and the way in which the archiphoneme is realised. Returning to our earlier illustrations, the [p] of Latin *scripsi* can now be explained by a similar suppression, before another consonant, of the oppositions between Voiced and Voiceless plosives. In Ancient Greek the pattern also extended to the Aspirates; it is in consequence of the neutralisations, we may then add, that *tʰríks*, *aíks* and *pʰýlaks* all have a phonetically identical [k].

Archiphonemes can also be established in vowel systems. In stressed syllables in Italian, Half-close [e] and [o] are phonologically opposed to Half-open [ɛ] and [ɔ]. The first two appear, for example, in the roots of *vendo* 'I sell' and *pone* '[he] puts' and the others (though spelled the same) in *sento* 'I feel' and *volge* '[he] turns'. But in an unstressed syllable neither pair is in contrast; each reduces to a single Mid Front or Mid Back archiphoneme. It follows that *vendiámo* 'we sell' (with the stress marked by the acute accent) must have an *e* identical to that of *sentiámo* 'we feel', and *ponéva* 'was putting' must have an *o* identical to that of *volgéva* 'was turning'. According to one account, their phonetic quality is in these environments more similar to the [ɛ] and [ɔ] than to the [e] and [o].[1] But this need not imply that the stressed roots [vend] and [pon] are to be related as allomorphs to the unstressed [vɛnd] and [pɔn]. Phonological statements alone can cope quite adequately. The harmony in our Turkish examples could, in principle, be brought under the same heading. Although Turcologists do not speak in these terms, we could say, for instance, that the oppositions between *i*, *ü*, *ı* and *u* are neutralised in any harmonic syllable; it is the resulting archiphoneme (Close) which was represented by the *I* in our basic forms of the Accusative morpheme (*-I*), Genitive (*-In*), and so on (Ch. VI).

So far, then, the 'morphophonemics' could be explained completely by the phonology. Of course, a morphological statement may also be helpful; a description is often clearer if different sections can look at the same phenomenon from different angles. But strictly there is no

[1] Hall, *La struttura dell'italiano*, p. 23.

need for it (unless, of course, we insist on the rigid application of Post-Bloomfieldian phonemics). Unfortunately, other forms of sandhi are less straightforward. For illustration, let us pick up again the forms of the Past Participle. In *morto* or *apparso* there is only the difference in suffixes; the roots *mor-* and *appar-* are in their normal form. In *spento* or *scelto* there is no problem that we have not already dealt with. Only the formation of root + *t* requires special statement. There are a few others that can be handled similarly. For example, the oppositions of geminated and single consonants (near minimal pair in *c*[o]*rro* 'I run', *c*[ɔ]*ro* 'choir') are neutralised except between vowels: hence the [ɾ] in *cor-s-o* 'run' (with root [korr]) is only a slightly different case from the [n] in *spento* (with root [spɛɲɲ]). But what of *volto* 'turned' or *chiuso* 'closed'? The Infinitive 'to turn' is *volgere* and 'to close' is *chiudere*. Basically, therefore, the stems are plausibly **volg-t-* (the *g* being a 'palatalisable' Velar – see below) and **chiud-s-*. Moreover, both *lgt* and *ds* are excluded by the rules of phonotactics: more generally, the language has no clusters of Velar (or Palatal) + *t* or Dental Occlusive + *s*. We may therefore say that the sandhi is **phonologically** (or more precisely **phonotactically**) **motivated**. It makes sense, at least, for reasons that can be stated independently of the morphological boundary. But is that enough? Do we not need, in addition, a specific rule by which *g* is dropped, and another by which *d* and *s* are fused together?

In terms of sandhi, each case forms part of a larger generalisation. To begin with the roots in Dentals, any junction of *d* + *s* reduces regularly to single *s*. Further examples are:

'killed' *uccid-s-o → ucciso

and also, with preceding *n*:

'taken' *prend-s-o → preso

A junction of *t* + *s* reduces, however, to double *ss*:

'shaken' *scot-s-o → scosso

and so do cases of *tt* + *s*:

'annexed' *annett-s-o → annesso

This does not dispose of certain irregularities: for instance, the Participle with root *chied-* 'call' is *chiesto* not *chieso*. But for these we must postulate basic differences (see later in this discussion). Turning to the class of *volto*, we find that in general a *c* or *g*+*s* (*c* in these examples being also 'palatalisable' – see below), reduces between vowels to double *ss*:

'I said'	*dic-s-i → dissi
'I erected'	*ereg-s-i → eressi

and *c* or *g*+*t* likewise to double *tt*:

'made'	*fac-t-o → fatto
'erected'	*ereg-t-o → eretto

The same applies if the root consonant is itself double, e.g.:

'I read'	*legg-s-i → lessi
'read'	*legg-t-o → letto

But if a Liquid or Nasal precedes, the *s* or *t* is again single. Hence, for example:

'turned'	*volg-t-o → volto
'I turned'	*volg-s-i → volsi
'won'	*vinc-t-o → vinto
'I won'	*vinc-s-i → vinsi

The same pattern holds with other root consonants: thus *v*+*s* and *v*+*t* again yield *ss* and *tt*:

'moved'	*mov-s-o → mosso
'written'	*scriv-t-o → scritto

– except in an example with *l* preceding:

'absolved'	*assolv-t-o → assolto

Here too we must note that there are irregularities: for example, *eressi* and *eretto* have an *e* where the Infinitive *erigere* 'to erect' has an *i*. Nevertheless a fair number of forms can be derived without further difficulty by the processes outlined.

How far, then, can they be explained by aspects of the phonology? Certain points are again straightforward. After another consonant there is no distinction between a geminate and non-geminate, and it is for that reason, we may say, that we have *volto* and not *voltto*. Moreover all the sandhi is phonotactically motivated: nowhere in the language are there clusters such as *nds* (as in the basic **prend-s-o*), *ggs* (**legg-s-i*), and so on. But why these particular sandhi modifications? Why, for example, should $g+s$ give double *ss* while $d+s$ gives single *s*? That there should be a difference is phonetically plausible: *g* has a different place of articulation from *s* (and is merely assimilated to it), whereas *d* has the same place of articulation (and therefore $d+s$ collapse completely). But there must be rules – morphophonemic rules as we have called them – which show that it happens. Again, why should $d+s$ (*chiuso*) reduce in a different way from $t+s$ (*scosso*)? It is doubtless significant that one has a Voiced and the other a Voiceless consonant. But we might still expect *chiuso* to be *chiusso* (or, alternatively, *scosso* to be *scoso*). There must be explicit rules to specify the forms correctly.

The problem, evidently, is that the phonology or phonotactics will only provide a PARTIAL explanation. In a form such as *spento* the sandhi is not only 'motivated' by the phonology (there being no cluster of the form [ɲɲt], but is also INFERRABLE: given a statement of neutralisation, and further statements for the phonetic realisation of the archiphoneme, the actual [nt] follows automatically. But in *volto* or *chiuso* the sandhi is not inferrable. The phonology makes clear that SOME adjustment of **volg-t-o* and **chiud-s-o* will be necessary, but not WHICH adjustment. That must still be specified by the techniques of description which we introduced in Ch. VI. In cases such as these the morphophonemics and phonotactics work together, but each requires its own separate mode of statement.

The case of *preso* 'taken' raises another complication. Although *nds* is contrary to the phonotactics, *ns* is certainly not: compare already *vinsi* 'I won'. Why then does the cluster reduce to *s*, instead of a simpler reduction to *prenso*? In effect, it is possible to state two successive rules, one motivated (though not also inferrable) and the other not. The first is the general rule for $d+s$, which we will already establish for forms such as *chiuso*. The second would specify a further reduction of $n+s$: this might also be proposed for *posi* 'I put' (Past) or *rimasi* 'I remained', the basic **pon-s-i* and **riman-s-i* being established with the roots of *pon-e* 'puts' or the Infinitive *riman-e-re* 'to remain'. So, by the first rule, basic **prend-s-o* → *pren-s-o* and, by the second, **pren-s-o* in turn → *preso*. In a generative treatment, this second rule might even be stated without exceptions;[1] certainly it applies to nearly a dozen Verbs (and more with basic *-d* than without). Nevertheless,

[1] Briefly, its specification would have to refer to the formative boundary: so **pren-s-o* → *preso*, but, for example, *denso* (with Adjectival root *dens-*) is not modified to *deso*. It would also have to be ordered (see Ch. XII) before the rule by which **vinc-s-i* → *vinsi*; otherwise this would be further modified to *visi*.

there is no reason in the phonology why **pon-s-i* or **pren-s-o* should not remain precisely as they are.

By other rules, a cluster might be reduced to a single consonant in some forms and a geminate in others. Occasionally, a suffix in *r-* directly follows a root: for example, *ved-r-à* '[he] will see' or *av-r-à* 'will have'. But in *porre* 'to put' we would expect a root *pon-* (compare again *pone* 'puts') and in *verrà* '[he] will come' we would expect *ven-* (compare *ven-i-re* 'to come'); it is therefore tempting to see in these the sandhi forms for basic **pon-re* (Infinitive suffix *-re* with no preceding vowel) and **ven-r-à*. A similar sandhi rule could be suggested for *condurre* 'to conduct, drive [a vehicle]'; where a basic root *conduc-* (with 'palatalisable' *c*) is established by *conduco* 'I drive', *conduce* 'drives', and so on. But what, in that case, of the further Infinitives *dire* 'to say', *fare* 'to do', or *bere* 'to drink'? If we consider these on their own, we might establish the basic formations **dic-re* (compare *dico* 'I say', *dice* '[he] says'), **fac-re* (this Verb is more irregular, but compare *fac-e-va* 'was doing') and **bev-re* (compare *bevo* 'I drink', *beve* '[he] drinks'). But of course we CANNOT consider them on their own. The rule for *bere* is already questionable: somehow, it would have to be formulated to exclude **av-r-à* → *arà* (presumably by limiting it to forms with a stressed vowel, as in **bév-re*, preceding). But, even then, why should *v*+*r* yield *r* while *n*+*r* yields double *rr* (*verrà*)? And why, above all, should **dic-re* yield *dire* while **conduc-re* yields *condurre*? The consonant is the same 'palatalisable' *c* in both roots; moreover *rr* is perfectly possible after *i* (compare *birra* 'beer'), just as *r* is perfectly possible after *u* (compare *duro* 'hard'). We have no alternative but to state specifically that one lexeme goes one way and the other the other.

With *bere*, in particular, we are coming close to a simple difference in morphological formations. However, there is still another possibility to be distinguished. In the roots with written *c* or *g* (*dic-*, *conduc-*, and earlier *volg-*, *vinc-*, etc.), there is an alternation between a Palatal phoneme before Front vowels (*dice* ['ditʃe] '[he] says', *volgi* ['vɔldʒi] 'you turn') and the corresponding Velar before Back or Open (*dico* ['diko] 'I say', Subjunctive *volga* ['vɔlga]). The same alternation can be found with double consonants (*leggo* ['lɛggo] 'I read' but *legge* ['lɛddʒe] '[he] reads'); nor is it confined to the Verbs (compare *ami*[k]*o* 'friend' but Plural *ami*[tʃ]*i* 'friends'; *astrolo*[g]*o* 'astrologist' but *astrolo*[dʒ]*i* 'astrologists'). The cluster [sk] also alternates, under the same conditions, with the phonetically double [ʃʃ]: thus *fin-i-sc-o* [fi'nisko] 'I finish', but *fin-i-sc-e* [fi'niʃʃe] '[he] finishes'. Obviously, an attractive solution is to treat this as a phenomenon of palatalisation. By the first and most important rule, basic Velar Occlusives would be modified to Palatals before a 'palatal' vowel: thus **di*[k]-*e* → *di*[tʃ]*e*, **vol*[g]-*i* → *vol*[dʒ]*i*, and also **fin-i-s*[k]-*e* → *finis*[tʃ]*e*. By a subsidiary rule, the [stʃ] of the last form (which is phonotactically excluded) would be further adjusted to [ʃʃ]. The basic morphological formations (1st Singular with suffixed -*o*, Noun Plural in -*i*, and so on) would remain quite regular.

Unfortunately, the first rule itself is not phonotactically motivated. A Velar can certainly appear before Front vowels (e.g. initially in *chilo* 'Kilo' or *ghiro* 'dormouse'). Nor is the alternation automatic (see Ch. V). For example, the Verb PAGARE 'pay' has 1st Singular ['pago] 'I pay' and likewise 2nd Singular ['pagi] 'you pay'; although these are spelled *pago* and *paghi*, the '*gh*' is merely a spelling convention for [g] before *i* and *e*. Again, the Noun LUOGO 'place' has Singular *luogo* and likewise Plural *luoghi* ['lwɔgi], CIECO 'blind' the Singulars *cieco* and *cieca* and the Plurals *cie*[k]*i* (*ciechi*) and *cie*[k]*e* (*cieche*), BOSCO 'wood' Singular *bosco* and Plural *bos*[k]*i* (*boschi*), and so on. How then should the cases of palatalisation be handled? One possibility, of course, is to ascribe the effect not to sandhi but to a morphological process (Ch. VII). *Amici* 'friends' might be derived directly from its root ([amik]-) firstly by the suffixation of *i* and, secondly, by the change of [k] to [tʃ]: AMICO would then be assigned qua lexeme to a 'palatalising' class whereas CIECO, BOSCO, etc., would be 'non-palatalising'. Similarly, the 2nd Singular *volgi* would be derived from [vɔlg]- firstly by suffixation and, secondly, by the change of [g] to [dʒ]. There would simply be 'palatalising' and 'non-palatalising' Verbs, with the -*sc*- of *finisco* and *finisce* (see the end of Ch. III) added as a 'palatalising' affix. The process would then belong to a different level; it would be taken away from sandhi or morphophonemics altogether.

However, there are two considerations which argue against this. Firstly, the alternation is not only recurrent (in the sense of Ch. V) but it also recurs in several morphological contexts. We would need a separate formation of Noun Plurals, also of the 2nd Singular of Verbs (-*i* with palatalisation versus -*i* without), also of the 1st Plurals (compare *volgiamo* 'we turn', also with [dʒ]), and so on. Although the process itself is identical, the formations in which it operates would each require their own statement. Secondly, the change is phonetically very plausible or natural. The fronting of velars is widespread before Front vowels (e.g. in English and still more in Turkish), and this readily leads to affrication. It is by just such a process (subsequently overlaid by analogy and other developments) that the alternation in Italian has historically arisen. Accordingly, we will still speak of a sandhi rule – but one which is lexically restricted (compare again Ch. V) as opposed to the unrestricted or automatic rules which are established, e.g., for **volg-t-o* → *volto* or (if necessary at all) for **spegn-t-o* → *spento*. In this way we establish just one rule, and its phonetically natural or 'euphonic' character (compare Ch. VI) is suitably brought out. Other cases in the same category are the Ancient Greek dissimilation in **tʰrikʰ-ós* → *trikʰós* (see again Ch. VI) and, once again, the Turkish rules involving the 'soft *g*' (Absolute *çocuk*, Accusative *çocuğ-u*, but Absolute *kök*, Accusative *kök-ü*) which we gave as our example of lexically restricted alternation in Ch. V.

The precise way of restricting the rule is perhaps less important. But a common technique would involve a special quasi-phonological unit called a **morphophoneme**. In Hall's Italian grammar, the roots for 'friend' and 'astrologer' are spelled *amiK-* and *astroloG-*, where *K* and *G* are basic units (units of the basic forms of morphemes) distinct from the phonemes /k/ and /g/ (written *c*/*ch*, *g*/*gh*) which are retained in the roots of *cieco* 'blind' or *luogo* 'place'.[1] Before Front vowels, *K* and *G* then have a palatalised realisation (**amiK-i* → *ami*[tʃ]*i*, **astroloG-i* → *astrolo*[dʒ]*i*) whereas /k/ and /g/ do not (*cie*[k]*i*, *luo*[g]*i*). The formative written as *-sc-* also has a morphophoneme which for our purposes may be identified with *K*: thus **fin-i-sK-e* '[he] finishes'. Accordingly it too can undergo palatalisation (more specifically to [ʃʃ]), whereas the phonemic /sk/ of *boschi* 'woods' is again unaffected. In terms of distinctive features /k/ and /g/ would be the normal phonemes: Voiceless and Voiced Velar Occlusives. The morphophonemes *K* and *G* could be the same, except that they would also have a special classificatory feature (called a 'diacritic feature' by the generativists) which we may label 'Palatalisable'. The sandhi rule would then apply without exception to any root which ends in a Palatalisable Velar Occlusive (e.g. *amiK-*, *astroloG-*), but not at all if it is 'Non-Palatalisable' (*cie*/k/-, *luo*/g/-). In standard Turkish the orthographic 'soft *g*' (*ğ*) might be

[1] Hall, *Op. cit.*, p. 52 (with further elaborations not here considered).

said to represent a morphophoneme, distinct from both normal *g* and *k*, which allows the special fusion which we have described.

Of the arguments which justify the rule of palatalisation, that of phonetic naturalness or plausibility is particularly important. Indeed it is crucial for sandhi in general; if the modifications do not make SOME phonetic sense, then why should we ever consider them at this level? Returning to the Participles, there are four Verbs which apparently share a formation in *-st-*. We have already mentioned *chiesto* 'called' (Infinitive *chied-e-re*); the others have roots ending before a vowel with *-nd* (*nascosto* 'hidden', Infinitive *nascondere*), or with *-n* (*rimasto* 'remained', Infinitive *rimanere*; *posto* 'put', 3rd Singular Present *pone*). Could this conceivably be treated as a case of sandhi? For the first two one might, perhaps, suggest a basic **chied-t-o* and **nascond-t-o*:(*n*)*dt*, which is phonotactically excluded, would then reduce to *st* while (*n*)*ds* reduces to *s* (as in *chiuso* or *preso*). Could there then be a further rule by which basic **pon-t-o* and **riman-t-o* are handled similarly? The answer, surely, is No. Not only would the sandhi be phonotactically unmotivated (as is also true, the reader will recall, for the Preterites *posi* and *rimasi*), but it is also most unnatural. Why on earth should a nasal change to a sibilant in this position? Short of an answer, we must simply accept the irregularity. Either the roots have a basic alternation between *-n* and *-s* (and the form in *-s* then appears in the Preterites also?), or there is indeed a formation with both *-s* and *-t* as formatives.

That is one proposal which is ruled out by its phonetic implausibility. But it would be easy to invent others. In *mor-t-o*, as we said, there is a suffix *-t-*, while in *appar-s-o* there is an *-s-*. However, the distribution of these suffixes follows, to some extent at least, the class of the final consonant of the root. Roots in *-gg* have the formation in *-t-* (*leggere*: *letto*, *figgere*:*fitto* 'fix', and so on). So do most roots in *-c* or *-g* generally: another important class are those in *-nc* or *-ng* (*vincere*:*vinto* or *spingere*:*spinto* 'push'). By contrast, those in *-d* or *-nd* generally have *-s* (e.g. *chiudere*:*chiuso*), and this holds for the few in *-t* or *-tt* (e.g. *annettere*:*annesso*). Is there any reason for this distribution (other than simple analogy)? Faced with just these examples, we might hazard the guess that *chiuso* or *annesso* are basically **chiud-t-o* and **annett-t-o*; that would leave us with just two formations, regular with *-t-* plus preceding vowel (as in *fer-i-t-o* or *and-a-t-o*) and irregular with *-t-* alone (e.g. both **legg-t-o* and **chiud-t-o*). But then it would be technically possible, by the use of morphophonemes, to force the same analysis on the remainder. Taking our original examples, APPARIRE might have a root *appaR-* in which the final consonant, *R*, is a special 'sibilant-forming' *r* which alters the *t* of **appaR-t-o* to yield *apparso*. MORIRE would naturally continue to have the 'normal' *r*; hence *mor-t-o* would not be altered to *morso*. By establishing other 'sibilant-forming' morphophonemes, any recalcitrant form in *-s-* could easily be transferred to the *-t-* formation. Thus *mosso* 'moved' would be basically **moV-t-o* (with 'sibilant-forming' *V*), and so on.

The objection to this, too, is that it is phonetic nonsense. If *R* is a sort of *r* (i.e. with Liquid and Trilled as its 'non-diacritic' features) then why should it be expected to convert a following *t* to an *s*? Even Sibilants themselves do not do so (compare the medial cluster of *pasta* 'pasta'). The change of *V-t* to *ss* is even odder. But if these are NOT a 'sort of *r*' or a 'sort of *v*', then why are they realised as *r* or *v* before vowels (Infinitives *appar-i-re* 'to appear', *muov-e-re* 'to move')? Because there is no answer to these questions we are forced to establish two irregular formations. 'Sibilant-forming' (or having a Participle in *-s-*) is a property of lexemes and not of the final elements of roots.

* * *

We have now come back to our starting-point. In the author's view, there is no simple boundary between alternations that can be explained by the phonology and those that cannot. There is a distinction (which one theory emphasises) between allophonic variation and cases of neutralisation. We can draw another between sandhi which is phonologically inferrable (from neutralisations, in particular) and sandhi which is motivated but not inferrable. For the latter we need specific rules, which for some linguists are 'morphophonemic' and for the generativists still 'phonological'. There is then a third distinction between rules that are motivated and those that can merely be stated by one device or another; the latter make no PHONOLOGICAL sense, but insofar as they make PHONETIC sense they may still be generalised beyond their morphological contexts. Finally, there are alternations which are purely morphological, with no explanation at all in terms of the phonological units which enter into them. That, then, is the range of 'facts' – at least as one theorist interprets them. Nor is Italian at all atypical in this respect. With such material, there is ample scope for theoretical argument.

RELATED READING

There is no general, up to date survey of phonological theory. Of the introductory textbooks, ROBINS, Ch. 4 is the clearest and most catholic, but it does not cover generative contributions. For a later survey which does, see E. C. Fudge's contribution to *New Horizons*, pp. 76–95; also his recent collection of readings (abbreviated FUDGE). Naturally, many other introductions are excellent on specific points or for particular schools (see below). For the problems raised in this chapter see in general *Inflectional Morphology*, §10.2 (also parts of Ch. 14). The survey of Italian may be compared with a more technical survey of Latin: cf. P. H. Matthews, 'Some reflections on Latin morphophonology', *TPhS*, 1972, pp. 59–78.

For Post-Bloomfieldian introductions to the phoneme see, for example, HILL, Ch. 4; GLEASON, Ch. 16. For earlier sources see BLOCH & TRAGER, Ch. 3; HARRIS, Ch. 7 (and generally Chs. 3–11); also many of the papers in *RiL*, in particular Hockett's 'A system of descriptive phonology' (originally in *Lg*, **18** (1942), pp. 3–21). One important paper which is too long for reprint collections is B. Bloch's 'A set of postulates for phonemic analysis', *Lg*, **24** (1948), pp. 3–46. For a characteristic description see Bloch's 'Studies in colloquial Japanese IV: phonemics' (in *RiL*, pp. 329–48). Of the later American introductions some give different definitions of the phoneme (e.g. HOCKETT, *Course*, Ch. 2), but none differ on the points considered here. It is important to realise that when the generativists attack 'the phoneme' (references below) it is THIS theory that they have in mind.

For Prague school phonology (indeed for phonology in general) a study of TRUBETZKOY is essential. For a very readable introduction see A. Martinet, *Phonology as Functional Phonetics* (Supplement to *TPhS*: Oxford, 1949); also MARTINET, Ch. 3 and the introductory chapters of his *Économie des changements phonétiques* (Berne, 1955). For distinctive features and neutralisation see also ROBINS, pp. 153–7, LYONS, pp. 115–17, 120–7. For the boundary between phonology and morphology see Martinet's 'De la morphonologie', *La linguistique*, 1965, 1, pp. 15–30 (partial translation in FUDGE, pp. 91–100). For a relevant Post-Bloomfieldian critique see Hockett's review of Martinet's 1949 monograph (*Lg*, **27** (1951), pp. 333–42); other criticisms of the concept of neutralisation are discussed by C. E. Bazell, 'Three conceptions of phonological neutralisation', in *For Roman Jakobson*, ed. M. Halle *et al.* (The Hague, 1956), pp. 25–30.

For generative phonology FUDGE, Section D offers a sensible and original selection. There is a recent textbook: S. A. Schane, *Generative Phonology* (Englewood Cliffs, 1973); however, it is naively didactic in tone and it is not yet clear whether it will be successful with students. For most readers, a far better introduction has now become available in French: F. Dell, *Les règles et les sons: introduction à la phonologie générative* (Paris, 1974). At a more technical level, the leading work is now CHOMSKY & HALLE; to understand the theory one must, however, begin with the same authors' earlier formulations and critiques of the Post-Bloomfieldians: see M. Halle, *The Sound Pattern of Russian* (The Hague, 1959), Part 1; N. Chomsky, *Current Issues in Linguistic Theory* (The Hague, 1964), §4.2–5; also Halle's 'Phonology in generative grammar', *Word*, **18** (1962), pp. 54–82, and Chomsky and Halle's joint 'Some controversial questions in phonological theory', *JL*, **1** (1965), pp. 97–138. For the argument against the phoneme see, in particular, Halle's Russian monograph, pp. 22ff.

For 'morphophonology' or 'morphophonemics' see Martinet's critique in the article already referred to; for the various senses of the term see the references in *Inflectional Morphology*, p. 54[1,4]. It must be noted, in particular, that I am not taking it in Trubetzkoy's sense (see the French edition of TRUBETZKOY, pp. 337ff.), or in that of Hockett and some other American scholars (see HOCKETT, *Course*, Chs. 16 and 32). For morphophonemics as a third level see the 'stratificational' proposals discussed in *New Horizons*, p. 101, and *Inflectional Morphology*, §10.1.1. For the use of 'morphophonemes' and 'diacritic features' see *Ibid.*, §14.2 (also references to CHOMSKY & HALLE in Ch. XII).

For phonotactics see HILL, Ch. 6. But the term itself is much less widespread than the concepts it refers to; it is interesting, for example, that Fudge uses it to translate 'prosodie' in one of his selections (see FUDGE, pp. 277ff. and the original in K. Togeby, *Structure immanente de la langue française*, 2nd ed. (Paris, 1965), pp. 8ff.). For the problems of phonotactic motivation, inferrability, etc., I can only refer to my own previous publications; among generative contributions I would, however, stress the importance of C. W. Kisseberth's 'On the functional unity of phonological rules' (reprinted in FUDGE, pp. 257–74).

XII
Morphology in generative grammar

The generative 'paradigm'.
Basic principles: sentences; creativity, 'rule breaking' and 'rule governed'; problems of semi-productivity; formal rules; structural descriptions; levels of representation; rôle of inflectional rules.
Possible systems: models of description; IA, WP, IP; generative formulation of IP (English vowel change); of WP (specimen Verb forms in German); sequencing of rules; disjunctive and conjunctive ordering; exceptions.
Value of generative approach.

This book has not been conceived within what is called the generative 'paradigm'. According to a fashionable work of the 1960s,[1] 'sciences' develop historically by fits and starts. In one period 'investigators' are working within one 'paradigm' or frame of reference (e.g. the geocentric paradigm of Pre-Copernican astronomy). Then the frame of reference is changed, typically by the insight of some major figure. After that, investigators work within the new paradigm (e.g. the Post-Copernican heliocentric paradigm) instead. The subject has undergone a 'revolution', and will continue under its dispensation until another 'revolution' comes along. In the recent development of linguistics, some writers have seen a 'paradigm change' which dates from the end of the 1950s. Before *Syntactic Structures*, linguists worked within a 'structuralist' paradigm: this particular notion of 'structuralism', referring in effect to the maximally atomistic theories of the Post-Bloomfieldians, is Chomsky's own. The science then underwent a 'Chomskyan revolution',[2] and ever since we are supposed to be working within the new paradigm of generative grammar. If not, we are simply clinging to old ways, etc., etc.

It would be impertinent to disparage Chomsky's achievements. They are without doubt more significant than anything the author himself is

[1] T. S. Kuhn, *The Structure of Scientific Revolutions*, 2nd ed. (Chicago, 1970). Of course, Professor Kuhn is not responsible for the way his book has been seized on in linguistics.

[2] 'Chomsky's revolution in linguistics' is the title of an essay by J. R. Searle, a philosopher, in *New York Review of Books*, 29 June 1972.

likely to accomplish. Nevertheless it would be a mistake to look at language solely through the eyes of one particular school. There are many notions that are common to all scholars in the field, and often other, non-generative schools have handled them better. Nor need this refer to structural linguistics only ('structural' now in its more usual and more proper sense). There is still food for thought in the earlier tradition (see Ch. IV). There is even more that the structural linguist may learn from the philologist: many concepts that belong to both their disciplines (for example, those of roots and stems, of inflections and word-formation) are used with more assurance in the manuals of Indo-European, Romance, and other specialist fields. In such circumstances, the generativist himself would be foolish to ignore the insights which have been won by earlier investigators. At present, many do ignore them, alleging that so-called 'structuralist' views belong to the history of the subject only. The theory of 'paradigms' is a wonderful excuse for what would otherwise be considered laziness and bad scholarship! But generative phonology, for example, has run into serious turmoil. Although a standard theory has been taken for granted in Ch. XI, it is in fact very difficult to see how generativists will view these problems in five years' or even one year's time. They should, therefore, be more receptive to ideas from elsewhere.

For this reason our own discussion has throughout been cast more widely. But within structural linguistics, generative grammar has now become a very important concept; for many linguists the term 'grammar' itself is scarcely intelligible in any other sense! Let us therefore end by narrowing (if we like) our vision. How would morphological relationships be handled within a theory specifically of this kind?

* * *

A **generative grammar** is a set of **formal rules** which **generate** the **sentences** of a language and assign to each a set of appropriate **structural descriptions**. It will be clear that the field of 'grammar' is here conceived in the broadest possible sense. Not only does it refer to the secondary as well as the primary articulation of language (see Ch. I), but it also includes a great deal of what is traditionally assigned to the dictionary. So already the concept differs – and differs controversially – from more conventional ideas of language description. In addition, each of the terms in bold face calls for more or less extended comment.

The notion of a **sentence** may for our purposes be taken as self-evident. If I say 'Shut up!' in Reading and my brother says 'Shut up!' in Manchester these two utterances are instances of the same sentence *Shut up!* It is with the properties of sentences, and not of utterances, that the grammar is concerned. Now of course the unit is problematic. For example, how far can one 'Shut up!' differ from another 'Shut up!' (in intonational or other characteristics) before we are prepared to distinguish them systematically? Nor are the problems matters of criteria only. For example, the notions of 'sentence meaning' and 'utterance meaning' form a serious philosophical crux. But these are not controversies that the student of morphology need enter into. He merely assumes that there is SOME larger unit within which his words or morphemes fit.

The sentences of a language form a set. Thus *Shut up!* is a member of the set of sentences in English, the test being that it may be uttered acceptably in an appropriate context. But *Up shut!* is not a member; it is not observed as an utterance, and if uttered experimentally a subject's reaction will show that it is not acceptable. Taking the lexicon as a whole (*Shut*, *up*, and so on), some sequences of items form English sentences and the others do not. To **generate** this set is simply one way of DEFINING it, of specifying what its members are. So, a grammar of English must generate a set comprising *Shut up!*, *I'm going out*, *Did he say he wasn't?*, etc., etc., while excluding *Up shut!*, *I'm outing go*, *Say wasn't he did he?*, and all other non-sentences of the sort.

This is controversial for more than one reason. But a layman may ask, in particular, what is meant by 'the lexicon as a whole'. I have just looked in a dictionary and found a word for a wood-pigeon, *cushat*,[1] which I didn't know; one imagines many readers will not know it either. Should a generative grammar of English include this in its lexicon – i.e. generate *I saw a cushat*, etc. – or not? The generativist will feel that this is perhaps not an important question. In the last resort sentence-hood must be verified for the individual speaker, and it is merely a matter of fact whether speaker *x* has *cushat* in his vocabulary, or sentences containing *cushat* in his grammar. It is evident, for example, that the writer has not. However, the student of lexical morphology can point to more interesting cases. In Ch. III we referred, for example, to a putative Noun PONTIFICATION: in the layman's terms, is there such a 'word' or isn't there? Again, the generativist will have

[1] 'Sc. and North Dial.' (*OED*). I am a Devonian.

to stand on his principles. His grammar of English must either generate, e.g., *His pontification gets on my nerves*, or it must exclude it. For verification speaker *x* and speaker *y* must again be invited to sit in judgment. But does this truly reflect the nature of the lexical formation?

The problem here is a problem in capturing the creative aspect of language. 'Creativity' is often invoked in Chomskyan writings: generative theory is said to explain it while earlier (notably 'structuralist') theories are said to ignore it. But we have to consider rather carefully the SORT of creativity which is intended. Perhaps the reader will think first of creative work in literature. In the lines from Yeats's poem (Ch. 1), the sentences are mostly shaped in a quite ordinary way. We could write acceptable prose while preserving their syntax perfectly. Nor are the collocations individually surprising; it is a straightforward thing to talk of *birds in the trees*, *monuments of intellect*, *sailing the seas*, and so on. But already *That is no country for old men* has an effect which, for example, *These are no surroundings for imaginative children* would never have. For most people, that is what is meant by the 'creative use' of language.

It is not, however, the sort of creativity which the linguist is called on to explain. The grammar will generate the sentences which are here instanced in writing, just as it will also generate *Shut up!*, etc. It is the business of other scholars to elucidate their literary quality. Nor is the grammarian concerned directly with 'poetic licence', or in general with the use of 'deviance' (the term is not meant at all pejoratively) for literary effect. In T. S. Eliot's 'The Dry Salvages', the phrase *and the gear of foreign dead men* (line 24) is deliberately awkward. It slightly 'deviates' from English grammar either in the successive ordering of Adjectives or, if we like, in the treatment of *dead men* as a Nominal compound.[1] In a pair of lines from Wilfred Owen:

> We wise, who with a thought besmirch
> Blood over all our soul

('Insensibility', Verse 5),[2] there is a striking – some would say a deviant – collocation of the lexemes THOUGHT and BESMIRCH, BLOOD and SOUL. Such examples display a form of creativity that is 'rule breaking'. In writing a generative grammar we can correctly exclude them, while generating other sentences which are similar in every non-deviant

[1] *Four Quartets* (London, 1944), p. 26.
[2] *The Poems of Wilfred Owen*, ed. E. Blunden (London, 1946), p. 64.

respect. It is because a 'deviant sentence' is similar to ones which are 'in' the grammar, but yet not precisely 'in' the grammar itself, that (a generativist would argue) we react to it in the way we do.

Of course, there may be 'rules' for 'rule breaking'. In a line picked out from Matthew Arnold:

> And with the country-folk acquaintance made

('Thyrsis', verse 4),[1] the ordering of members follows an established pattern of licence (and one which a grammarian in the traditional sense will naturally notice). However, there is a more banal form of creativity which lies within the rules entirely. The first sentence of this chapter, let us say, is nothing very remarkable. But I do not think I have written it before, and I doubt very much if I have ever uttered it. Equally, you may never have read or heard it. Again, I might visit someone tomorrow and say *Heavens, why have they put purple paint on the ceiling?* Neither I, nor the person I am speaking to, may have heard this specific sentence before; it is something created, from the resources of the language, for the particular occasion. This sort of creativity is so commonplace that it has at times been overlooked. As Hermann Paul remarked at the beginning of this century, 'It was a fundamental error in earlier linguistics, that any utterance (so long as it did not depart from current usage) was regarded as something simply reproduced from memory'.[2] This is indeed an error, as Chomsky in his turn has emphasised. At the same time, an original sentence is uttered and understood as easily as one that can be instanced five times a day. If we pause and think, that is rather an interesting datum. A linguistic theory must explain it, if the 'resources of the language' are to be accounted for correctly.

It is to creativity in this sense that generative theory is addressed. By generating all POSSIBLE sentences – and not merely those that a given linguist may have observed or elicited – a grammar defines the limits within which new instances can arise. The creativity is 'rule governed' (creation within the rules which the grammar must set out). Since it is the grammar that is also 'known' to the speaker – and not merely the utterances which he may previously have heard or spoken – the rules will accordingly help to explain the phenomenon. It is on the

[1] *Poetical Works* (London, 1890), p. 282.

[2] 'Es war ein Grundirrtum der älteren Sprachwissenschaft, dass sie alles Gesprochene, so lange es von dem bestehenden Usus nicht abweicht, als etwas bloss gedächtnismässig Reproduziertes behandelt hat' (PAUL, p. 109).

basis of this 'knowledge' (his linguistic **competence**), and not from the memory of previous utterances (of linguistic **performance**), that he 'performs' on any given occasion.

So far this is quite attractive, but can it also account for semi-productivity (in the sense of Chs. III and X)? The construction, say, of *old men* is fully productive, any Adjective going with any Noun provided that the collocation makes sense. That a generative grammar handles beautifully: the rules of syntax give the order of parts of speech (e.g. by the transformations of Ch. X), and the rest is up to the lexicon. By contrast, the formation of *breadth* is wholly non-productive (see Ch. III). The items which belong to it are fixed, and if we try to extend them (e.g. *thickth* alongside *thickness*, *rigidth* alongside *rigidity*) the forms obtained are unacceptable. Here too a generative grammar is in no difficulty: although the pattern will be stated in general – as part of syntax according to the transformationalist view (again Ch. X) – the actual Nouns of the structure Adjective + *th* will be restricted to a handful of roots which are marked accordingly in the lexicon. However, the formation in *-ion* (e.g. *pontification*) is in neither category. Nor, for instance, is the formation in *-ness*. *Thickness* or *whiteness* are established English Nouns; so perhaps is *broadness* (cf. *the broadness of his views*). But what, say, of *rigidness* or *pinkness*, of *puceness* or *purpleness* (*the purpleness of this passage*?), of *frigidness* or *strongness* (*the strongness of his views*?), of *creamness* or *magentaness*? To the writer, the last pair are far less acceptable than the first; but where exactly is the line between items which are 'in' my lexicon (and therefore 'in' my grammar) and those which are not?

Generative theory forces us to answer such questions. The grammar is a device for separating sheep (sentences) from goats (non-sentences), and does not allow gradation between the species. For borderline cases we are left with two ways to jump. The first is to generate them all, adding, however, that speakers are in some way unhappy with their 'use'. Their awkwardness belongs to linguistic performance and not to linguistic competence. But WHY should speakers be 'unhappy with their use'? It may seem at first that there are answers: for example, *rigidness* is awkward because there is the established word *rigidity*, *puceness* more awkward than *whiteness* because the colour is mentioned less frequently, and so on. But these are points which the generativist is unable to make. If both *rigidity* and *rigidness* are generated, then why should it be the latter which is awkward? Why is it not *rigidity* instead ('because it conflicts with *rigidness*')? The reason is precisely that *rigidity* is an established word, while *rigidness* is not. That is, their status in the lexicon cannot be the same. And if *the purpleness of the ceiling* is less secure than *the whiteness of the ceiling*, then why is *a purple ceiling* every bit as acceptable as *a white ceiling*? The answer is that Adjective + Noun is fully productive, whereas Adjective + *ness* is only semi-productive. But the essence of semi-productivity is that the rule itself allows borderline instances.

The other expedient would be to generate established items only: e.g. *rigidity* but not *rigidness*, *automation* and not *pontification*, and so on. If we SAY one of the others, then it is an instance of 'rule breaking creativity' (compare *foreign dead men*) and not the 'rule governed creativity' which the grammar explicates. But why is *rigidness* or even *magentaness* still on a different plane from *rigidth*? In general why is there frequent 'rule breaking' with *-ness* and none with *-th*? The answer, presumably, is that there is a 'rule' for it (as with the line from Arnold). But then the grammarian must state it; to ignore it is like drawing a map which makes no distinction between ordinary hills and volcanoes. Nor does it belong to some special variety of English (as with literary usage). It is part of the ordinary speaker's 'competence'. So surely we need a theory of grammar that can cope with it.

Here then is the gist of one controversy (not yet resolved) which affects morphology directly. However, it is only the lexical branch that is in question: of its nature, inflectional morphology does not raise similar problems of 'word creativity'. And the lesson, perhaps, is that 'generative grammar' should indeed deal with 'grammar' and not with matters which properly belong to the lexicon. To return then to our original definition, we said that a generative grammar should consist of 'formal rules'. **Formal** means, for our present purposes, little more than 'explicit': anyone who consults it must be able to tell, without prior knowledge, exactly what a rule is intended to say. For example, it must not be ambiguous, or interpretable only by guess-work or charity. To this end, a theory of grammar will lay down in detail what a grammar may look like – how it will be divided into sections, how sentences will be represented at different levels, what is the format of a possible rule (or a possible rule in each particular section), how the rules are to be read in relation to each other, what effect each type may have on its input, and so on. Briefly, the theory specifies in full the metalanguage (see Ch. IV) in which the object language (e.g. English) is to be described.

In principle (though it need not concern us here), the system ought to have a mathematical formalisation.

Finally, the grammar assigns 'structural descriptions'. Taking the transformational theory for illustration (Ch. X), *old men* has a deep structure which we would sketch as follows:

['men' ['The men are old']]

More precisely, '*men*' (the structure corresponding to *men*) might be the sequence of morphemes MAN and PL (short for Plural), '*the*' a morpheme DEF (for Definite), '*are*' the Verb BE, and '*old*' simply the morpheme OLD. In a slightly less sketchy way, the structure is therefore:

[MAN PL [DEF [MAN PL] BE OLD]]

In addition, '*men*' or [MAN PL] will in each case be classed as a Noun (N), likewise OLD as an Adjective (A), and the entire structure as a Noun phrase (NP) consisting of a smaller Noun phrase (the first '*men*') with a subordinate Sentence (S). Within this sentence, '*the men*' is another Noun phrase and '*are old*' is a Predicate (Pred). By bracketing each sequence of morphemes so classified (e.g. [OLD]), and subscripting the class label to the second bracket (thus $[\text{OLD}]_A$), we may give a fuller (though still incomplete) representation:

$$[[[\text{MAN PL}]_N]_{NP}\ [[\text{DEF}\ [\text{MAN PL}]_N]_{NP}\ [\text{BE}\ [\text{OLD}]_A]_{Pred}]_S]_{NP}$$

Such a structure will naturally be specified by a corresponding section of the grammar: the phrase will be generated, that is, by rules which state that a Noun phrase may consist of a smaller Noun phrase and subordinate Sentence, that a Sentence consists of a Noun phrase followed by a Predicate, that a Noun phrase may also consist of a Noun with or without the morpheme DEF. In this sense it is part of a total **structural description** assigned to *old men* (or any sentence containing it) by the grammar as a whole.

In other sections, other rules will deal with other aspects of its derivation. Continuing with the same theory, the transformations will assign a partial surface structure:

$$[[\text{OLD}]_A\ [\text{MAN PL}]_N]_{NP}$$

and it is this, together with the deep structure to which it is linked, that forms a description of the phrase at the level of syntax (its 'syntactic description'). Then, just as the deep structure can be said to form the input to the transformations (their output being the surface structure), so the surface structure – or something essentially like it – is in turn the input to a final section of the grammar, whose rules assign the corresponding phonetic description or 'phonetic representation'. This whole section is usually called 'phonology' (see Ch. XI). So, for instance, the surface structure of *old men* will be linked by phonological rules with the phonetic description:

['ould 'men]

(using IPA symbols for purposes of illustration). In the light of Ch. VII we can see at least two ways in which this might be done. In either case the partial input OLD would correspond to the partial output [ould]; the precise details depend on the nature of the phonetic representation and the exact way in which morphemes are represented in surface structure. In one treatment the partial output [men] would then correspond to MAN alone, PL being related to a so-called 'zero'. In the other treatment [men] would be related to [MAN PL] as a whole, by means of a 'Pluralising' process which directly affects the vowel of [mæn]. Detailed correspondences such as these – which we called relations of exponence in Ch. VIII – must also form part of the total structural description assigned to a phrase or sentence.

A commitment to generative grammar does not also commit us to the particular theory which we have taken for illustration. In principle, we COULD refuse to distinguish surface and underlying structures; the reasons for rejecting any such theory (according to actual generativists, that is) is that it is empirically wrong. Again, the surface structures might conceivably have words instead of morphemes as successive elements; we will illustrate from just such a variant later in this chapter. Another obvious alternative would be to separate morphology from phonology. Most actual generativists have lumped them together, but (they would agree) this is not entailed by the generative principle itself. Such points are matters for substantive argument, for them as indeed for everyone else.

Broadly, however, the rôle of inflectional rules is always to relate two different levels of representation. Traditionally, *men* has as one of its representations:

'The Plural of MAN'

– a Word and Paradigm formula in which MAN is a lexeme and Plural a morphosyntactic property (see Ch. VIII). This could form part of a structural description at the surface structure level. In reading the grammar one would then ask how this is phonetically realised (in traditional terms 'What IS "the Plural of MAN"?'). The answer would be given by some other level of structural description – in the first instance, perhaps, by a representation of successive phonemes. In generative grammar the inflectional rules (whether 'morphological' or 'phonological' or what we please) are those which supply the answer to this sort of question. More technically, they define a correspondence between one set of representations ('The Plural of MAN' or [MAN PL], 'The Singular of MAN' or simply MAN, 'The Comparative of HOT' or HOT followed by the morpheme COMPARATIVE, and so on) and another set which represents the same forms at another level ([men], [mæn], [hɔtə], etc.). The exact way of doing this is, as we said, a substantive problem.

* * *

Generative grammars are written in a fairly complex notation. There are good reasons for this, stemming partly from the need for mathematical formulation and also from a wish to measure the value of alternative solutions. But it is easy to become befuddled with notation, and to forget (or never work out) what one is actually saying about the language. For this reason a preliminary **model of description** is very helpful. A 'model' (as we have used the term) provides a blueprint for a particular type of structural description: it will show that sentences are to be represented on levels *x* and *y* (e.g. syntax and phonology), that their elements are to be of types *a* or *b* (e.g. lexemes or morphosyntactic properties), that units in representation *i* (e.g. words) are to be related in such and such a way to units in representation *j* (e.g. word-forms), and so on in whatever detail we choose. We have to consider the sort of structural description we want (what we want to say about the sentences of the language), before we decide what form of rule, and still more what notation, is appropriate.

For morphology in general, three such blueprints have been widely discussed. They were distinguished three years before *Syntactic Structures*, in the article by Hockett which we first mentioned in Ch. I (HOCKETT, *Models*). But it is a contribution which Chomsky mentions several times (CHOMSKY, *Structures*, fnn. to pp. 50, 86, etc.) and which in spirit is close to a generativist's preoccupations. For our purposes it is still the best starting-point.

The clearest of Hockett's models was the one to which he gave the label **Item and Arrangement** (normally abbreviated **IA**). This took the morpheme as its basic unit – 'morphemes' (as in Ch. V) including roots, inflections, derivational affixes, everything. These 'items' form an 'arrangement' in what will now be called the surface structure: typically (though for many writers of the 1950s not always), the arrangement was a sequence. Thus, as we have seen, *men* may be represented as MAN+PL, *the men* (so far as the morphemes are concerned) as DEF+MAN+PL, and so on. In Hockett's original formulation, IA was a model of grammar (i.e. morphology plus syntax) as a whole. It was therefore concerned with the structure of phrases and sentences (e.g. *the men* as more specifically, say, $[\text{DEF}\ [\text{MAN}\ \text{PL}]_{\text{N}}]_{\text{NP}}$) as well as the morphemes within words. But the study of syntax has indeed been revolutionised by Chomsky's theory (see also Ch. I for other developments), and only the morphological aspect need concern us here. In an IA morphology, we could envisage rules assigning allomorphs (again as in Ch. V) to each item. Some would specify the individual basic alternants (basic in the sense of Ch. VI); in normal generative practice, such forms would be given directly by the lexicon (the set of 'lexical rules' within the total 'grammar'). Other rules would deal with recurrent alternations: for example, in *waited* the alternant of *-ed* might be given (in part) by a rule extending [d] to [id] when the preceding morph ends in an Alveolar. In the resulting structural description, morphemes correspond to morphs in what we may call the allomorph-relation (morphs *a* or *b* being assigned as allomorphs to morphemes *x* or *y*).

At the other extreme stood a model which we have already labelled **Word and Paradigm** (abbreviated **WP**). Hockett only mentioned this in passing (which is why HOCKETT, *Models* has the title 'Two models...' instead of 'Three models...'), but it has since been taken further in an important article by Robins and in a series of studies by the present writer.[1] The difference lies, firstly, in what may again be reformulated as the surface structure. Categories of the word which are arranged sequentially in IA (e.g. *sailed* with the Tense morpheme following the Verbal morpheme) are 'arranged', as it were, simultaneously in WP (Past Tense neither preceding nor following SAIL – see Ch. VIII). We will illustrate the simplest type of 'simultaneous representation' below. Secondly, their exponents may extend throughout the word-form,

[1] References in Reading for Ch. VIII.

overlapping each other where necessary. The analysis of Greek *elelýkete* in Ch. VIII (summarised by the table on p. 143) provides a sketch of the sort of structural description which might be assigned.

Hockett's third model was called **Item and Process** (or **IP**). By this he meant a description which included morphological processes (Ch. VII): for example, English *take → took* alongside *bake → baked.* But such a description may vary in other important ways. The surface structure might be based on words (as in WP) or morphemes (as in IA); the rôle of processes is logically independent of the form of syntactic descriptions. In Hockett's treatment *bake* as a word is apparently not distinguished from *bake* as a root; this is compatible both with the classical word-based model (Ch. IV), and with a morpheme-based model (Ch. V and at one point in Ch. VII). It is not surprising that the term 'IP' has since been used in several slightly different ways. For some writers, it simply refers to any kind of 'process' formulation. If a rule has an input and an output (e.g. input *bake*, output *baked*) then already it presents a process picture of language. Since most generative rules are precisely so interpreted, IP is sometimes identified with a generative description as such. For others its reference is more specific (though still we will not find consistency). It is generally fatuous to ask if such and such a treatment 'IS' IP as opposed to WP or to IA.

Nevertheless it is an illuminating term for one approach that generativists have widely adopted. In this model, surface structure is again made up of morphemes; in the generative school these are among the elements called 'formatives' (not, unfortunately, our sense of 'formative' in earlier chapters). So *teeth*, for example, will be crudely TOOTH + PL. Less crudely, the first morpheme TOOTH will have from the lexicon both a basic phonological representation ([tu:θ]) and, let us say, an inflectional feature (the marker of an inflectional class) 'Vowel Change'. The other morpheme, PL, will be unanalysed. We might sum this up with a representation as follows:

$$[\ \begin{bmatrix}\text{Vowel Change}\\ \text{tu:}\theta\end{bmatrix} + \text{PL}\ ]_{\text{N}}$$

where the whole word is in addition classed as a Noun ($[\ldots]_N$). Similarly, the Past Participle *bent* might have a representation:

$$[\ \begin{bmatrix}\text{Basic } t\\ \text{bend}\end{bmatrix} + \text{PP}\ ]_{\text{V}}$$

where PP = Past Participle, V = Verb, and 'Basic *t*' is again an inflectional feature associated, by lexical rules, with the basic [bend]. Naturally, each structure could form part of larger syntactic descriptions.

These, then, would be the input to the 'phonological rules' (see above and Ch. XI). As a preliminary step, PP will be given its own appropriate phonological spelling:

$$[\ [\text{bend}]+[\text{t}]\ ]_V$$

– the rule stating that this must be [t] whenever a morpheme marked as 'Basic *t*' precedes. This would be the same as the procedure in IA (the [t] being a morphologically conditioned allomorph). But with *teeth* there is a different form of rule, adding what has already been called a 'diacritic feature' (see again Ch. XI) to the vowel of the basic [tu:θ]. Let us label this feature simply 'Change':

$$[\ \text{t}\begin{bmatrix}\text{Change}\\ \text{u:}\end{bmatrix}\theta\ ]_N$$

– meaning, more precisely, that the vowel so marked must be altered according to a rule 'Change' which will be specified later. Such a feature will be introduced whenever the morpheme PL coincides, in the representation of a word, with the feature 'Vowel Change'. In that way, PL can be said to spark off a process (Ch. VII) by which its exponent – eventually [i:] – lies within the form which would otherwise emerge as [tu:θ].

The PL morpheme, like PP, has now been disposed of; in addition, neither 'Vowel Change' nor 'Basic *t*' plays any further part. Of the remaining rules, one must deal with the sandhi (the 'joining' in the sense of Ch. VI) of [bend] and [t]. This would be subject to no restriction, stating simply that whenever [t] is preceded by [nd] or another [t] (compare **hit-t → hit* in Ch. VII), the two Plosives fuse together to a single [t]. This yields a continuous sequence of elements:

$$[\ \text{bent}\ ]_V$$

which is as far as we need go towards the eventual phonetic representation. The other rule ('Change') would then pick up the diacritic feature attached to [tu:θ]. For this particular effect, the vowel must be Back or Close Back specifically (compare also *goose → geese* or *foot → feet*), the Non-Back vowel in [mæn], which would also be marked for 'Change', being modified to [e] instead. Naturally, too, the diacritic feature must be present; Singular *tooth* or the regular Plural *truths* must not be affected. But finally the rule could also refer to the overall syntactic classification ($[\ldots]_N$) in the surface structure; Verbs which we might also mark for 'Change' (e.g. *shoot* → *shot*) are affected in a different way. By such means, the same feature 'Change' could be used to activate both sets of processes:

$$[\ldots[\text{u:}]\ldots]_N \rightarrow [\text{i:}],$$
$$[\ldots[\text{u:}]\ldots]_V \rightarrow]\text{ɔ}],$$

and so on. Under this range of conditions, the representation of *teeth* is finally (so far as we need be concerned) derived as:

$$[\ \ \text{ti:θ}\ \ ]_N$$

This illustration is not taken from any specific account of English 'phonology' (and certain details will be disputed). Most generativists would also express themselves a little differently (for example, Chomsky and his followers do not generally use the term 'sandhi'). But the spirit of the analysis will be sufficiently clear. As in Chs. VI and VII, it is DYNAMIC rather than STATIC: starting from a sequence of self-contained units (TOOTH followed by PL, BEND followed by PP), the rules fashion a continuous phonological representation ([ti:θ], [bent]) by successive interactions between its members. At one stage [tu:θ] and PL interact to yield what must subsequently be [ti:θ]. This effectively recapitulates our account of processes based on morphemes (the least traditional model in Ch. VII). At another stage the forms of BEND and PP join together to form [bent].

For most generativists the surface structures, as here, remain in the IA (morpheme-based) format. The whole notion of 'surface structure' is, indeed, their most obvious legacy from Bloomfield and their more immediate Post-Bloomfieldian predecessors. But in some European work the model is more similar to the classic form of WP. For illustration, let us look in greater detail at a recent study of German by W. U. Wurzel.[1] Although the title refers to 'Sound Structure', the first of its four parts is entirely devoted to morphology (including a transformationalist sketch of 'word formation') and most of the second deals with the Umlaut (as in the Nouns cited at the end of Ch. VIII). It is therefore a work of particular importance for our field.

We may again take two examples: first, the Verb form *redeten* '[they] spoke'. Grammatically, this has the following properties.

[1] *Studien zur deutschen Lautstruktur* (Berlin, 1970).

Firstly, it is Past Tense: since Past is the marked term in this category (as for Modern Greek in Ch. VIII), it is represented as '+Past' as opposed to '−Past' or Present. Secondly, it is 3rd Person and Plural: the Number is likewise represented as '+Plural' (as opposed to '−Plural' or Singular), and the Person simply as '+3rd'. Thirdly, it is Indicative (let us say): since this is the unmarked term in the category of Mood it is represented as '−Subjunctive'. Finally, the Verb itself is 'weak' (i.e. it does not have Ablaut) and is in general Regular: these properties are represented as '−Strong' (i.e. it is NOT a 'strong Verb') and '+Regular'. For Wurzel, as for the ancient grammarians (Ch. IV), such properties are of a single theoretical type. In Chomsky's terms, they are all **syntactic features** – features rather than 'formatives' in surface structure. Taking the root as [re:d], the surface representation is thus established as follows:

$$[\ \begin{bmatrix} +\text{Past} \\ +\text{Plural} \\ +\text{3rd} \\ -\text{Subjunctive} \\ -\text{Strong} \\ +\text{Regular} \\ \text{re:d} \end{bmatrix}\ ]_V$$

(V again = Verb) where, as in WP, each of the properties is assigned simultaneously to the same structural position.

The inflectional rules will then supply a Tense suffix (thus *redet-*) followed by the Person/Number termination. The former is basically [t]:

$$[\ \begin{bmatrix} +\text{Past} \\ \vdots \\ +\text{Regular} \\ \text{re:d} \quad\quad \text{t} \end{bmatrix}\ ]_V$$

– the rule stating that whenever a Verb is '−Strong' and '+Past' (i.e. when both these features form part of its surface structure), the form classified as '$[\ldots]_V$' has this affix added to it. As a result, the various syntactic features (+Past, +Plural, etc.) are also extended to the derived form **red-t-* as a whole. The second rule will then add to this a basic [n] as follows:

$$[\ \begin{bmatrix} +\text{Past} \\ \vdots \\ +\text{Regular} \\ \text{re:d} \quad \text{t} \quad \text{n} \end{bmatrix}\ ]_V$$

– the conditions for this last suffix being, firstly, that the Verb must be '+Plural' and, secondly, that it must NOT be '+2nd'. In this way, the same rule can derive both the 1st and the 3rd Plurals (*redeten* is also the form for 'we spoke'), as opposed, e.g., to the 2nd Plural *redetet* (with basic -[t]).

The basic [reːd]-[t]-[n] is then adjusted, by sandhi processes, to the actual [reːdətn̩]; briefly, Wurzel has a rule writing in *e* or [ə] as in the spelling (thus [reːdətən]), followed by another which eliminates it in more restricted environments. In a sense, the rules for inflection might be said to resemble formally the first of these rules for sandhi. Just as the process of epenthesis 'adds an *e*' under specified conditions (in writing, *red-t-n* → *redeten*), so the processes of suffixation 'add a *t*' or 'add an *n*' (e.g. *red-* → *red-t*, *red-t* → *red-t-n*) under others. But the conditioning factors are of a different sort. The former refers specifically to the surrounding phonological units – though also to the formative boundary (p. 172) – whereas the latter (pp. 66, 68) refer only to syntactic features. For this reason Wurzel maintains a clear distinction between the morphological section of his grammar and the usual generative 'phonology' or morphophonemics.

For the second example, let us take a form with Ablaut or vowel change: say, *gehoben* 'lifted'. In its surface structure this is a Verb ('$[\ldots]_V$') classified as a Past Participle (+PP), as strong (+Strong), but otherwise again as regular (+Regular). Within the strong class it also belongs specifically to a class whose Participle has the same vowel as the Past Tense (*hob* 'lifted') but a different vowel from the root (as in *heben* 'to lift'); this Wurzel marks with the features '+Past=PP' and '−PP=Root'. The input to the morphological rules is thus as follows:

$$[\ \begin{bmatrix} +\text{PP} \\ +\text{Strong} \\ +\text{Past}=\text{PP} \\ -\text{PP}=\text{Root} \\ +\text{Regular} \\ \text{he:b} \end{bmatrix}\ ]_V$$

Basically, three processes must then apply. Firstly, the prefix and suffix (*ge-* and *-en*) must be added by rules which are similar to those already illustrated for *redeten*. For the suffix, Wurzel again establishes a basic [n] – the phonetic alternation between [ən] and [n̩] being handled, as before, by subsequent adjustments. This suffix is added to any form that is both '+PP' and effectively (see below) '+Strong'. For the prefix ([ge]), the condition is simply that the form must be '+PP' (p. 66). Of course, many Participles in German do not have the *ge-*: for example, the compound meaning 'translated' is *über-setz-t* and not *ge-über-setz-t* or *über-ge-setz-t*. But Wurzel posits a later rule of 'phonology' by which it is deleted under specified conditions.

If that were all, these processes would accordingly yield a representation as follows:

$$\left[\begin{bmatrix} +\text{PP} \\ \vdots \\ +\text{Regular} \\ \text{ge} \quad \text{he:b} \quad \text{n} \end{bmatrix} \right]_{V}$$

– the prefix naturally being added to the beginning of the form which is classified as '$[\ldots]_V$' just as the suffix is added at the end. But before this can be derived, there must also be a further rule which introduces a Back vowel in place of the Front vowel in [he:b]. In the system of Ablaut variations (pp. 69ff.), an *o* can replace a Root vowel of various qualities: compare *flieg-en* and *ge-flog-en*, *lüg-en* and *ge-log-en*, etc. Accordingly, Wurzel's rule does not require an [e:] specifically as input. In addition, the *o* is related closely to an *u* appearing under complementary conditions: e.g. in *find-en* and *ge-fund-en* (where the root ends in a consonant with nasal preceding) or in derived Noun stems such as *Hub* '[action of] lifting' or *Flug* 'flight'. Wurzel accordingly treats them by the same rule, taking *u* as basic. Thus, for our example, the output of the morphological rules will be as follows:

$$\left[\begin{bmatrix} +\text{PP} \\ \vdots \\ +\text{Regular} \\ \text{ge} \quad \text{hu:b} \quad \text{n} \end{bmatrix} \right]_{V}$$

– [hu:b] being subsequently altered to [ho:b] by a rule applying only to Participles and Past Tenses derived by Ablaut (hence not to *Hub* nor, for example, to the unchanged vowel of *ge-ruf-en*) and then not, for example, before *-nd*.

That, then, is the way these forms would be derived from their surface structures. But in generative work a problem, naturally, is to ensure that the right rule always applies at the right time. For example, we do not want the *-n* of *redeten* to be added before the *-t* – yielding *redenet* instead. Nor, for that matter, would we want the *-t* to be added twice – yielding *redeteten*. To avoid such results, the rules must be read in a determined **order**. Taking the surface structure as input, the FIRST to be consulted must be those which derive the stem of the Past Tense: although the Terminations COULD be added to *red-* itself (the rules merely referring to a Verb with certain syntactic features), and ARE added to it when the Verb is '–Past' (thus *red-en* '[they] speak'), they do not come into play until after the inflectional stem, if any, has been formed. So, at that stage, we must derive *redet-* in any case where *red-* is classified as '+Past'. THEN, when these rules have been consulted once, they cannot possibly be consulted again. We must move on to the next group, which will be those concerned with the terminations. Accordingly, *redeten* must be derived if *redet-* is classified as '+3rd' and '+Plural'. At each point in the sequence only one rule can apply to any given input.

Such sequencing obtains between GROUPS of rules (e.g. those dealing with Past Tenses or Past Participles and those dealing with Person/Number terminations). But within each group the rules are also ordered, rather differently, amongst themselves. Where *ge-hob-en*, as we have seen, has the suffix *-n*, Participles such as *über-setz-t* 'translated' have a *-t* as in the Past Tense (compare *redet-*); the former is regular for strong Verbs (+Strong) and the latter for weak (–Strong). Wurzel accordingly has two alternative rules, which we may call A and B. Rule A states that *t* must be added, both for '+PP' and '+Past', whenever the form is '–Strong'; it is this alternative which is stated first. Rule B then adds the *-n* effectively, as we have said, when the input is both '+PP' and '+Strong'. But of these conditions, only '+PP' is explicitly stated. In consulting the grammar, we are directed first to look at rule A: if that can apply (i.e. if the input meets its conditions) then the *-t* is added and we must move at once to the next group altogether. We then look at rule B only for forms where rule A has in fact proved inapplicable; but since none of these can be '–Strong' as well as '–PP' (these being conditions, as we said, for rule A), there is no need to refer to '+Strong' specifically. Rule B simply applies to ANY OTHER Past Participle, not already dealt with.

In technical terms, the alternatives within the group are said to be **ordered disjunctively** as opposed to **conjunctively**. In the case of groups a rule from one may apply, or a rule from another, or possibly a rule from each: *redeten*, as we have seen, is derived by the CONJUNCTION of the rules which suffix *-t* and *-n*. But within groups either the first applies, or if not the second, but NOT both: the suffixes for Past Participles are the DISJUNCTION of *-t* or *-n*. Naturally, a group of three or more rules may be ordered in this way. In dealing with Ablaut, Wurzel sets out five successive sets of conditions, of which the set applicable for *gehoben* is the last (p. 72). By that stage in the succession, only the features '+Strong', '+PP' and '−PP=Root' need to be mentioned explicitly. Where such forms do not have the Back vowel they have already been dealt with at earlier stages or as exceptions in the lexicon.

This is getting technical, maybe. Moreover, we must stress that many applications of rule ordering are controversial even within the narrowly generative school. But the disjunctive technique, in particular, is far from foreign to conventional grammars. For the English Plurals, a generative account might FIRST give the rules deriving *oxen*, *children*, *teeth*, *knives* (with root consonant Voiced, [v]), and so on. It would THEN have the general rule ('Plurals are derived regularly by adding *-es*'), which would be understood to apply to 'all other' Nouns (all Nouns except OX, CHILD, TOOTH, KNIFE, etc.). This is equivalent to the conventional statement that *children*, *teeth*, and so on are **exceptions** – the general rule being understood to apply to ALL NOUNS BAR the exceptions specified. Similarly, the English Past Participle in *-en* is an exception to the Past Participle in *-ed*; in a generative treatment, the rules for *shown*, *begotten*, etc., could thus be ordered disjunctively BEFORE the rule for *towed* or *waited*. In the latter we would not need to refer to the inflectional class of TOW or WAIT specifically, but merely to 'all other' lexemes whose forms were still in play. Wurzel, it will be seen, does not employ the device in quite this way; Participles in -(*e*)*n* are surely an exception to those in -(*e*)*t* rather than vice versa. But perhaps one may legitimately wonder WHY not. Certainly, many rule orderings (at all levels of generative grammar) are established for just such familiar reasons.

* * *

It is hard to satisfy all potential readers of this book. Some will feel that this final chapter has ground to a halt too quickly; the author can only refer them to, for example, other things that he himself has written. Others may feel that the last few pages already lead beyond their interests. But the majority, perhaps, will at least find their interest aroused. Generative grammar is not the only approach to linguistic description. Indeed on many points it can be criticised (as in the lexical context earlier). But for inflectional morphology experiments with formal rules can only be a gain.

RELATED READING

For the basic notion of a generative grammar compare CHOMSKY, *Structures*; also N. Chomsky, 'A transformational approach to syntax', in *Third Texas Conference on Problems of Linguistic Analysis in English*, ed. A. A. Hill (Austin, 1962), p. 152 (§10). The latter is reprinted, but without the ensuing discussion (pp. 158–86), in *The Structure of Language*, ed. J. A. Fodor & J. J. Katz (Englewood Cliffs, 1964). For the term 'generate' see also GLEASON, p. 181f.; for a mathematical characterisation of the notions 'language' and 'grammar' see R. Wall, *Introduction to Mathematical Linguistics* (Englewood Cliffs, 1972), p. 166. In the course of the 1960s 'generative grammar' acquired a number of looser senses; for discussion see LYONS, pp. 155ff. (possibly clearer in *New Horizons*, pp. 23ff.). For Chomsky's later formulation see, e.g., CHOMSKY, *Mind*, pp. 126f. (paper reprinted as part of the second edition).

For competence and performance see CHOMSKY, *Aspects*, Ch. 1; there is a brief but standard formulation, e.g., in CHOMSKY & HALLE, p. 3. It is important to realise that this is only loosely similar to Saussure's distinction of 'langue' and 'parole' (SAUSSURE, Chs. 3–4); for example, Saussure would not have shared Chomsky's notion of the sentence. For relevant criticisms see C. F. Hockett, *The State of the Art* (The Hague, 1968); E. M. Uhlenbeck, *Critical Comments on Transformational-Generative Grammar, 1962–72* (The Hague, n.d. [1973]); U. Weinreich, W. Labov & M. I. Herzog, 'Empirical foundations for a theory of language change', in *Historical Linguistics*, pp. 95–195. For lexical semi-productivity see S. C. Dik, 'Some critical remarks on the treatment of morphological structure in transformational generative grammar', *Lingua*, **18** (1967), pp. 352–83; K. E. Zimmer, *Affixal Negation in English and Other Languages* (Supplement to *Word*: New York, 1964), especially Weinreich's preface; briefly in P. Schachter's review of Lees, *Grammar of English Nominalizations*, *IJAL*, **28** (1962), pp. 145f. See also the general references for Ch. III; as often, BOLINGER (p. 66, for syntax v. compounds) puts his finger straight on the main point. For a useful restatement of the generativist position see Botha, *Function of the Lexicon . . .*, §4.3.

For the rôle of inflectional rules see *Inflectional Morphology*, §2.2. For the generative formulation of IA see *Ibid.*, §5; compare again the stratificational proposals outlined in *New Horizons*, pp. 100–3. For IP see again *Inflectional Morphology*, §7.4.2; *New Horizons*, pp. 103–7. For the detailed generative technique the reader must work through CHOMSKY & HALLE,

Part 2; the illustration with *teeth* and *bent* is naturally very simplified. For 'diacritic features' see *Ibid.*, pp. 373–80; for their rôle in morphological processes compare the feature '+F' in rule 33 (*Ibid.*, p. 243; cf. p. 201).

For 'syntactic features' v. 'formatives' see CHOMSKY, *Aspects*, p. 82; for their application to a WP-type morphology see *Ibid.*, pp. 170ff. Wurzel's study of German may profitably be compared with an earlier and independent study of Old English by K.-H. Wagner, *Generative Grammatical Studies in the Old English Language* (Heidelberg, 1969). For an alternative formulation see again *Inflectional Morphology*, Ch. 9 (and earlier articles); although 'generative', this is otherwise more directly traditional than Chomskyan in inspiration.

For ordered rules in morphology and morphophonemics see *Inflectional Morphology*, §§9.3.4, 10.3 (with discussion of earlier references). For disjunctive v. conjunctive ordering see CHOMSKY & HALLE, pp. 61–4 (and other references in their index); also Schane, *Generative Phonology*, pp. 89–90.

INDEX

Page numbers in italics refer to the sections of 'Related Reading' at the end of each chapter.